A Spare Capacity Planning Methodology for Wide Area Survivable Networks

by

Adel A. Al-Rumaih

ISBN: 1-58112-046-X

DISSERTATION.COM

1999

PATENT PENDING

ISBN: 1-58112-046-X

Dissertation.com
1999

www.Dissertation.com/library/112046xa.htm

A SPARE CAPACITY PLANNING METHODOLOGY FOR WIDE AREA SURVIVABLE NETWORKS

By

Adel A. Al-Rumaih

[B.S. in Computer Science and Engineering, University of Petroleum and Minerals], 1986

[M.S. in Electrical Engineering, King Saud University], 1993

Submitted to the Graduate Faculty of

Department of Information Science and Telecommunications at

School of Information Sciences

in partial fulfillment of the requirements of the degree of

Doctor of Philosophy

University of Pittsburgh

1999

University of Pittsburgh
Department of Information Science and Telecommunications

Dissertation Defense

Name of Student: **ADEL AL-RUMAIH**

Dissertation Title: **"A Spare Capacity Planning Methodology for Wide Area Survivable Networks"**

Committee:

Name	Signature	Accept	Department
Dr. Paul Munro		yes	DIST
Dr. James G. Williams		Yes	DIST
Dr. Marek Druzdzel		YES	DIST
Dr. Bryan Norman		Yes	Engineering

Major Advisor:

Dr. David Tipper		Yes	DIST

Date: January 13, 1999

DIST Chair: ______________ **Date:** 1/15/99

To my parents

Dr. David Tipper
Research Advisor

A SPARE CAPACITY PLANNING METHODOLOGY FOR WIDE AREA SURVIVABLE NETWORKS

Adel A. Al-Rumaih, Ph. D.

University of Pittsburgh, 1999

ABSTRACT

In this dissertation, a new spare capacity planning methodology is proposed utilizing path restoration. The approach is based on forcing working flows/traffic which are on paths that are disjoint to share spare backup capacity. The algorithm for determining the spare capacity assignment is based on genetic algorithms and is capable of incorporating non-linear variables such as non-linear cost function and QoS variables into the objective and constraints.

The proposed methodology applies to a wider range of fault scenarios than most of the current literature. It can tolerate link-failures, node-failures, and link-and-node failures. It consists of two stages: the first stage generates a set of network topologies that maximize the sharing between backup paths by forcing them to use a subset of the original network. The second stage utilizes a genetic algorithm to optimize the set of solutions generated by the first stage to achieve an even better final solution. It can optimize the solution based on either minimizing spare capacity or minimizing the total network cost. In addition, it can incorporate QoS variables in both the objective and constraints to design a survivable network that satisfies QoS constraints.

Numerical results comparing the proposed methodology to Integer Programming techniques and heuristics from the literature are presented showing the advantages of the technique. The proposed methodology was applied on 4 different size networks based on spare capacity optimization criteria and it was found that it achieved solutions that were on average 9.3% better than the optimal solution of the IP design that is based on link-restoration. It also achieved solutions that were on average 22.2 % better than the previous heuristic SLPA.

The proposed methodology is very scalable. It was applied on networks with different sizes ranging from a 13-node network to a 70-node network. It was able to solve the 70-node network in less than one hour on a Pentium II PC. The curve-fitting of the empirical execution time of the methodology was found to be $O(n^3)$.

KEYWORDS

Survivable networks, spare capacity, capacity assignment, mesh restoration, genetic algorithm, capacity placement, network design, path restoration, quality of service, delay calculations

Acknowledgements

All thanks are due to Allah for showing his mercy and grace to me in this life. Allah gave me the chance and the means to do this work.

I would like to express my deepest gratitude to my advisor, Dr. David Tipper, for his support, encouragement, invaluable guidance throughout the course of this work, and most of all, for being a good friend. His knowledge, dedication, and work ethics have been a constant source of inspiration. Without his patience and understanding in difficult times, it would most probably not be possible to complete this work.

My thanks to Dr. Bryan Norman, a member of my Ph.D. committee, for his constructive criticism, and useful suggestions to improve the genetic algorithm implementation. I would also like to thank the other members of my Ph.D. committee, Dr. Jim Williams, Dr. Marek Druzdzel, and Dr. Paul Munro for their invaluable comments, useful suggestions and for taking the time to make sure this work was a quality one.

I gratefully acknowledge the financial support I received from the Ministry of Defense and Aviation, Saudi Arabia. I am grateful to General Saad Al-Rumaih and Dr. Ibrahim Al-Nasser for their personal support regarding this matter. There are many other people who have helped me. I apologize for not naming them all, but I would like to thank them all.

I will always be grateful to my parents, for their du'aa, love, understanding, help, and continuing support throughout the years. My brothers deserve special thanks for their encouragement, concern, and for only being a phone call away when I needed them.

I save my final, insufficient word of gratitude for my wife, Maha, for her help, patience, and for sacrificing her time throughout the course of my Ph.D. study. I am indebted to my wife and my kids, Fatmah, Albatul, Omar, and Norah for providing me with the moral support that has made it possible to accomplish the work presented in this dissertation.

Table of Content s

List of Figures

List of Tables

Chapter 1

Introduction

1.1 Introduction

Due to the widespread use of telecommunication networks and society's increasing dependence upon the exchange of information, reliable network services have become essential for societal growth and survival. Many organizations and individuals now rely heavily on voice (e.g., phone calls), data (e.g., Internet resources, facsimile transmission, electronic fund transfer), and video (e.g., video conferencing) services in their day-to-day activities. Disruption of telecommunication services may result in both short-term and long-term effects. Short-term effects would be things like the loss of emergency services (e.g., 911), or airport traffic-control. The long-term effects of such disruptions include things like a company's loss of business (e.g. an Internet service provider) to competitors due to unreliable telecommunication service.

Survivability has become a critical issue in telecommunication networks due to the growing society reliance on telecommunications, on the one hand, and the increasing importance of information exchange, on the other hand. This vital relationship between society and telecommunications reflects the importance of having stable and secure telecommunication networks. Previous studies of network reliability identified network failures and classified them into the following categories:

- Architectural / Implementation defects
- Human errors
- Environmental hazards
- Accidents
- Sabotage
- Operational disruptions

Architectural/implementation defects: include designing and manufacturing defects, software bugs, database errors, etc. Human errors: include maintenance and procedural errors, errors during upgrades, and rearrangement of equipment. Environmental hazards: include floods, fires, lighting, earthquakes, and hurricanes. Accidents: include things like cutting of underground cable by a construction activity. Sabotage: includes things like vandalism, software break-ins, etc. Operation disruptions: include things like intentional breaking of links to carry out networks' expansion or maintenance operations [1, 2].

Because of the recent advances in the technology of computer equipment, communication devices, and software systems, telecommunication networks have become a major part of the national infrastructure of civilized countries. Thus, many structures of society including business, finance, air traffic control and reservation, education, medicine, security, and government agencies are among those who are critically dependent on reliable telecommunication networks. Hence, telecommunication networks are identified as one of the nations' most critical infrastructures. Because of its importance, telecommunication incapacity or destruction would have a debilitating impact on the national defense or economic security of any modern country. Threats to these critical infrastructures can be classified into two categories: "physical threats" (tangible) to the telecommunication network facility, and "cyber threats" which include computer-based attacks on the information or communication components that control the critical infrastructures. In this regard, the U.S. government took three major actions to overcome these threats: first, establishing the Reliability and Vulnerability Working Group (RVWG), as part of the Information Infrastructure Task Force (IITF) of the National Information Infrastructure (NII). RVWG aims to develop a survivable and reliable national telecommunication architecture that satisfies the requirements of the national security and emergency preparedness of the nation [3]. Secondly, the establishment of the "information survivability" program by the Department of Defense (DoD), which aims to create affordable, verifiable, scalable technologies for reliable defense infrastructure [4]. Thirdly, the formation of the president's commission on critical infrastructure protection to formulate a comprehensive national strategy for protecting the nation's critical infrastructures. These infrastructures include: telecommunications networks, electric power systems, gas and oil production, storage and transportation, banking and finance, transportation, water supply systems, government services, and emergency services [4].

One of the main reasons for the increased focus on telecommunication network survivability is that economies of scale over the last ten years have caused network providers to deploy optical fibers (with high bandwidth capability), to provide higher throughput for the network, resulting in a higher average traffic cross-section for a given cable [5]. Deploying more optical fibers in telecommunication networks tends to make the network topology sparser (the connectivity of the network topology graph decrease). As a result, a failure in a network link will have larger impact on network reliability since an optical transmission link can carry a significant amount of traffic.

Network survivability has recently attracted many researchers to investigate it [1, 6-14], and it recently became an area of interest by itself [15]. There is no standard definition for the term "survivability"; however, it is defined in some literature as "the capability of a network where a certain percentage of the traffic can still be carried immediately after a failure" [16]. In [17], the researchers defined it as "the ability of a network to cope with facility outages, capacity overloads, and national disasters." Network survivability was also defined in [18] as: (1) the ability of a network to maintain or restore an acceptable level of performance during network failures by applying various restoration techniques, and (2) the mitigation or prevention of service outages from network failures by applying preventive techniques.

Survivability procedures are essential to recover the lost service of the network that occurs due to a network component failure. To start with, survivable network design generally has three stages: physical topology configuration, path distribution between each node-pair, and spare capacity assignment. Physical topology configuration will be discussed in section 1.2.1 (Survivable Network Design, page 6), path distribution will be discussed in section 1.2.2 (Traffic Flow Management, page 15), and spare capacity assignment in survivable networks will be presented in Chapter 2 (This chapter presents a review of previous work presented in the literature for solving the spare capacity problem in survivable networks. The two approaches in solving the spare capacity problem are discussed in details in the first section. The problem considered in this dissertation is presented in the second section).

The organization of this dissertation is as follows: in this chapter, a background of survivable network techniques will be presented which include: (1) survivable network design, and (2) traffic flow management in survivable networks. In the second chapter, (1) a survey of the spare capacity planning research in survivable networks (reviews and discussions) is presented, and (2) the problem considered in this research is identified with the research objectives. In the third chapter, the proposed new methodology for economical spare-capacity planning for a large-size survivable network with link, node, both link and node failure tolerances, and quality of service (QoS) is discussed and illustrated. Chapter 4 discusses the implementation details of the proposed methodology with its sensitivity analysis. In the fifth chapter, there is a comparison between the proposed methodology and previous approaches with numerical results and discussions. In the sixth chapter, the scalability of the proposed methodology and the incorporation of QoS constraints are illustrated. Finally, a conclusion with the main contributions of this dissertation and future work is presented in the last chapter.

1.2 Background

Telecommunication networks consist mainly of links and nodes. Links are the transmission media between nodes. Nodes are the processing units (e.g. switches, routers, digital cross-connect switches) of the network. Links can be of any type of transmission media such as fiber, copper, coax, microwave, and satellite [19]. Network failures can be classified into link failures, node failures, link and node failures. Link failures include things like cable cut, and interface card failures. Node failures include things like hardware malfunctions, software bugs, and operational failures. Link and node failures include both the failures of links and nodes.

Survivable network design includes the capability of the network to tolerate network failures. In order for the network to tolerate failures, it should have many characteristics in terms of topology, link capacities, and working and backup traffic routing. In this section, survivable network design will be discussed with its different architectures, in addition to the traffic management of survivable networks.

1.2.1 Survivable Network Design

Network survivability depends mainly on the network architecture. Network architecture design determines which survivability mechanism could be used to restore the network from different failures. All network failure discovery and restoration procedures are designed to take advantage of the architecture of the network. In order to have a survivable network, we should have some kind of redundancy in network resources. The excess resources are utilized to recover the lost network service due to a failure. These extra resources can be links, bandwidth, buffers, or a combination of them. In order for the network to be survivable in case of failures, its topology should have specific characteristics. For a single-link failure tolerance, the connectivity of the nodes should be at least of degree two. However, not all networks with degree 2-connectivity nodes can mitigate single-link failures (see Figure 1.1a for an example). In Figure 1.1a, if the link between nodes 4 and 5 fails, the network will be separated into two disconnected sub-networks.

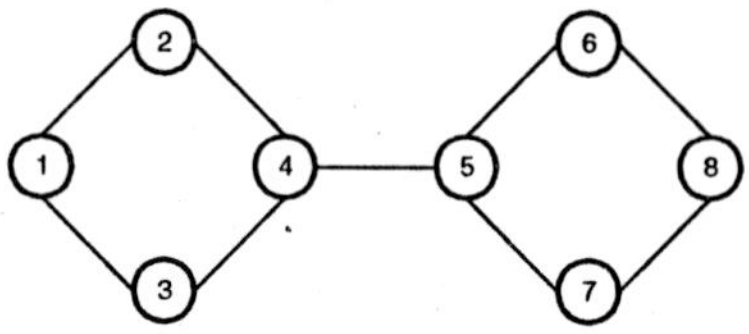

a) 2-connectivity node network

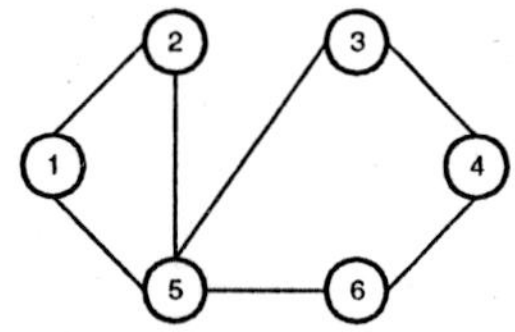

b) Single-link failure tolerant network

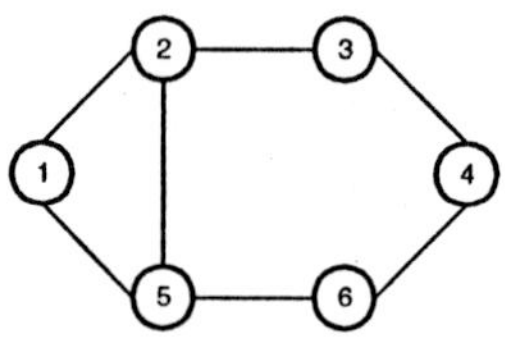

c) Single-node failure tolerant network

Figure 1.1 Network Topologies with Different Levels of Failure Tolerance

Another way to verify if a given network is survivable for single-link failures, is by testing if there are at least two link-disjoint paths between each node-pair of the network. Figure 1.1b shows a network that is single-link failure tolerant, but not single-node failure tolerant. For the single-node failure survivability, we should have at least two node-disjoint paths between each node-pair of the network. Figure 1.1c shows a network which is both single-link and single-node failure tolerant [1]. For a simultaneous two-link failure tolerant network, we should have at least three link-disjoint paths between each node-pair of the network. Similarly, for a simultaneous three-link failure tolerant network, we should have at least four link-disjoint paths between each node-pair

[1] Any network with n-node failure tolerant is also n-link failure tolerant

of the network, and so on[2]. As a result, the number of links, the connectivity of nodes, and the capacity of links required are increased for multiple failure survivable networks.

The traffic load between each pair of nodes is the amount of traffic (voice, data, or video) that should be sent across the network per unit time. The network should have adequate capacity on its links to handle all the traffic load of each node-pair of the network according to some quality of service (QoS) constraints. The QoS constraints can be a connection blocking requirement, and/or delay constraints such as maximum link delay, average path delay, maximum path delay, average network delay, or a combination of two or more of them. In packet-based networks, one is also concerned with QoS metrics like packet loss rates and path delay jitter. In addition to providing a QoS level for a normal operation, a survivable network should have additional (spare) capacity on the links to use for rerouting traffic around any failed link/node. Since this spare capacity is redundant and may be reserved for use in case of failures, an important goal in survivability research is to minimize spare capacity as much as possible without affecting the survivability level of the network [11-13, 20, 21].

Survivable network architectures are generally classified into two categories: dedicated facility restoration and dynamic facility restoration [22]. Dedicated facility restoration uses standby resources that are dedicated for failure restoration, and not used during normal operation of the network, such as an automatic protection switch (APS) and self-healing rings (SHRs). Dynamic facility restoration uses spare resources within working facilities to restore lost services in case of failures. Dynamic facility restoration

---

[2] For an n node-failure tolerant network, there should be at least n+1 node-disjoint paths in the network

includes techniques such as dual homing and dynamic routing with mesh-type network architectures. We briefly illustrate these concepts.

1.2.1.1 Automatic Protection Switch (APS)

APS is a technique used in case a cable is cut between two nodes (which are connected by a link). One type of APS is 1:1 that means there is one standby cable for each working cable between any two nodes connected by a link [22, 23]. In case of a failure in the working cable, the traffic will be switched to the standby cable almost immediately (within 50 msec.[24]) and the service will be restored without any serious interruption.

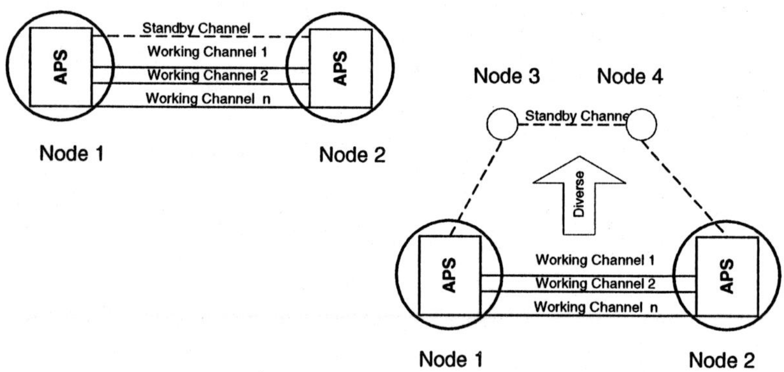

Figure 1.2 Automatic Protection Switch (APS) and APS with Diverse Protection (APS/DP)

Another type of APS is 1:N, which means that there is one standby cable for N working cables. In this case, the survivability has decreased since only one of the working cables could be recovered in case of failures; however, the standby facility has been reduced by a factor 1/N. The standby facility could be physically on a different route than the working facility, which in this case is called APS with diverse protection (APS/DP). 1:1 APS/DP means that there is a standby cable for each working cable, but the standby cable is placed physically on a diverse route other than the working cable. 1:N APS/DP means that there is only one standby cable for each working cable in a diverse physical route. The problem with APS (without DP) is that a cable cut may result in cutting both the working and standby cables at the same time, while this does not occur in the case of diverse protection (DP). 1:1 APS/DP provides 100 % survivability level, while 1:N APS/DP provides only 100/N % survivability level. However, 1:1 APS requires more facility and equipment (cost) than 1:N [22].

A fully restorable APS/DB system requires 100% capacity redundancy (total spare to working capacity ratio) in the network. In addition, it is limited to link-failure tolerance only, it can not alone tolerate node-failures, or line card failure [25].

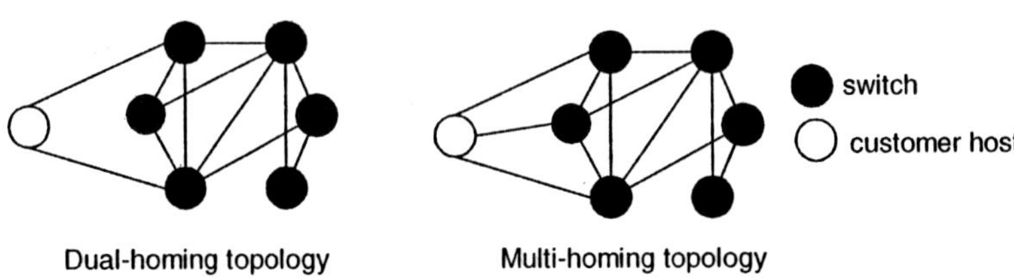

Figure 1.3 Dual-homing and Multi-homing Architectures

1.2.1.2 Dual Homing and Multi Homing

Dual homing is a concept that connects a customer host to two switches, as in Figure 1.3. The traffic from the customer host is split between the two switches; one called the primary and the other the secondary. In case a failure occurs on a link between the customer host and one of the switches, the other switch can take over and reroutes all the traffic of the customer host. A dual homing customer host doesn't accomplish the restoration automatically by itself; it needs to coordinate with the switches dynamically to restore services at the path level [22]. Dual homing is capable of providing 100% survivability in case a failure occurs in one of the switches or in the connection to either switch. Multi-homing is connecting a customer host to more than two switches, which results in more survivable architecture in case of failures of more than one switch [26].

1.2.1.3 Self-healing Rings (SHRs)

SHR is a topology connecting a set of nodes by one (or more) rings. Each node is connected to all the ring(s). For each ring, each node is connected to two Add/Drop multiplexers (ADM), one to read from the ring on one direction and the other to write to the ring on the other direction. There are two types of rings, uni-directional ring (USHR) consisting of a single cable, and bi-directional ring (BSHR) consisting from two cables. In Figure 1.4, the two types of SHR with 4 nodes are shown.

In USHR, all the traffic goes in one direction in the normal state (in case of no failures); while in BSHR all the traffic goes in one direction on the first ring and in the reverse direction on the second ring in the normal state. 1:1 USHR uses two rings, one working and the other standby; while 1:1 BSHR uses 4 rings, two working and two standby. An important distinction is that USHR utilizes path protection switching, while BSHR utilizes link protection switching according to the requirements of ANSI T1X1 and Bellcore [24, 27].

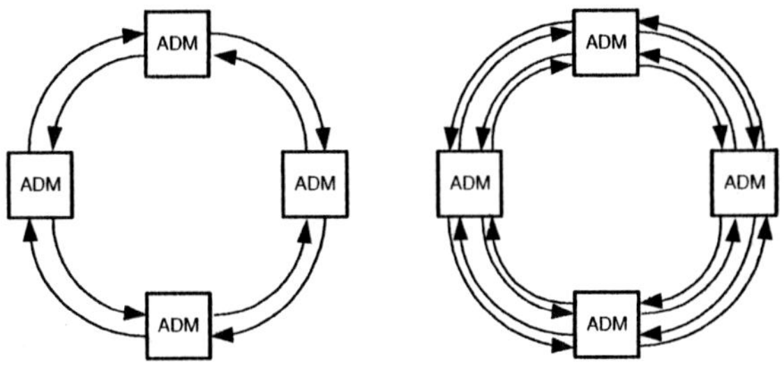

1:1 Uni-directional self-healing ring (USHR)

1:1 Bi-directional self-healing ring (BSHR)

Figure 1.4 Types of Self-healing Rings

In USHR, the capacity of the ring is determined by the sum of the traffic load between all node-pairs. However, in BSHR, the spare capacity of each link around the ring can be shared between working paths since the traffic between each node-pair has the same route [28]. SHRs can be visualized as an extension to 1:1 APS [25]. SHRs provide 100% restoration capability for single link or ADM failure. In addition, it is fully automatic and provides a fast restoration process [22].

SHR architecture requires at least 100% capacity redundancy for full restoration [25]. However, it is limited in restoring failures that occur in its ring(s) or its ADM(s). In other words, it can not accommodate failures that occur in network nodes such as line card failures, or software failures.

1.2.1.4 Mesh-Network with Dynamic Routing

A mesh-network with dynamic routing utilizes digital cross-connect switches (DCS) to reroute the traffic around a failed link (or node). Unlike APS or SHR, DCS does not require dedicated facilities. It utilizes the spare capacity of the links and working resources to restore the affected traffic. Figure 1.5 shows a mesh network with dynamic routing. When the link between DCS 1 and DCS 2 in Figure 1.5 fails the traffic between DCS 1 and DCS 2 is rerouted to the 1-3-4-2 route. The routing strategy can be either centralized or distributed; in the former, all the routing tables are calculated and stored in a central control location (CL). When a failure occurs, the adjacent nodes to the failed link inform the CL, which in turn distributes the new routing tables to the affected nodes. While in the latter strategy, distributed routing, the routing tables, for each failure scenario, are stored in each node. It is the job of the adjacent nodes of the failed link to inform all the other nodes of any failure in order to take an action for rerouting the traffic around the failed link. These rerouting tables can be precomputed, for each link failure, in a central location and then distributed to all the nodes. Alternately, the routing tables can be computed dynamically after the occurrence of a failure and then the traffic is rerouted according to the available spare capacity in the other links of the network.

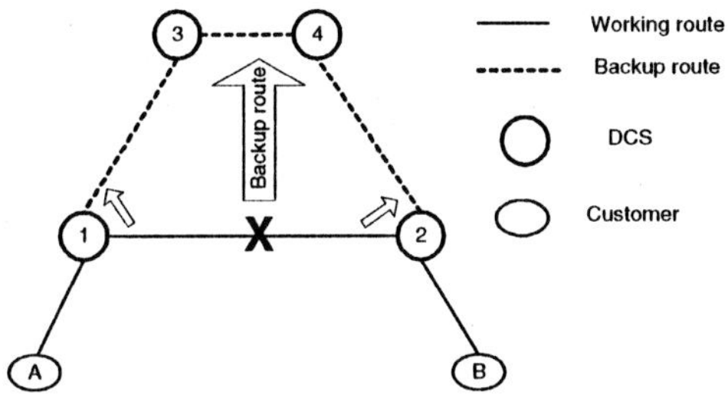

Figure 1.5 Mesh Network with Dynamic Routing

The AT&T telecommunications network is composed of 114 nodes which form a logically fully-connected mesh network. It has over 114 logical ways to route a call between each pair of nodes [29]. Two different logical routes may use the same physical route. The AT&T network is centrally controlled from three locations (Bedminster, New Jersey; Conyers, Georgia; Denver, Colorado) with dynamic restoration procedures when a failure occurs [30].

Mesh network restoration procedures tend to utilize the available capacity of the network more efficiently than APS or SHR [15, 25] since it doesn't require dedicated restoration facilities. Pervious studies showed that the savings in network redundancy for a small-size survivable mesh network with link-failure tolerance can be up to 50% more than APS or SHR [7, 20]. This shows that mesh network restoration procedures have an advantage in redundancy savings over dedicated restoration systems (e.g. APS or SHR).

The work proposed here is based on wide area survivable mesh networks, centrally controlled with precomputing routing distributed on the network's nodes. The network switches from its normal to its restoration state dynamically when a failure occurs.

1.2.2 Traffic Flow Management

Traffic routing strategies in survivable networks are generally classified into two categories: link-restoration[3] routing and path-restoration[4] routing. Link restoration routing reroutes all the traffic on the failed link from one of the adjacent nodes to the other adjacent node of the failed link using the spare capacity of the other links around the failed link. While path restoration routing reroutes all the working paths, on the failed link, to backup paths from source to destination (end-to-end node-pair routing) utilizing the spare capacity of the links of the network. Table 1.1 shows a comparison between link-restoration and path-restoration.

Table 1.1 Comparison Between Link-restoration and Path-restoration

	Link-Restoration	Path-Restoration
Efficiency	Not optimal	Can be optimal
Restoration speed	Fast (since it reroutes between two nodes)	Slow (since it routes between each node-pair)
Location of computing	Normally, it is locally computed at the node	Normally, it is centrally calculated, then distributed
Backup Path length	Usually, shorter	Usually, longer
Recovery from node failure	No	Yes
Computation	Less	More
Formulation	Single-commodity flow	Multi-commodity flow

[3] Sometimes called line-restoration, local-restoration, or patch restoration.
[4] In some literature, it is also called point-to-point restoration, or end-to-end restoration.

Restoration routing (whether it is a link or a path restoration) can be either computed centrally or computed in a distributed manner. Centrally computed routing implies that there is a CL that oversees the whole network and maintains an active status of the network at all times. The CL is notified by affected nodes in case of failures to take the proper actions to reroute the traffic around the faulty link and restores the lost services. The CL may either precompute these actions (including routing tables) for each failure scenario to provide faster recovery, or it may compute the backup paths dynamically based on the available spare capacity in the network. The advantage of the preplanned computation is the speed of the restoration process, while the advantage of the dynamically computed approach is the efficiency in utilizing the available capacity.

Routing criteria used in survivable networks is generally either k-shortest path (KSP) or maximum flow (MF). These two criteria are explained in the next section.

1.2.2.1 Routing Criteria in Survivable Networks

The two main routing criteria used widely in the literature of survivable networks are k-shortest path (KSP) and maximum flow (MF) [25, 31, 32]. Both of them aim to find the maximum disjoint paths between any node-pair in the network. KSP is simpler computationally than MF, but it does not always generate the optimal disjoint path set, on the one hand. On the other hand, MF is guaranteed to produce the maximum number of possible disjoint paths but it does not produce the actual path set. The difference in their effectiveness in practical network topologies is very small (less than 0.3 %) according to an extensive empirical study reported in [31]. Since the difference between them is so small and the computational complexity between them is substantial (O (n log (n)) vs. O

(n^3) + path-set calculation), some researchers argue that KSP can be used in practice instead of MF with virtually no penalty [31].

1.2.2.2 K-Shortest Disjoint-Path criteria (KSP)

KSP aims to find the K shortest disjoint paths from a source node A to a destination node B in the network. It works by successively applying the shortest path algorithm K times. The first path found is the shortest path between A and B. In the second iteration, it finds the second shortest path between A and B that is disjoint with the first path found. In the Kth iteration, it finds the Kth shortest path between A and B that disjoint with all the previous K-1 paths. The way that this algorithm is implemented is that after finding the first shortest path, all the links of the first shortest path are removed from the network. Then, the shortest path algorithm is applied again to find the second shortest path. Next, the second shortest path is removed and the shortest path algorithm is applied to find the third shortest path, and so on.

The reason that KSP may sometimes be not optimal (which means that it sometimes does not find the maximum possible number of disjoint paths between every node-pair) is that when the topology of the network contains a special structure called a "trap" topology as shown in Figure 1.6.

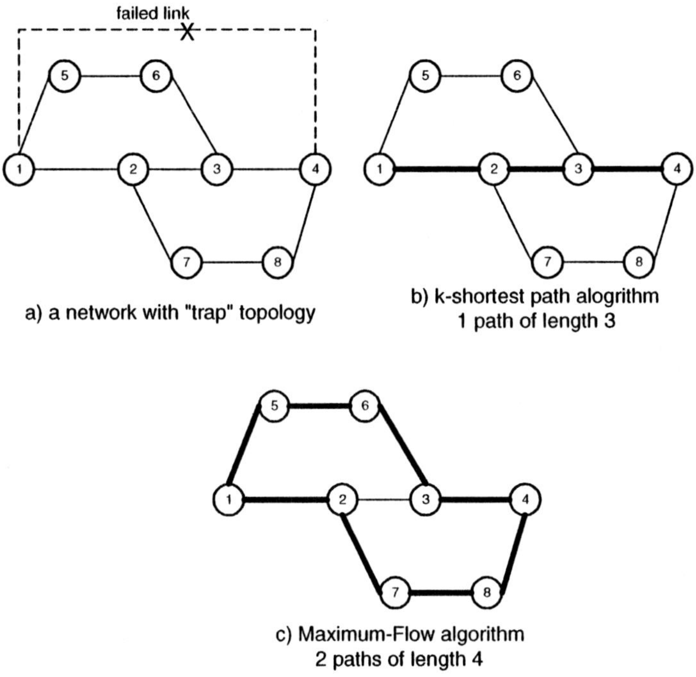

Figure 1.6 Network with "trap" Topology

When KSP finds the shortest path between node 1 and node 4 (as the path 1-2-3-4) in the first iteration and removes the links of the path from the network, no other disjoint path exists between node 1 and node 4. MF is superior in this case since it can discover that there are 2 possible disjoint paths between node 1 and node 4. Then, the disjoint path set can be found (they are 1-5-6-3-4 and 1-2-7-8-4) by another procedure. Other than the "trap" topology, the two algorithms generate equivalent results [31].

The complexity of a shortest path algorithm such as Dijkstra's algorithm is O (n^2); however, some variations of the Dijsktra algorithm such as the binary-min-heap are of order O (n log(n)) [31], where n is the number of nodes in the network. KSP has the same time complexity as the shortest path algorithm used in its implementation since it runs the shortest path algorithm K times for each node-pair. Applying KSP on each node-pair of the network will require time complexity of O $(L*n^3 * \log(n))$, where L is the number of links and n is the number of nodes.

1.2.2.3 Maximum Flow (MF)

The MF routing criterion aims to find the maximum number of possible paths that exists between two nodes of the network. MF is based on the min-cut max-flow theorem [33]. The theorem indicates that the maximum possible number of paths between any two nodes is equal to the minimum cut in the network that isolates the network into two disconnected sub-networks (the first node is in one sub-network and the other node is in the other sub-network). In Figure 1.7, the maximum number of possible backup paths between node 1 and node 4 is equal to the minimum sum of the available spare capacity on any cut in the network, excluding the capacity of the failed link between node 1 and 4. A cut is any set of links that if removed from the network, will divide the network into two disconnected sub-networks. MF produces the optimal (maximum) possible number of backup paths. However, it does not generate the path set of the backup paths. Producing the path set is another problem that takes exponential time in the worst case [25]. However, for the average case, there exist linear programming (LP) algorithms that can run in polynomial time [25]. Finding the path set of the MF algorithm can be modeled as a multicommodity maxflow problem [25].

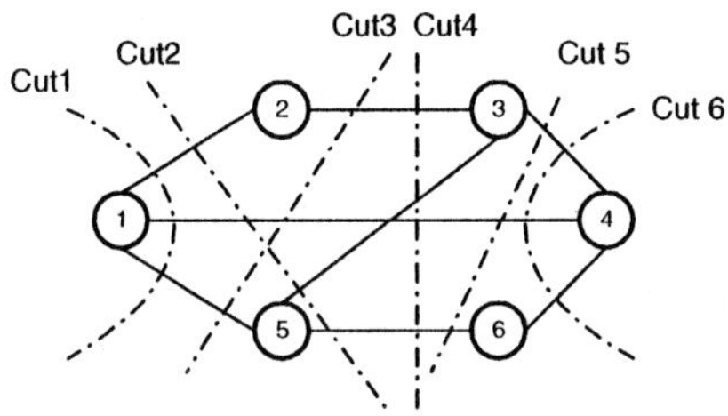

Figure 1.7 Cuts of Max-flow algorithm

Because of the complexity of computing the MF algorithm and the importance of speed in the restoration process, MF, if implemented, is best used in a centrally controlled network utilizing a preplanned routing calculation strategy. The restoration process then can be either centrally controlled or distributed to all nodes. A rough comparison between KSP and MF is shown in Table 1.2.

Table 1.2 A Rough Comparison between K-shortest Path and Max-flow Algorithms

	KSP	Max-flow
Computation	Simple	Complex
Time limit (2 second)	Possible	Not likely
Restoration efficiency	=< 100%	= 100%
Best calculated	Dynamically (when failure occurs)	Preplanned
Computing location	At node (distributed on nodes)	Centrally (in a central location)
Changing network environment	More suitable	Less suitable

The proposed work in this dissertation is based on path-restoration rather than link-restoration since the path-restoration approach tends to utilize the available capacity more efficiently than the link-restoration approach. In addition, KSP is used in this dissertation rather than MF, because the traffic in the backup paths of the proposed methodology uses one route between each node-pair.

Chapter 2

Previous Work

This chapter reviews the literature which deals with the spare capacity problem in survivable networks. The two approaches of solving the spare capacity problem are discussed in detail in the first section. The problem considered in this dissertation is presented in the second section.

2.1 Previous Work in Spare Capacity Planning

Previous research on optimizing the spare capacity assignment of survivable networks used either one of the following two strategies. The first approach is to use linear programming (LP) techniques [13, 20, 21, 34]. The other strategy is to use heuristic techniques to find semi-optimal solutions [11, 32, 35, 36]. Linear programming approaches formulate the backup paths for each link failure scenario into an LP model with an objective function to minimize the spare capacity required for a full restoration from a single link failure. Some LP approaches use an integer programming (IP) model such as in [13, 20, 34], while others try to reduce the complexity of the IP model by an approximate LP model as in [21].

In [10, 21], a two-part procedure to solve the spare-capacity assignment in survivable networks with a hop-limit path length was proposed. It is based on link-restoration with a distributed routing scheme. The procedure starts with predefined path-sets for each link failure (that satisfy the hop-limit criteria), and a given working capacity for each link. Part I of the procedure relies on an LP model (Min-Max) that is formulated as an integer programming (IP) problem. The objective of Part I is to produce a feasible flow for each restoration path-set of every link failure with minimum spare capacity. Part II applies more optimization techniques on the resulting network of Part I to reduce the excess redundancy of the network without reducing the restoration level achieved in Part I. Part II relies on an LP model (Max-flow) to find the links that have more spare capacity than what is needed for the restoration level. Each link with excess capacity is reduced until no more reduction is possible without affecting the restoration level. The output of Part II is the capacity needed for each link, and the path-sets of each link failure with their associated traffic flow.

In order to significantly reduce the complexity of the IP model, the approach taken in [10, 20] is to use a link-restoration (not path-restoration) scheme which usually results in less efficient solution than path restoration approaches [9, 36]. The feasible solution produced by this approach depends mainly on the path-sets chosen. If larger path-sets are chosen (increasing the hop-limit per path), then they may result in a better solution at the expense of a more complex LP formulation. This approach requires a prohibitively larger LP formulation model for large networks, which may not be solvable by the computation ability of today's computers.

In another study [21], an LP approach, to approximate an IP model, is also used for the spare capacity assignment, but it is based on a partial cut-sets of the network for each link failure. It is equivalent to the maximum-flow minimum-cut theorem [33], which places constraints on restorability based on the set of minimum cuts in the network. A cut-set is a set of links that when removed divide the network into two disconnected sub-networks. The input to this approach is the topology of the network and the working capacity of each link, and the output is the spare capacity required for each link that results in a network with a single-link failure tolerance. The objective function of the LP model is to minimize the total spare capacity of the network.

In this approach, a partial set of the cut-sets for each link failure scenario is generated, and then an LP model of these partial cut-sets is formulated. Then, the LP model is solved by the simplex method. After that, a max-flow procedure for each link failure scenario is checked to ensure that the spare capacity is adequate for the 100% restoration level. If the solution of the max-flow is not feasible (not 100% restorable), then an update to the spare capacity is done and the simplex method is reapplied again until a feasible solution is achieved. The main drawback of this approach is the generation of the partial cut-set, since the complete cut-sets could require $O(L+2^N)$ [5]. Identifying the proper partial cut-set is an essential part of this approach, which alone is a significant problem. In addition, the complexity of the LP model makes this approach not scalable to large-size networks.

5 Where L is the number of links, and N is the number of nodes in the network.

In [11], a heuristic for spare capacity placement in mesh survivable networks was proposed. It is based on a greedy algorithm that aims to maximize the restorability and minimize the redundancy of the network by applying successive operations of addition, removal, and rearrangement of spare capacity. It is based on link-restoration and it uses a two-stage heuristic that designs a restorable network in the first stage. Then it optimizes the network in the second stage to reduce the assigned spare capacity while maintaining the same restorability level. The heuristic starts initially with a network that has enough working capacity. It also has one spare capacity unit in each link. In addition, there are routing tables between each node-pair of the network that satisfy the hop-limit criterion. In stage I, called Forward Synthesis (FS), it iterativily adds one spare capacity unit to the link that results in maximum restorability increase. If the network reaches a state where no single addition of spare capacity to a link would result in an increase in the restorability of the network, double links are used where a spare capacity is added to two links at the same time which they produce the maximum restorability increase. If the network reaches a state where no double link addition would result in any restorability increase, a spare capacity is added to a complete path between the node-pair that generate the maximum increase in restorability. Stage I continues until 100% restorability is achieved. Then, stage II, called Design Tightening (DT), tries to reduce the spare capacity while maintaining the 100% restoration level by applying addition and deletion operations on spare capacity. Stage II tries to remove a spare capacity unit denoted (rem1) on a single link without affecting the restoration level. If it does not find any single spare capacity unit on a link to remove, then it tries to remove two spare capacity units (one from two different links) and add one spare capacity unit (rem2_add1) at the same time (to a third link), while maintaining the same restoration level. If no rem2_add1 was found, it then tries to remove three spare capacity units (one each from three different links) and add two spare capacities (rem3_add2) at the same time (one to two different links), while maintaining the same restoration level. The heuristic stops when no rem3_add2 is found in the entire network, and the final network is the output of this technique.

There are a number of comments about the efficiency of the above heuristic. It is based on link-restoration (and not path restoration) which tends to generate less efficient results than path-restoration schemes. The routing strategy used in case of failures employs the KSP algorithm with a hop-limit, which generates a subset of all the possible path-set between each node-pair. The final result depends mainly on how this path-set is chosen and on the limit of path-length, on the one hand. On the other hand, this approach is more scalable to large networks than LP models since it can run in a polynomial time [32]. As a result, the above approach needs more investigation to show its effectiveness on large-size survivable network design.

In a more recent study, another IP approach is presented [13, 34]. The approach aims to find the optimal capacity assignment for both the working and backup paths in a full restorable mesh network using diverse backup routing. It starts by finding the working paths and the alternate disjoint-diverse backup paths for each node-pair using the successive KSP algorithm. Since the number of alternate backup paths is exponential ($O(2^L)$, where L is the number of links), it chooses a subset of them using a limit criterion. The limit criterion used in this approach is the maximum allowable number of hops and the distance limit for each path. The working path and the subset of the backup paths are formulated into an IP model. The model formulation is prohibitively large in both the number of constraints and the number of variables [13, 34], even for a network of 20-nodes. Both, link-restoration and path-restoration with a limited set of predefined paths, are formulated. The link-restoration solution is much simpler since the restoration paths are only between the node-pair adjacent to the failed link. However, for the path-restoration, the solution is much harder to achieve because the rerouting needs to be done on end-to-end basis of each node-pair for each link failure. Because of the complexity of the IP model, a global optimal solution can only be achieved for a network of size 20 nodes with link-restoration [13, 34]. It was not possible to find a global optimal with path-restoration for a 20-node network due to the large increase in the number of constraints and memory space needed [13, 34]. The semi-optimal solution for larger networks was achieved based on a small selected subset of predefined paths.

The above study, although it was comprehensive, didn't find the global optimal solution for link-restoration for a moderate-size network. In addition, it does not generate a global optimal solution based on the path-restoration scheme. This approach produce an optimal solution based on a subset of predefined backup paths (which is not a global optimal solution since it does not include all possible backup paths). The complexity of the IP model is large (in both the number of variables and constraints) which prohibits applying it on large-size networks, even for line-restoration only. In addition, the IP model should be modified each time that a change occurs in routing technique, link capacity, or topology which makes it difficult to apply in practice for short-term plans.

The above study showed some benefit to joint selection of working and backup routes in the IP formulation based on link restoration. It also showed some benefit to considering the stub release (the surviving portions of a cut working path and make those links available to the restoration process) in the optimization of the IP formulation based on path restoration.

In [37], a heuristic, called Add/Delete (AD), for spare capacity assignment was proposed. It was based on link-restoration technique using the shortest path for both working and backup paths with hop limit. The heuristic starts by finding all the working paths between each node-pair using the shortest path algorithm. Then, it finds the backup path sets for each link failure scenario based on the shortest path algorithm. With each backup path set, it tries to remove the ones that are redundant. It does that by successively removing each backup path from the set temporarily, and then tests for the restoration ratio of the network. The backup path that results in the smallest reduction of the restoration ratio is permanently removed. This operation is repeated until no more paths can be removed without reducing the restoration ratio below the objective design restoration ratio. After all the backup path sets are tested, the final network with its spare capacity assignment is the output of the heuristic. In [37], it was shown that the heuristic generates roughly 85% redundancy for a 10-node network and about 53% redundancy for a 100-node network while satisfying 100% restoration ratio for any single link failure.

The above heuristic has a number of shortcomings such as: it is based on link-restoration (and not path-restoration) which tends to produce less efficient results. Furthermore, the sharing of spare capacity between backup paths is solely based on the results of the shortest path algorithm, which may not always result in a large reduction in spare capacity. In addition, the objective function of the heuristic is linear with respect to the capacity cost since it tries to reduce the total length of the backup paths, which is not very accurate in reality.

In [35], another heuristic called Increment Decrement Assignment (IDA), to find the spare capacity assignment was proposed. It is based on a path-restoration technique using an LP-like formulation model. This heuristic utilizes an LP model with an objective function to minimize the spare capacity subject to constraints for flow conservation and capacity limitation. An additional constraint for backup paths based on an end-to-end restoration using a shortest path algorithm is added to the formulation which makes the formulation model not an LP model. A heuristic approach is used to solve the formulated model in two phases. The first phase tries to find the backup path with the maximum possible spare capacity decrease without violating the model constraints. Then, it tries to decrease the backup path capacity as much as possible without violating the model constraints, in the second phase. These two phases are repeated until no more reduction can be found. The final network with its spare capacity assignment is the output of the heuristic.

The above heuristic, while overcoming the limitation of the LP models by incorporating a routing strategy (in this heuristic, it is the shortest path algorithm) is still limited to solving small-size survivable networks as shown in the figure of the time calculation of the heuristic in [35]. In addition, the final solution depends mainly on the set of backup paths chosen as the input to the heuristic.

In a recent research paper [12], another approach was proposed that helped to expedite the restoration process in case of failures by optimizing the cross-connection of the nodes. This technique does not reduce the spare capacity of the links, but it aims to preconfigure the connections of the backup paths in such a way to maximize the network preparedness in case of failures. Since for each link failure there is a backup path-set that is used to reroute the traffic around the failed link, the switches need time to setup the backup paths for the cross-connections. This time is very important to be minimized as much as possible (less than 2 seconds [12]) to avoid a significant loss of traffic which results from the transition period between the discovery of faults and the switching to the backup paths. One way to reduce the setup time of backup paths is to cross-connect these backup paths in such a way that results in a minimum dynamic setup time for backup paths after the occurrence of a failure. This can be accomplished by finding the best set of backup paths that can be cross-connected together to provide the maximum overall restorability for all link failures statistically. The approach in [12] uses IP to formulate the problem and solve it to produce the best preconfigurable set of backup paths that provide the maximum network readiness. In [12], it was reported that in a 10-node network with 22 links, 30-40% working capacity can be restored through preconfigured paths, and the rest of the working capacity can be restored using the normal dynamic restoration technique.

In the above approach, link-restoration was used (and not path-restoration) to reduce the complexity of the IP formulation model. Applying the same technique using path-restoration on large network requires a very complex IP model that may not be possible to formulate and solve using today's computers.

Other approaches that dealt with problems related to the spare-capacity assignment were proposed [16, 38, 39]. These problems include the incorporation of both the physical (transmission layer) and logical (traffic layer) network design into a unified approach [16], and the transient congestion problem that happens immediately after a network failure [38, 39]. The approach in [16], unlike all the studies mentioned earlier where the logical and physical network topology are considered to be the same, aims to design a survivable network where the logical and physical network topology are taken to be different. In the logical network topology, one or more diverse routes may use the same underlining physical topology route. A failure of a physical link in the physical network topology may affect one or more logical link(s) in the logical network topology. In [16], a heuristic for designing a survivable network was proposed. It incorporates both the logical and physical network layers into its model. The input of the heuristic are the physical and logical network parameters and traffic loads. The heuristic works as follows: for each physical link failure scenario, an LP model is formulated (that incorporates both the physical and logical layers), and solved. Then, the capacities of the physical links are updated. After all single link failure scenarios are examined, the final network topology is the output of the heuristic. This heuristic is designed for a circuit-switched network with maximum path length of two logical links. Furthermore, the cost function is taken to be linear to fit in the LP formulation model used.

In [38], a study of the network performance during the transient congestion period (which starts immediately after the occurrence of a failure) was presented. All the studies mentioned earlier solve the spare-capacity assignment based on the steady state of the network after the occurrence of a failure. The failure scenario in survivable networks can be described as follows: after the occurrence of a link failure and before establishing the backup paths, all the traffic that was supposed to go through the failed link is stored for restoration. Then, after establishing the backup paths, a transient congestion period will occur because both of the stored traffic (and the lost traffic due to the link failure), in addition to the new traffic are all competing to go through the backup paths which results in a transient congestion period. In the study, different routing schemes for the transient congestion period such as minimum-hop and load-distributed among paths were analyzed and simulated on a 10-node sample network. In [39], a parameter for the transient congestion time was proposed as one of the quality of service for the network design framework. It was observed in the study that designing a survivable network with 2 seconds transient threshold costs roughly 50% higher than the same survivable network without the transient threshold taken into consideration.

In this dissertation, a new methodology is proposed consisting of a two-stage heuristic that overcomes the limitation of application to only small-size networks of the LP approaches mentioned earlier. Unlike previous heuristics in [11, 37], which are based on link-restoration and limited to single link-failure tolerance, it is based on the path-restoration technique and capable to tolerate not only link-failures, but also node, and both link and node failures for large-size survivable networks (which none of the previous heuristics found in the literature is capable of). It takes advantages of the economies of scale of the spare capacity assignment to produce an economical survival network design with non-linear capacity cost function. Non-linear capacity cost function is used in much of the literature [40, 41] to solve different network problems. The proposed heuristic aims to maximize the sharing of the spare capacity among backup paths in order to reduce the overall spare capacity required for a full restorable network with link, node, and both link and node failure tolerance.

It is worth mentioning that the survivable network design is a very complex problem with a large number of variables that only a few of them can be taken into account. Mentioning just a few of them are: traffic priority class, quality of services, service categories, delay constraints, reliability constraints, and admission control. As a mater of fact, survivable network design includes many sub-problems that are alone complex problems such as: congestion control techniques (traffic shaping, flow specification, resource restoration), routing strategies, unicast and/or multicasting, transient congestion control, and fair scheduling techniques.

2.2 The Problem Considered

The problem considered in this dissertation is how to find an economical spare capacity assignment for large-size survivable networks with link, node, and both link and node failure tolerances while satisfying QoS constraints before and after failures. Previous work on this problem using LP was limited to small-size networks due to the complexity of the formulation [13, 20, 21, 34]. In addition, previous heuristics proposed in the literature are all limited to single link failure tolerance (they can not accommodate node failures) and are based on the link-restoration approach [11, 32]. The objective of the proposed dissertation is to formulate, develop, and implement a generic survivable network capacity design model which provides specific QoS under specific failure conditions. The methodology proposed here overcomes the limitations noted previously of the current literature based on LP approaches or heuristics. In addition, the proposed methodology incorporates a non-linear capacity cost function to produce survivable network design based on either of the two criteria: minimum spare capacity, or minimum network cost while satisfying QoS constraints (QoS constraints which are considered here, such as maximum path delay and average network delay, were not considered before in the current literature of this problem).

In the next chapter, the methodology proposed to solve the above problem is presented and illustrated in both flowcharts and tables.

Chapter 3

A New Approach to Spare Capacity Planning

This chapter presents the proposed methodology to solve the spare capacity problem in survivable networks. The proposed methodology is presented in the first section and consists of a two-stage algorithm as detailed below. Stage I of the proposed methodology is presented in the second section, and Stage II is presented in the third.

3.1 The Proposed Methodology

A basic challenge in communication networking is meeting user demand for reliability and fault tolerance in a cost-effective manner. One component in meeting this challenge is designing the physical network with enough spare capacity to allow rerouting of flows/connections in the event of a failure, that is to make the network survive a specified failure scenario. Here, we consider the problem of given a network topology, traffic demand, QoS requirements, and capacity allocation to meet the normal traffic demand, how much spare capacity should be provisioned and where should it be located in order for the network to tolerate a specified set of failure scenarios (e.g., loss of any single link). Optimal spare capacity assignment in a mesh restorable network is an NP-hard problem [32]. Previous research on optimizing the spare capacity assignment of survivable networks uses either linear programming techniques [10, 13, 20, 21, 34] or heuristics [11, 32, 35, 36]. The previous work did not consider the incorporation of non-linear variables, unlike the proposed methodology which considers non-linear variables in both the objective and constraints that make the spare capacity problem even more difficult. Since the linear programming approach can not include non-linear variables, we are therefore interested in a heuristic approach that can yield near-optimal spare capacity assignment in less than exponential time (and preferably in polynomial time).

As previously noted, the goal of this dissertation is to develop a new methodology that aims to optimize the spare capacity assignment in large-scale networks while satisfying QoS objectives (e.g. maximum path delay, average overall network delay, and restorability ratio) for specific failure scenarios (e.g. link, node, and both link and node failures). The proposed methodology overcomes the limitations of LP approaches of considering only small-size networks and its inability to include non-linear variables. In addition, it overcomes the limitation of previous heuristics of single link-failure tolerance capability and the use of link-restoration methods. An overview of the problem of optimizing spare capacity considered in this dissertation is illustrated in Figure 3.1 as a process with objectives, input requirements, methodology, and output of the target results. The objectives aim to optimize the spare capacity assignment with one of the following two criteria: minimum spare capacity, or minimum network cost. They also aim to design survivable networks considering the reliability constraints of either link-failure, node-failure, or both link and node failure tolerances. The quality of service considered includes maximum path delay between each node-pair, average overall network delay and restorability level (the ratio of the recovered backup traffic to working traffic).

The input requirements to the process include network topology and node locations, traffic load between each node-pair, reliability level specification, quality of service requirements, and cost elements. Table 3.1 (on page 41) briefly describes the various factors associated with the input issues.

The target output results of the suggested process are the distance between nodes, network topology with backup routes, working and backup traffic paths, network flow in each link, working and spare link capacities, network performance, and total network cost. Table 3.2 describes various factors of these outputs.

For obtaining the target output results considering the objectives, and given input parameters, a new design methodology was developed, consisting of a two-stage algorithm as shown in Figure 3.1. The algorithm uses the concept that working connections/flows which travel over disjoint routes may be able to share a backup path since it is unlikely that more than one failure will simultaneously occur. Thus, the algorithm tries to reduce the amount of spare capacity needed for a full restorable network by finding the set of backup paths that maximize the amount of spare capacity *shared* among them. Since the spare capacity is idle during the normal operation of the network and not used until a failure occurs, forcing these backup paths to share the spare capacity (when their working paths are disjoint) will result in reducing the overall spare capacity needed in the network. This can be achieved by forcing the backup paths to use a subset of the links of the network. This approach tends to concentrate the backup paths on certain routes of the network, unlike all the previous approaches [11-13, 20, 21, 32, 34] where they tend to distribute the backup paths uniformly on the available routes. Concentrating backup paths on certain routes results in other advantages such as:

- Reducing the total cost due to the economies of scale of spare capacity[6].
- Making the network restoration speed more consistent since there are fewer backup routes between each node-pair.
- Minimizing the spare capacity needed due to path route sharing using a two-stage methodology (the first stage uses a Force-sharing algorithm, and the second stage uses a Genetic Algorithm).

So, the main three factors (restoration time, restoration ratio, and spare capacity) in survivability performance [42] are all taken into account in the design of the proposed methodology. The proposed methodology normally reduces the restoration time by assigning one backup route between each node-pair of the network, and reducing the spare capacity required by maximizing the spare capacity sharing among backup paths, in addition to achieving a100% restoration ratio.

In the following, we illustrate some of the details of the general methodology. Table 3.3 (on page 43) gives various factors with the necessary equations used in the proposed methodology. The algorithm for implementing the shared spare capacity approach is based on the use of genetic algorithms. Genetic algorithms have received considerable attention in recent years for use in solving various combinatorial optimization problems, including the solution of integer programming problems [43] and computer network topology design [40]. Here, we apply the genetic algorithm approach with a two-stage algorithm. Stage I determines an initial population for the genetic algorithm using a k-successive shortest path approach over a modified topology. Stage II then tries to improve the spare capacity assignment resulting from Stage I via a genetic algorithm.

[6] The capacity cost function is typically non-linear. For example, the cost of the capacity of a 45 Mbps link may cost only 4 times 6 Mbps link, and 150 Mbps link may cost only 9 times 6 Mbps link per distance unit [43].

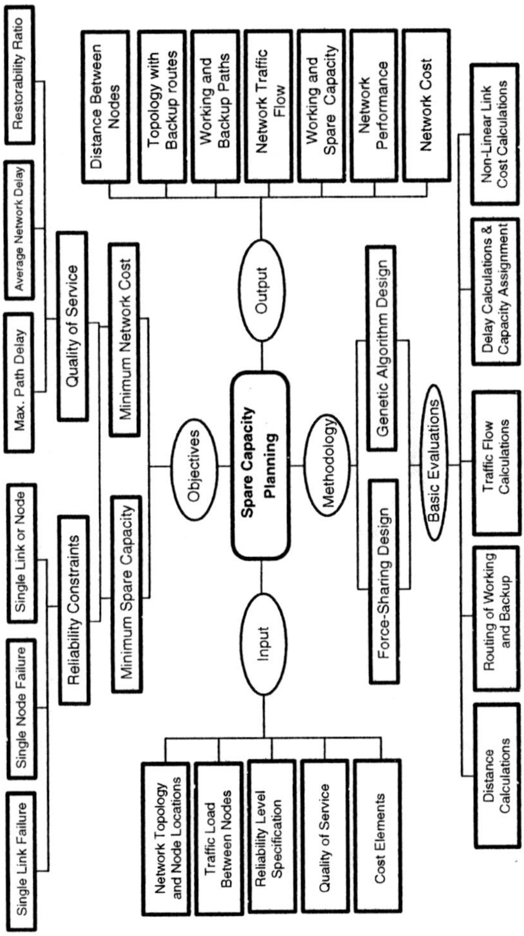

Figure 3.1 Spare Capacity Planning Methodology

Table 3.1 Input Issues and Factors Concerned with the Proposed Methodology

ISSUE	FACTOR	SYMBOL	DESCRIPTION
NETWORK TOPOLOGY AND LOCATION OF SITES (NODES)	Number of Sites (nodes)	N	Number of sites where nodes are placed
	Site (Node) Longitude	L[i]	Angular distance east or west of Greenwich for node i [radian]
	Site (Node) Latitude	G[i]	Angular distance north or south of the Equator for node i [radian]
	Network Topology	Top[i,j]	Top[i,j] = 1 if the link exists, =0 if the link does not exists
TRAFFIC LOAD BETWEEN NODES	Number of Traffic Streams	NS	NS $\leq$ N(N-1)
	Message rate of a stream	S[i,j]	Traffic rate from node i to node j (messages/sec)
	Average Message Length per Stream	M[i,j]	Average message length for the stream of traffic from node i to node j (bits)
	Message Length Distribution	e.g. Message length may be fixed, exponentially distributed or following other distributions. (In our investigation message length will be assumed to follow an exponential distribution)	
RELIABILITY REQUIREMENTS	Link-Failure Tolerance	To ensure continuous communication between each node-pair even if one of the links fails.	
	Node-Failure Tolerance	To ensure continuous communication between each node-pair even if one of the nodes fails	
	Link-or-Node-Failure Tolerance	To ensure continuous communication between each node-pair even if one of the links or nodes fails	
QUALITY OF SERVICE (QoS)	Path Delay	PD	Maximum acceptable message delay through a path (sec)
	Average Network Delay	ND	Maximum acceptable message average delay through the network (sec)
	Restorability Ratio	RR	Ratio of restored backup traffic to working traffic
COST ELEMENTS (for a link)	Capacity Modularity	CM[i]	Different line rates (e.g. CM[1,2,3,4,5,6] = 622-,150-, 45-, 12-, 3-, 1-Mbps
	Capacity Cost Factors	CLC[i]	Cost per 1 km for link capacity of CM[i]

Table 3.2 Output Issues and Factors Concerned with the Proposed Methodology

ISSUE	FACTOR	SYMBOL	DESCRIPTION
DISTANCE BETWEEN NODES	Distance Between A Pair of Nodes	D[i,j]	Distance between node i and node j (meters)
	Total Distance	TD	TD = $\sum_{i=1}^{N}\sum_{j=i+1}^{N} D[i,j]$
NETWORK TOPOLOGY (with links used in backup routes)	Number of Links	NL	Total Number of links that interconnect the nodes
	Link Used in Backup Routes	BL[i,j]	BL[i,j] = 1 if the link used in backup routes, =0 if the link was not used in backup routes
	Link Length	LL[i,j]	Length of link from node i to node j
	Total Length of Links	TL	TL = $\sum_{i=1}^{N}\sum_{j=1}^{N} LL[i,j]$
NETWORK PATHS (Routes)	Working Path of Traffic Stream	H[i,j]	Path of the working traffic stream from node i to node j (specified by the proposed methodology)
	Number of Hops in a Path	NH[i,j]	Number of hops in the path from node i to node j (specified by the proposed methodology)
	Backup Path of Traffic Stream	BH[i,j]	Path of the backup traffic stream from node i to node j (specified by the proposed methodology)
NETWORK TRAFFIC FLOW	Data Flow through a Link	DF[k]	Data flow through link [k] (bps)
	Message Flow Through a Link	F[k]	Message flow through link [k] (message/sec.)
	Average Message Length through a Link	M[k]	Average message length through link [k] (bits)
	Average number of Hops per message	AH	Average hop count of paths
CAPACITY OF LINKS	Working Capacity of a link	C[k]	Capacity of link [k] (bits/sec.)
	Total Working Capacity of all links	C	C = $\sum_{k=1}^{NL} C[k]$
	Backup Capacity of a link	BC[k]	Backup Capacity of link [k] (bits/sec.)
	Total Backup Capacity of all links	BC	BC = $\sum_{k=1}^{NL} BC[k]$
NETWORK PERFORMANCE	Link Delay	LD[k]	Delay through link [k] (sec.)
	Path Delay	PD[i,j]	Delay through the path from node i to node j (sec.)
	Overall Average Network Delay	AD	Average message delay at the network overall level (sec.)
COST	Cost of a Link	CL[k]	Cost of link [k]
	Total Cost of Links	CL	CL = $\sum_{k=1}^{NL} CL[k]$

Table 3.3 Basic Calculations Required by the Proposed Methodology

Calculation	Factor	Equations
DISTANCE	D[i,j]	D[i,j] = ARCCOS {{SIN[L(i)*SIN[L(j)]}+{COS[L(i)]* COS[L(j)* COS[G(j) – G(i)]}} * (6371.256) (km) [41]
TRAFFIC FLOW	DF[k]	$DF[k] = \sum_{i=1}^{N}\sum_{j=1}^{N} S[i,j]M[i,j]$ (bps) For k ∈ H[i,j]
	F[k]	$F[k] = \sum_{i=1}^{N}\sum_{j=1}^{N} S[i,j]$ (mbps) For k ∈ H[i,j]
	M[k]	$M[k] = \frac{DF[k]}{F[k]}$ (bits)
	AH	$AH = \frac{\sum_{i=1}^{N}\sum_{j=1}^{N} NH[i,j]S[i,j]}{\sum_{i=1}^{N}\sum_{j=1}^{N} S[i,j]}$
	C	$C = \sum_{k=1}^{NL} C[k]$
DELAY	LD[k]	$LD[k] = \frac{\{F[k]M[k]\}/C[k]}{\{C[k]/M[k]\} - F[k]} + \frac{M[k]}{C[k]} + \frac{D[k]}{V}$ (sec.) Where: D[k] : distance of link [k] (meters) V : propagation speed (meter/sec.)
	PD[i,j]	$PD[i,j] = \sum_{k=1}^{NL} LD[k]$ (sec.) For k ∈ H[i,j], PD[i,j]=0
	AD	$AD = \frac{\sum_{i=1}^{N}\sum_{j=1}^{N} PD[i,j]S[i,j]}{\sum_{i=1}^{N}\sum_{j=1}^{N} S[i,j]}$ (sec.)
COST	CL[k]	$CL[k] = D[k] \bullet (C[k] + BC[k]) \bullet$ Capacity Cost per km (unit price)

Before the methodology is applied, the working paths and their capacity requirement, and the set of possible backup paths are calculated based on a specific routing strategy (e.g. shortest path). Figure 3.2 shows a flowchart for calculating the working and disjoint backup paths between each node-pair of the network. Factors involved in this calculation are shown in Table 3.4. The steps of the flowchart are explained as follows:

STEP 1 is concerned with finding working paths (WP[i,j]) between every pair of nodes in the topology using the routing strategy (e. g. shortest path algorithm).

STEP 2 is concerned with finding backup paths (BP[i,j]) for every pair of nodes. Each backup path BP[i,j] is disjoint with its corresponding WP[i,j]. The methodology finds the backup path BP[i,j] by applying the following steps:

> **STEP 2-1**: Removing the working path WP[i,j] between node i and node j temporarily. This is done by deleting all the links of WP[i,j] from the topology matrix (TOP).
>
> **STEP 2-2**: Finding a backup path BP[i,j] between node i and node j in the topology matrix (Top) using the routing strategy (e.g. shortest path algorithm).
>
> **STEP 3-2**: Returning the links of the working path between node i and node j (WP[i,j]) back to the topology matrix (Top).

STEP 3 is concerned with repeating STEP 2 for every pair of nodes.

STEP 4 is concerned with calculating the average path length (ABPL), the total capacity reserved (TCR) for the backup paths, and the topology cost (TC). In spare capacity optimization criteria, TC is the amount of spare capacity that satisfies the QoS constraints. While it is the network cost that satisfies the QoS constraints in case of network cost optimization criteria.

Table 3.4 Factors involved in working and backup path calculation

Symbol	Description
N	Number of nodes
P[i,j]	Path.from node i to node j
Top[i,j]	Top[i,j] = 1 , if there is a link from node i to node j = 0 , otherwise
Top	Matrix of Top[i,j] that represents the network topology
WP[i,j]	Working path from node i to node j
WP	Matrix nXn of WP[i,j]
BP[i,j]	Backup path from node i to node j
BP	Matrix nXn of BP[i,j]
ABPL	Average backup path length
TCR	Total capacity reserved
TC	Topology cost

3.2 Stage I Generate a Set of Topologies with Backup paths of Shared Spare Capacity

Stage I is concerned with generating a set of topologies that have backup paths with shared spare capacity. Table 3.5 shows the factors involved in this stage, and Figure 3.3 shows how to generate the set of topologies that contains backup paths with shared spare capacity. With reference to Figure 3.3, the steps used are described below:

STEP 1 involves randomly choosing an existing link (SL) in the topology matrix (Top), then temporarily deleting it and checking if the topology of the network is still connected. If the topology is no longer connected, then the deleted link is returned and Step 1 is repeated.

STEP 2 enacts the successful repetition of STEP 1, until the number of deleted links equals a specified input parameter (delete).

STEP 3 determines the backup paths (BP[i,j]) for every pair of nodes. Each backup path BP[i,j] is disjoint with its corresponding WP[i,j]. The methodology finds the backup path BP[i,j] by applying the following steps:

> **STEP 3-1**: Remove the working path WP[i,j] between node i and node j temporarily. This is done by deleting all the links of WP[i,j] from the topology matrix (TOP).
>
> **STEP 3-2**: Find a backup path BP[i,j] between node i and node j in the topology matrix (Top) using the routing strategy (e.g. shortest path algorithm) and determine the spare capacity requirements.
>
> **STEP 3-3**: Return the links of the working path between node i and node j (WP[i,j]) back to the topology matrix (Top).

STEP 4 calculates the cost of the current topology (CTG[i]). The capacity assignment procedure (shown in Figure 3.5) is invoked to calculate the link capacities that satisfy QoS constraints.

STEP 5 is concerned with returning the deleted links of STEP 1 into Top. So, Top is the same as the original topology.

STEP 6 asks for the repetition of STEP 1-5, until the number of topologies generated equals a specified input parameter (NTop).

Table 3.5 Factors Involved in Generating the Set of Topologies

Symbol	Description
SL	Chosen link to be deleted
Connected	= 1,if the topology is connected and it contains two disjoint paths between every pair of nodes = 0, otherwise
NPop	Number of generated topologies
CTG[i]	Cost of the generated topology[i] $1 \leq i \leq NPop$
GTop[x]	Matrix nXn of the generated topologies
Gtop[x,i,j]	= 1 , if there is a link from node i to node j = 0 , otherwise
DelStr	Delete strategy (e.g. randomly, or any other criterion)

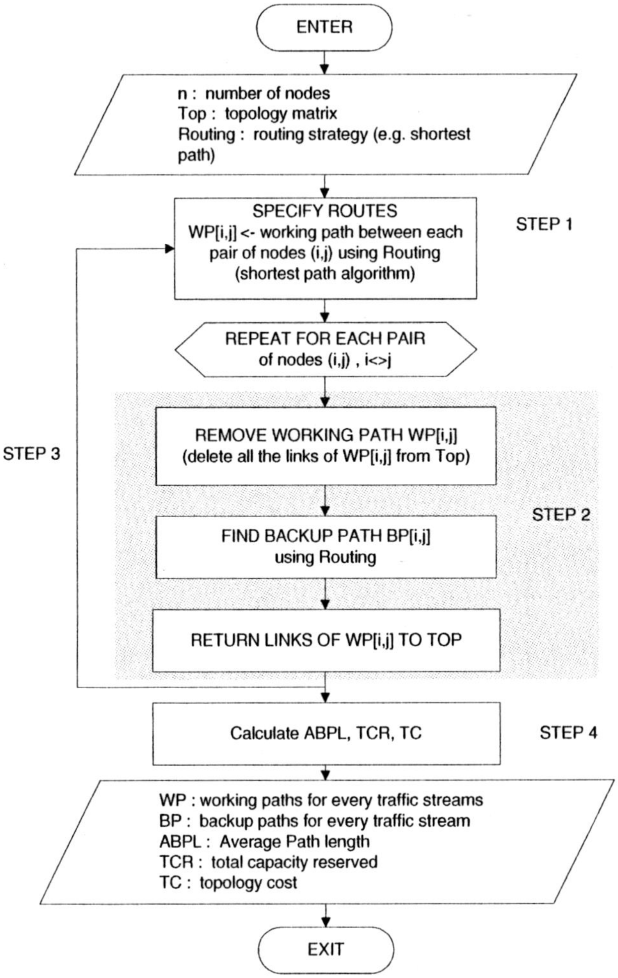
ENTER
n : number of nodes
Top : topology matrix
Routing : routing strategy (e.g. shortest path)
SPECIFY ROUTES
WP[i,j] <- working path between each pair of nodes (i,j) using Routing (shortest path algorithm)
STEP 1
REPEAT FOR EACH PAIR of nodes (i,j) , i<>j
STEP 3
REMOVE WORKING PATH WP[i,j]
(delete all the links of WP[i,j] from Top)
STEP 2
FIND BACKUP PATH BP[i,j] using Routing
RETURN LINKS OF WP[i,j] TO TOP
Calculate ABPL, TCR, TC
STEP 4
WP : working paths for every traffic streams
BP : backup paths for every traffic stream
ABPL : Average Path length
TCR : total capacity reserved
TC : topology cost
EXIT

Figure 3.2 Calculating working and backup paths

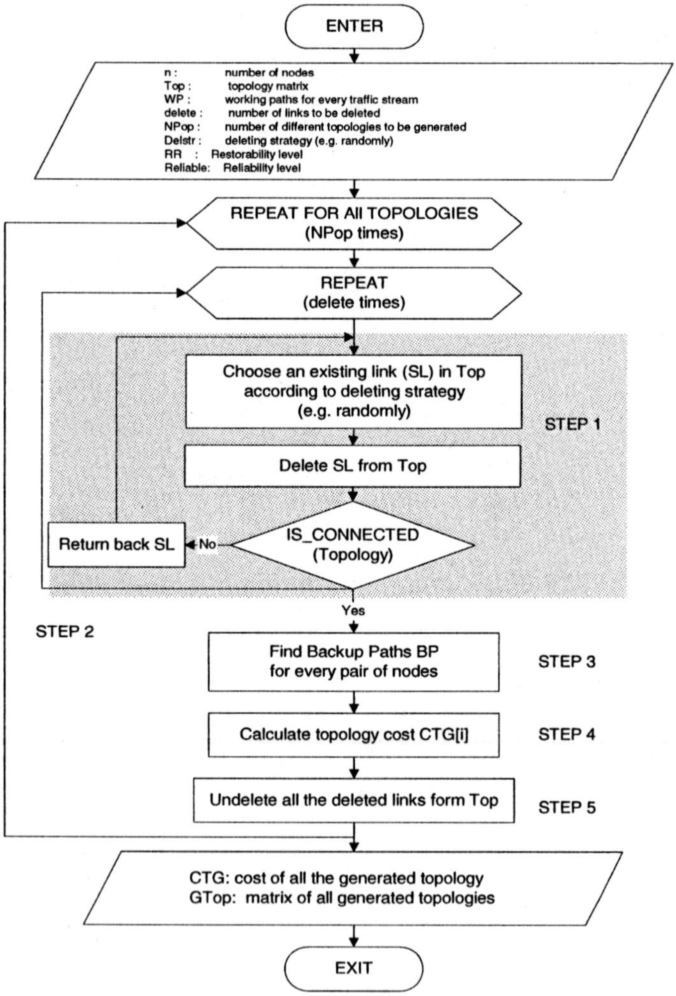

Figure 3.3 Stage I of the Methodology (Generating the Set of Topologies)

3.3 Stage II Applying a Genetic Algorithm (GA) on the Set of Topologies

Stage II is concerned with applying a GA on the set of topologies generated from Stage I, until the most economical survivable network is found. Table 3.6 shows the factors involved in this stage, and Figure 3.4 shows how the GA is applied on the set of topologies that contains backup paths with shared spare capacity. The following steps describe how the GA is applied on the set of topologies (more information about GA can be found in [44, 45]):

STEP 1 is concerned with sorting the generated topologies GTop in ascending order according to their costs (CTG). The first (NPop) topologies are the population that is used in this stage of the methodology.

STEP 2 involves splitting the population (first NPop topologies from STEP 1) into pairs (GETopP).

STEP 3 is concerned with choosing four links from GETopP[m,1] and GETopP[m,2] randomly.

STEP 4 involves switching chosen links between the elements of each pair, according to the rules below:

- switch selected links of GETopP[m,1] with links of GETopP[m,2]
- Check network connectivity (are the resulting networks still connected?)

If the topologies are not connected, then the deleted links are returned, and STEP 3-4 repeated. The steps 3 and 4 are called Cross-Over steps in genetic algorithm terminology. These steps produce two new topologies that are added to the population PGETop.

STEP 5 asks for repetition 3-4 for all pairs of GETopP.

STEP 6 calculates CTG for all the new topologies. The capacity assignment procedure (shown in Figure 3.5) is invoked to calculate the link capacities that satisfy QoS constraints.

STEP 7 arranges the topologies by sorting PGTopP in ascending order according to the cost CPGETop and selects the first half of PGETop to be the population for the next generation. The other half dies since it is less significant.

STEP 8 asks for repetition of STEP 2-7, until the improvement is less than E or the number of the successive generations exceeds (rot) times. Both E and rot are input parameters.

Table 3.6 Factors Involved in Stage II (Genetic Algorithm)

Symbol	Description
NPop	Number of the desired population
rot	Number of successive generations with improvement less than E
GETop[x]	Topology matrix nXn of the generated population (living) $1 \le x \le NPop$
GETop[x,i,j]	= 1 , if there is a link from node i to node j = 0 , otherwise
PGETop	All topologies of one generation of the genetic algorithm (GA)
PGETop[y]	Topology y of the population $1 \le y \le 2$ NPop
GETopP	Set of pairs of topologies of a generation of GA
GETopP[m,n]	The nth element of the mth pair in GETopP $1 \le n \le 2, 1 \le m \le NPop$
CPGETop	Cost of all topologies of the population in a generation
CPGETop[z]	Cost of topology z of the population

One important part of the proposed methodology is concerned with the link capacity assignment considering the delay criteria of the design objectives. Figure 3.5 gives the flowchart used for the link capacity assignment.

The capacity assignment procedure is based on the M/M/1 queuing model in which we have exponential interarrival times, exponential service time, and a single server. Traffic is assumed to form a Poisson process with a mean S[i,j] between each node-pair. All messages between a node-pair are assumed to have lengths that are drawn independently from an exponential distribution with a mean M[i,j] (more information about the queuing model can be found in [46]). The steps of the capacity assignment procedure are as follows:

STEP 1 is concerned with specifying the working and backup paths for every traffic stream. Then, it calculates the traffic flow through each link.

STEP 2 is concerned with initializing the capacity of each link. This is done by assigning one capacity unit for each link.

STEP 3 is concerned with adding capacity to different links until the delay of each working path is less than the specified maximum path delay. This is done by applying the following steps for each working path:

STEP 3-1: Compute the path delay of the working path.

STEP 3-2: If the path delay is larger than the specified maximum path delay, then increment the capacity of the link that has the greatest link delay by one capacity unit.

STEP 3-3: Repeat STEP 3-2 until the path delay is less than the specified maximum path delay.

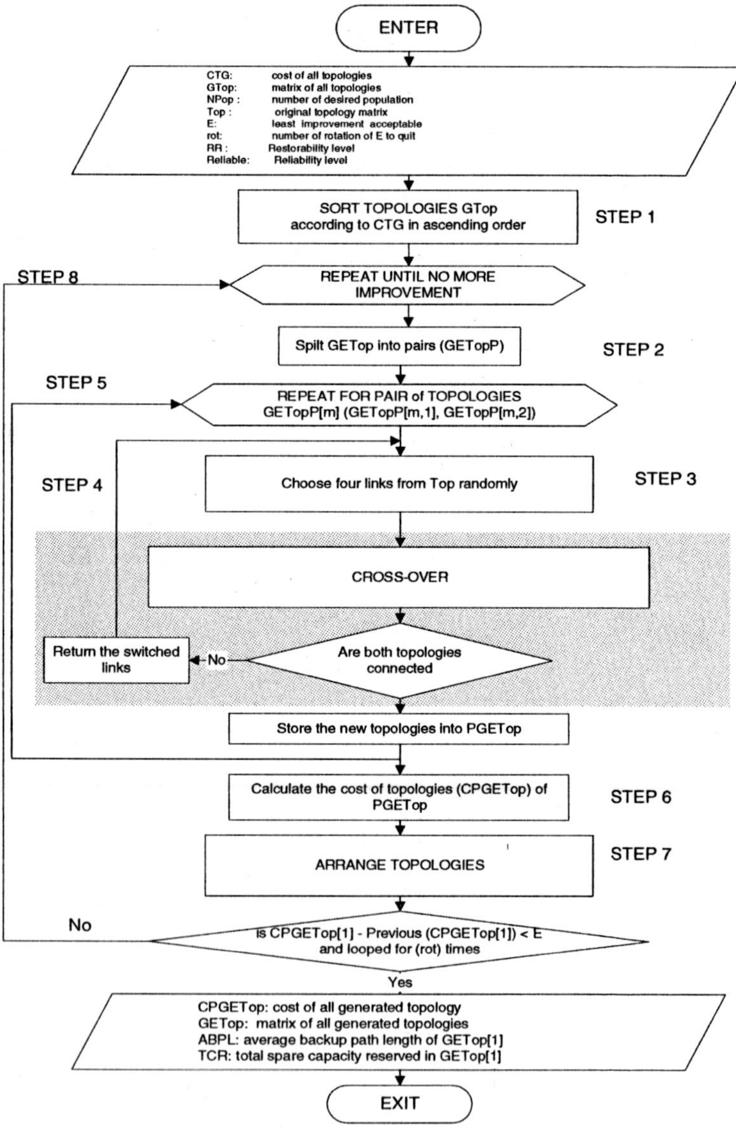
ENTER
CTG: cost of all topologies
GTop: matrix of all topologies
NPop : number of desired population
Top : original topology matrix
E: least improvement acceptable
rot: number of rotation of E to quit
RR : Restorability level
Reliable: Reliability level
SORT TOPOLOGIES GTop according to CTG in ascending order
STEP 1
STEP 8
REPEAT UNTIL NO MORE IMPROVEMENT
Spilt GETop into pairs (GETopP)
STEP 2
STEP 5
REPEAT FOR PAIR of TOPOLOGIES GETopP[m] (GETopP[m,1], GETopP[m,2])
STEP 4
Choose four links from Top randomly
STEP 3
CROSS-OVER
Return the switched links
No
Are both topologies connected
Store the new topologies into PGETop
Calculate the cost of topologies (CPGETop) of PGETop
STEP 6
ARRANGE TOPOLOGIES
STEP 7
No
is CPGETop[1] - Previous (CPGETop[1]) < E and looped for (rot) times
Yes
CPGETop: cost of all generated topology
GETop: matrix of all generated topologies
ABPL: average backup path length of GETop[1]
TCR: total spare capacity reserved in GETop[1]
EXIT

Figure 3.4 Stage II of the Methodology (Applying Genetic Algorithm)

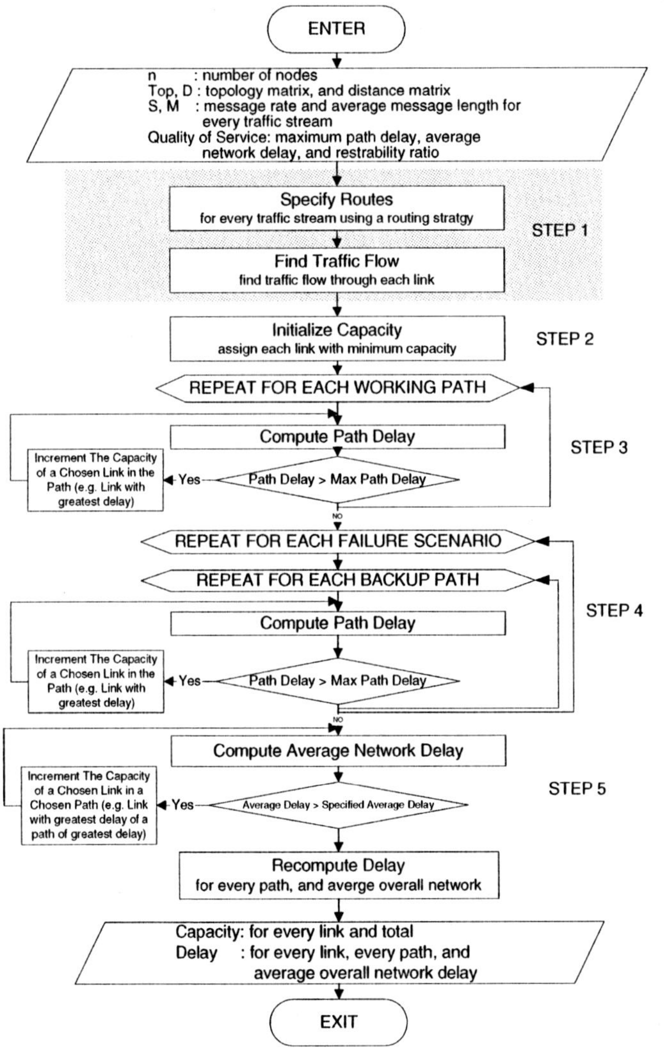

Figure 3.5 Link Capacity Assignment Procedure

STEP 4 is concerned with adding capacity to different links until the delay of each backup path is less than the specified maximum path delay. This is done by applying the following steps for each backup path of each failure scenario:

STEP 4-1: Compute the path delay of the backup path

STEP 4-2: If the path delay is larger than the specified maximum path delay, then increment the capacity of the link that has the greatest link delay by one capacity unit.

STEP 4-3: Repeat STEP 4-2 until the path delay is less than the specified maximum path delay.

STEP 5 is concerned with adding capacity to different links until the average path delay (of both working and backup paths) is less than the specified overall network delay. This is done by applying the following steps:

STEP 5-1: If the average path delay is larger than the specified overall network delay, then increment the capacity of the link that has the greatest link delay in the path that has the greatest path delay by one capacity unit.

STEP 5-2: Repeat STEP 5-1 until the average path delay is less than the specified overall network delay.

In the next chapter, the implementation of the proposed methodology will be illustrated in detail.

Chapter 4

Methodology Implementation and Sensitivity Analysis

This chapter presents the details of the methodology implementation in addition to the sensitivity of the proposed methodology to the input parameters. In the first section, the performance measures used by the proposed methodology are presented, and in the second the data structure adopted is described. Stage I of the proposed methodology is analyzed in the third section with respect to time complexity, memory usage, and its sensitivity analysis. The fourth section presents the analysis of Stage II of the proposed methodology, and genetic algorithm concepts in addition to the steps of Stage II are illustrated. Finally, the memory usage and time complexity of Stage II is discussed.

4.1 Performance Measures

Two typical metrics for estimating the survivability of mesh networks are restorability and redundancy. Restorability is the ratio of the restorable working capacity to the total working capacity in the network. A link-failure is fully restorable if the amount of the restored working capacity of the link is equal to (or greater than) the amount of working capacity C[k] that passes through that link. Link restorability can be defined as:

$$RR[k] = \frac{\min(C[k], r[k])}{C[k]}$$ k =1,...,NL (NL is number of links) **Equation 4.1**

where r[k] is the restored working capacity.

The restorability of the network as a whole (over all possible link-failures[7]) is the ratio of the amount of restored working capacity to the total working capacity of the network. Network restorability is defined as:

$$RR = \frac{\sum_{k=1}^{NL} \min(C[k], r[k])}{\sum_{k=1}^{NL} C[k]}$$ **Equation 4.2**

Restorability ranges from 0 to 1 (or 0% to 100%). 100% restorability means that the network can tolerate any link-failure without losing any working traffic, while 50% restorability means that the network can, on the average, restore 50% of the working capacity of any link-failure. Here, we target the 100% restorability level for all solutions to show the ability of the methodology to achieve a 100% restorable network design.

The other factor in the mesh network survivability measures is network redundancy. In order to have a survivable network, there must be some redundancy in the

[7] Throughout this chapter, we are using link-failure. However, it also applies to node-failure and link-and-node failure based on the reliability level (which is an input to the methodology).

network capacity. Network redundancy measures the amount of spare capacity in the network compared to the working capacity. Network redundancy can be defined as:

$$Redundancy = \frac{\sum_{k=1}^{NL} BC[k]}{\sum_{k=1}^{NL} C[k]}$$ **Equation 4.3**

where BC[k] is the backup capacity of link k.

Network redundancy is a good measure to evaluate different survivable network designs. Reducing network redundancy is an important objective in designing survivable networks. Network redundancy is a ratio of spare capacity and working capacity as shown in Equation 4.3. It can be reduced by either increasing the denominator or decreasing the numerator. Increasing the denominator means choosing a routing criterion for the working traffic that results in total path length for all node-pairs longer than the shortest path criteria. As a result, to consider the network redundancy as a good measure to evaluate different network designs, Equation 4.3 should be normalized to the amount of working capacity required by the shortest path criteria. So, Equation 4.3 is rewritten as:

$$Redundancy = \frac{\sum_{k=1}^{NL} BC[k]}{\sum_{k=1}^{NL} (C[k], shortest\ path)}$$ **Equation 4.4**

Where C[k],shortest path is the amount of working capacity on link *k* where all the working paths are routed using the shortest path criteria.

As discussed in Chapter 3, the proposed methodology is capable of optimizing the network design based on one of the following criteria:

1. minimizing spare capacity; or
2. minimizing network cost.

The proposed methodology is based on spare capacity optimization and evaluates different network designs based on network redundancy. It tries to minimize the network redundancy while maintaining the required restorability level. In the network cost optimization criteria, it tries to minimize the network cost while maintaining the restorability level. It evaluates the total cost of each network design using the following equations:

$$Total\ Cost = CL = \sum_{k=1}^{NL} CL[k]$$

where

$$CL[k] = (\sum_{i} LOC[k,m[i]] * CLC[i]) * D[k]$$

and

$$LC[k] = c[k] + BC[k]$$

$$LOC[k,m[i]] = \mathrm{mod}((LC[k] - \sum_{q=1}^{i-1}(LOC[k,m[q] * CM[q])), CM[q])$$

where

$$\mathrm{mod}(x,y) = \left\lfloor \frac{x}{y} \right\rfloor$$

The data structures, time complexity and memory usage will be covered in the next section.

4.2 Data Structure

As shown in Chapter 3, a network can be represented by a two-dimensional matrix (Top) where Top[i,j]=1 if there is a link between node *i* and node *j*, and Top[i,j]=0 otherwise. Representing a network of *n* nodes requires a matrix of size n*n (called an adjacency matrix). Top is an input to Stage I of the proposed methodology as shown in Table 3.1 and Figure 3.3. The working paths are calculated based on the shortest path criteria and they are represented by a three-dimensional matrix H[i,j,k], where H[i,j] is a vector of nodes that represent the shortest path from node *i* to node *j*.

4.3 Stage I Analysis

Stage I of the proposed methodology is called "Force sharing" (FS). It aims to generate a set of network designs that maximizes the sharing between the backup paths. It does that by restricting the backup paths to use only a subset of the original network while maintaining the desired restorability level. Each generated network design is a different subset of the original network (contains a different subset of links of the original network). We will call each network design a "Backup Network."

The input to Stage I is the original network topology, working paths, population size (number of different network designs to be generated by Stage I), and the number of links to be deleted (*delete*) in each network design from the original network. An example of Stage I on a sample network is shown in Figure 4.1. Figure 4.1 shows how Stage I generates one network design based on the original network which is shown in Figure 4.1(a). Stage I starts with the original network shown in Figure 4.1(a), then Stage I chooses an available link randomly from the network; then the chosen link is deleted. Next, Stage I tests the reduced network if there is a disjoint backup path for each working path. If not, the deleted link is returned and another link is chosen randomly. If yes, then the above process of link deletions is repeated until the number of deleted links equals to *delete*.

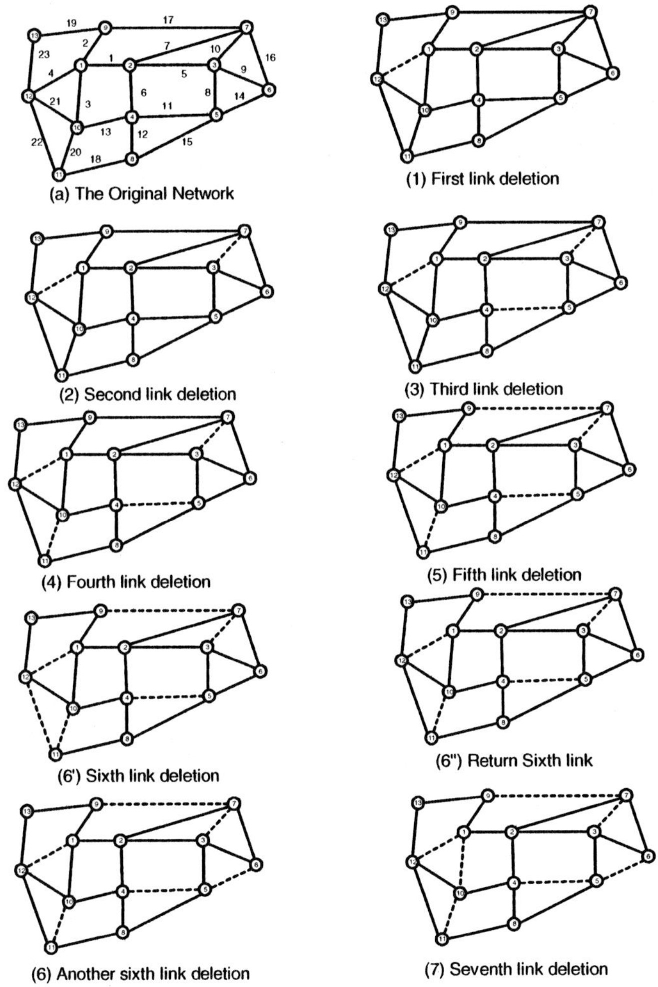

(a) The Original Network
(1) First link deletion
(2) Second link deletion
(3) Third link deletion
(4) Fourth link deletion
(5) Fifth link deletion
(6') Sixth link deletion
(6") Return Sixth link
(6) Another sixth link deletion
(7) Seventh link deletion

Figure 4.1 Example of Stage I of the Proposed Methodology

Figure 4.1 shows the steps of the above process. The original network is shown in Figure 4.1(a). Stage I chose a link randomly, and then tested for its feasibility in Figure 4.1(1). Since it is a feasible solution, it continued to delete links until it reached step (6') where the link chosen resulted in an infeasible solution. That link was returned as shown in step (6'') of Figure 4.1. Then another link was chosen and the process continued until the total number of deleted links was equal to a specific value stored in variable *delete.* The above process generated one feasible solution of the network design as in Figure 4.1(7). Then, the cost of the network (or the amount of spare capacity required) is calculated for this generated network design. Stage I continues applying the above procedure until it generates *NPop* network designs.

4.3.1 Time Complexity of Stage I

The most execution intensive part of Stage I is testing the feasibility of the network design. In other words, testing if there is a disjoint backup path for each working path. This is achieved by removing all the links (or nodes in case of node-failure level) temporarily of the working path between node i and node j from the generated network design, and testing if a path exists from node i to node j. Since finding a path between two nodes is done by applying a shortest path algorithm, the testing of the existence of two disjoint paths between each node-pair takes the time complexity of the shortest path O(n log n) multiplied by the number of node-pairs. The time complexity is shown in the following equation:

$$\frac{n(n-1)}{2} * O(n \log n)$$

Note that the above equation is the time complexity to find the backup paths between each node-pair. The working paths are calculated once and stored in the H matrix.

Since the testing is done after each link deletion, then the time it takes to generate each network design is

$$Mdelete * \frac{n(n-1)}{2} * O(n \log n)$$

Where *Mdelete* is the average number of link deletion attempts (whither it is successful or unsuccessful link deletion). *Mdelete* is normally less than 2**delete*. Since Stage I generates NPop network designs, the time complexity of Stage I is

$$NPop * Mdelete * \frac{n(n-1)}{2} * O(n \log n)$$

Since *Mdelete*, and NPop are constant, the above equation is reduced to

Stage I Time Complexity = O (n^3 log n)

4.3.2 Memory Usage of Stage I

The input of Stage I is the original network which is represented by a matrix of size n*n, and working paths between each node-pair takes a matrix of size n*n*n. The output of Stage I is the *NPop* generated network designs which take a three-dimensional matrix of size NPop*n*n. Since the number of links is much lower than n^2 (mesh networks usually have node-degree between 3 and 4), the matrix of the generated network designs can be reduced to a two-dimensional matrix GTop of size NPop * NL where NPop[i,j]=1 if the link number j in the network design i is used by backup paths. Figure 4.1(a) shows the numbering of network links that matches its adjacency matrix (left-to right, top-to-bottom, above diagonal). If the network design shown in Figure 4.1(7) is *i, then* the vector NPop[*i*] is equal to {1,1,0,0,1,1,1,1,1,0,0,1,1,0,1,1,0,1,1,0,1, 1,1}. The cost of all generated networks *CTG* takes a vector of size *NPop* elements where *CTG[i]* is the cost of the network design *i* (which is corresponding to the ith row of *GTop* matrix).

4.3.3 Stage I Sensitivity

Stage I has two input parameters *NPop* and *delete* in addition to the network topology. To investigate how Stage I is sensitive to these parameters, it was applied on two networks: the 13-node network (*Network 1*) shown in Figure 4.1(a) and the 15-node network (*Network 2*) shown in Figure 4.2. Table 4.1 shows the result of the methodology for both stages on *Network 1* with *delete*=3,4,5,6,7,8; *NPop*=100, and five runs were executed for each case. The traffic load is considered to be one traffic demand between each node-pair. The variables *rot* and ξ are considered to be 10 and 0.0001 respectively[8].

[8] The variables *rot* and ξ are considered to be 10 and 0.0001 respectively for all runs in the dissertation. The reason for taken *rot* large and ξ so small is to ensure that the GA reaches its best possible solution.

Table 4.2 shows the result of the methodology for both stages on *Network 2* with *delete*=4,5,6,7,8;9; *NPop*=100, and five runs were executed for each case[9].

From the results shown in Table 4.1 and Table 4.2, it is obvious that the methodology achieved better solutions when *delete* = 6 or 7 for Network 1 and delete=8 for Network 2. Deleting less number of links results, on the average, in network designs that cost higher in both stages of the methodology. In addition, deleting more links (than delete) will also result in network designs that cost higher. In the first case, deleting a small number of links will result in less spare capacity sharing between backup paths. While in the second case, deleting large number of links will limit the operations of GA. In other words, the result of crossover operations of GA will result in more infeasible solutions.

[9] Throughout this chapter, we are considering link-failure in all runs. However, the sensitivity analysis applies to node-failure and link-and-node failure reliability level. The time complexity and memory usage for all reliability levels are the same.

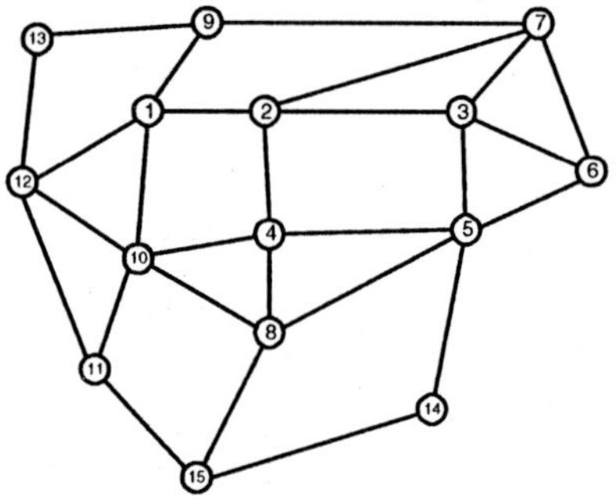

Figure 4.2 15-Node Sample Network (Network 2)

Table 4.1 13-Node Network with Different Number of Links Deleted

		Links Deleted	Runs				
Working Capacity			324				
			1st Run	2nd Run	3rd Run	4th Run	5th Run
Spare Capacity	Stage I	3	182	196	190	190	184
	Stage II		172	176	168	176	174
			6th Run	7th Run	8th Run	9th Run	10th Run
Spare Capacity	Stage I	4	184	190	188	190	188
	Stage II		168	164	164	168	162
			11th Run	12th Run	13th Run	14th Run	15th Run
Spare Capacity	Stage I	5	182	178	188	184	176
	Stage II		160	162	164	170	168
			16th Run	17th Run	18th Run	19th Run	20th Run
Spare Capacity	Stage I	6	184	178	182	178	172
	Stage II		162	160	158	162	172
			21st Run	22nd Run	23rd Run	24th Run	25th Run
Spare Capacity	Stage I	7	172	186	180	178	176
	Stage II		168	162	170	178	158
			26th Run	27th Run	28th Run	29th Run	30th Run
Spare Capacity	Stage I	8	172	174	174	172	174
	Stage II		172	174	174	172	174

Table 4.2 15-Node Network with Different Number of Links Deleted

		Links Deleted	Runs				
Working Capacity			464				
			1st Run	2nd Run	3rd Run	4th Run	5th Run
Spare Capacity	Stage I	4	264	272	272	274	270
	Stage II		238	228	224	238	220
			6th Run	7th Run	8th Run	9th Run	10th Run
Spare Capacity	Stage I	5	262	266	268	268	256
	Stage II		232	220	234	230	238
			11th Run	12th Run	13th Run	14th Run	15th Run
Spare Capacity	Stage I	6	262	266	254	254	266
	Stage II		234	220	224	234	232
			16th Run	17th Run	18th Run	19th Run	20th Run
Spare Capacity	Stage I	7	250	248	248	252	250
	Stage II		220	230	230	218	236
			21st Run	22nd Run	23rd Run	24th Run	25th Run
Spare Capacity	Stage I	8	248	256	244	250	242
	Stage II		218	218	234	234	224
			26th Run	27th Run	28th Run	29th Run	30th Run
Spare Capacity	Stage I	9	244	242	252	230	248
	Stage II		234	236	236	230	220

Looking to the connectivity requirements of survivable networks: For a network of 13 nodes and 23 links (such as *Network 1*) to be survivable, it should have a backup network of at least n links. Since there is no guarantee that we could have a survivable backup network of n links for some network topologies[10], the backup network should have NL' links where $n \le NL' \le NL$. To estimate the number of links in the best backup networks generated by Stage I of the methodology, NL' can be estimated by

[10] Finding a backup network of n links is similar to finding a Hamiltonian cycle in the graph. Not every graph has a Hamiltonian cycle. In addition, finding a Hamiltonian cycle in a graph is a classic NP-Complete problem [47].

$$NL' = n + \left\lfloor \frac{NL - n}{2.5} \right\rfloor$$

And *delete* can be estimated by

$$delete = NL - (NL') = NL - (n + \left\lfloor \frac{NL - n}{2.5} \right\rfloor)$$

The above equation takes into account the size of the network and the connectivity degree of the network since it includes both the number of nodes and the number of links. The other input parameter of Stage I is population size. Since population size is common to both stages of the methodology, population size will be analyzed in the coming section.

4.4 Stage II (GA) Analysis

Stage II applies Genetic Algorithm (GA) on the set of backup networks generated by Stage I (*GTop*). GA has a number of parameters which will be discussed in this section. These parameters include:

- Selection: parents' selection operator (e.g. random, roulette-wheel, quadratic)
- Reproduction rate: the percentage of the population that will be copied from one generation to the next. It can be set from 0 to 100%
- Mutation rate: the percentage of the population that will be mutated
- Crossover operator: crossover operator type (e.g. one-point, two-point, uniform, position-based, two-position random crossover, etc.)
- ε : least improvement acceptable between generations

- rot : stopping criteria. If the improvement between *rot* successive generations < ε

The input to Stage II includes the following:

- NPop : population size
- RR : restoration ratio
- Reliable : reliability level objective (link-failure, node-failure, link-and-node failure)

In Section 4.4.1, GA concepts that briefly introduce the above parameters will be presented.

4.4.1 Genetic Algorithm Concepts

Genetic Algorithms (GA) are a global heuristic search technique that tends to achieve near optimal solutions to complex problems. GA were first proposed by Holland in the early 1970s [48, 49] and were inspired by the mechanism of the natural evolution process [50]. In nature, members of a population compete to survive and only the best members continue to breed thus making a new generation from the current population. Breeding of the best members makes the good trails of a species be passed from one generation to the next. In a similar fashion, GA members of a population breed to form new members and only the best of the new members (based on an evaluation criterion; in GA terminology it is called a fitness function) survive in the hope that the good genetic features in their chromosomes are passed on to the next generation. The breeding process is repeated to generate successive generations until it reaches an optimal (or semi-optimal) solution. The roots of this expectation lie in schema theory [45, 51-53].

The mechanism of GA has several steps, the first one is the creation of the initial population and the evaluation of its members. This initialization step is done by Stage I of the proposed methodology. The initial population (the output of Stage I) is used to generate a new population which forms the next generation by combining pairs of members (parents) from the initial population to generate new members (children). Each member of the parents is chosen probabilistically based on the parent's rank in the population (which is proportional to each member fitness relative to the average fitness of the population). This step is called *Selection.* Each chosen pair is bred via a crossover operator that creates a pair of children from the genetic material contained in the parents. This step is repeated until an entire new population is generated. This step is called C*rossover.*

A portion of the new population is chosen (based on *mutation rate*) randomly and some of their alleles (a single piece of genetic material that determines the status of a particular link in the network) are mutated. This step aims to introduce new genetic material into the population (this step is called *mutation* in GA terminology). Then, the best members of the old population are copied to the new population (based on reproduction rate) to maintain the progress of the search between successive generations. This step is called *reproduction.* The new population is evaluated and sorted. The new generation is chosen from the best members of the population (which is equal in size to the original population). The above steps are repeated until some stopping criterion is met such as no progress is found for a number of successive generations or the population converges (when all the members have the same chromosome, or the same fitness value). The best member of the last generation is the final solution of the GA. Figure 3.4 shows the structure of GA and Figure 4.3 shows the transition between two successive generations in GA.

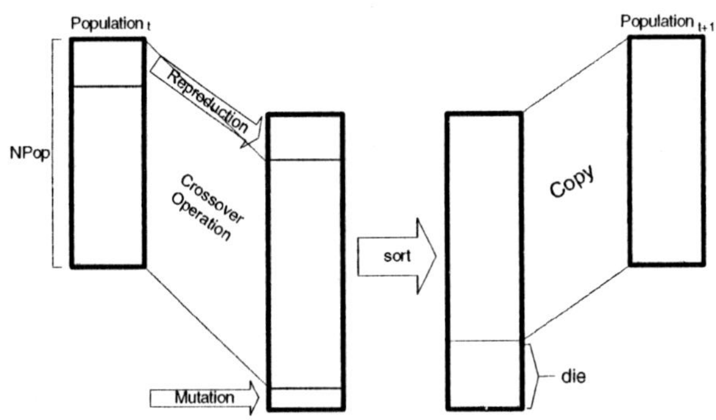

Figure 4.3 Transition between Two Successive Generations in GA

4.4.2 Description of Stage II GA and Its Sensitivity

In this section, the details of Stage II GA of the proposed methodology are described. GA has several parts such *seeding*, *selection* of parents, *crossover* (breeding), and *mutation*. There is a great deal of flexibility in the choice of how (and when) to select, breed, and mutate members of the population. It usually depends on the particular choice of encoding of the members of the population and the application domain of the problem being optimized [52]. Based on the domain of the network spare capacity problem, the details of the GA operators will be explained in this section.

4.4.2.1 Seeding

Seeding is the process of creating the initial population. In typical GA implementation, the initial population is generated randomly to keep the solution technique as general as possible. However, random seeding makes the GA take a longer time to reach the solution. In the proposed methodology implementation, seeding is achieved by Stage I which produces good initial feasible solutions. The main factor used in this step is the size of the population. Two sample networks (*Network 1* and *Network 2*) were used in our experimentation to choose the right size of the population in our problem domain. Table 4.3 shows the results of 30 runs of the proposed methodology on *Network 1* with *population size* = 60,80,100,120,140,160. Table 4.4 shows the results of 30 runs of the proposed methodology on *Network 2* with *population size* = 60,80,100,120,140,160. From both tables, a population size of 100 was enough to reach the fittest network design possible. For the remainder of the dissertation, a population size of 100 was chosen for all applications of the proposed methodology.

4.4.2.2 Reproduction

Reproduction occurs through copying the best members from the current population to the next. The number of members copied depends on the *reproduction rate* chosen (e. g. 50% reproduction rate means that the best 50% of the current population is copied to the next population).

Table 4.5 shows the results of 25 runs of the proposed methodology on *Network 1* with *reproduction rate* = 20%, 40%, 60%, 80%, and 100%. Table 4.6 shows the results of 25 runs of the proposed methodology on *Network 2* with *reproduction rate* = 20%, 40%,

60%, 80%, and 100%. Note that for each run in Table 4.5 and Table 4.6, Stage I is kept constant. In other words, the initial population for each run is the same for each case of Stage II with different *reproduction rate*. In Table 4.5, the spare capacity result with the reproduction rate of 20% was lower than the reproduction rate of 100% in 19 runs of the 25 runs. While the result of the reproduction rate of 100% was lower than the reproduction rate of 20% in only one run of the 25 runs. The 100% and 20% reproduction rates yield equivalent results in 5 runs. In Table 4.6, the spare capacity result of the reproduction rate of 20% was lower than or equal to the reproduction rate of 100% in 18 runs of the 25 runs. While the result of the reproduction rate of 100% was lower than the reproduction rate of 20% in only 7 runs of the 25 runs. From Table 4.5, Table 4.6, and our experimentation, the best results were achieved with a reproduction rate of 20%. This can be explained as follows: reproducing a large number of members between one population and the next may reduce the diversity of the new population, since a good solution may be bred by two less-promising parents. A *reproduction rate* of 20% was chosen for all applications of the proposed methodology throughout this dissertation.

4.4.2.3 Selection of Parents

Selection of parents in the proposed methodology is done as follows: all parents in the population are ordered according to their level of fitness (amount of spare capacity, or network cost) with 1 being the highest level of fitness. Each parent is chosen by applying the following equation:

$y = \lceil SQR(x) \rceil$ where x is a real random number and $0 \le x < \sqrt{NPop}$

The above equation is called the quadratic procedure and was proposed in [52]. The good feature of the above equation is that it is biased towards choosing the better solutions in the current population, unlike random selection where all members of the population have the same probability. After all of the population is chosen into pairs of parents, the crossover (breeding) operator is applied to each pair.

Table 4.3 13-Node Network with Different Population size

		Population size	Runs				
Working Capacity			324				
			1st Run	2nd Run	3rd Run	4th Run	5th Run
Spare Capacity	Stage I	60	186	180	178	172	176
	Stage II		168	176	168	172	170
			6th Run	7th Run	8th Run	9th Run	10th Run
Spare Capacity	Stage I	80	182	184	172	180	188
	Stage II		162	162	158	174	172
			11th Run	12th Run	13th Run	14th Run	15th Run
Spare Capacity	Stage I	100	180	180	178	168	182
	Stage II		172	170	168	168	158
			16th Run	17th Run	18th Run	19th Run	20th Run
Spare Capacity	Stage I	120	178	182	176	180	182
	Stage II		172	158	162	164	166
			21st Run	22nd Run	23rd Run	24th Run	25th Run
Spare Capacity	Stage I	140	180	176	170	182	180
	Stage II		162	170	158	158	158
			26th Run	27th Run	28th Run	29th Run	30th Run
Spare Capacity	Stage I	160	172	182	178	172	180
	Stage II		158	158	160	162	168

4.4.2.4 Crossover (Breeding)

Breeding is the application of the crossover operator to each pair of parents to generate a new pair of offspring. There are many types of crossover operators proposed in literature. Four of them are shown in Figure 4.4. One-point crossover is applied by choosing a crossover point randomly in the chromosome as shown in Figure 4.4(a). The portions of the two parents that lie beyond the crossover point are exchanged to form two new offspring. Two-point crossover is done by choosing two crossover points randomly, and the portions of the two parents that are between the two crossover points are exchanged to form two new offspring as shown in Figure 4.4(b). Uniform crossover is done by randomly picking an allele from one of the parents to form the corresponding allele of the child. This is done for each allele of the child with equal probability choosing from one of the parents as shown in Figure 4.4(c). Position-based crossover is done by choosing two alleles randomly from one of the parents and exchanging them with the corresponding alleles of the other parent to form the two offspring [50, 54] as shown in Figure 4.4(d). Two-Position random crossover is done by choosing two alleles randomly from one of the parents and exchanging them with two alleles (chosen randomly) from the other parent to form the two offspring as shown in Figure 4.4(e). Other types of crossover were proposed in the literature, such as multi-point crossover [51], order crossover, and cycle crossover [54].

In our experimentation, different types of crossover were tested to find the best suitable crossover operator for our problem domain. The crossover operator that was chosen for our methodology is the two-position random crossover. The good feature of the two-position random crossover is that it produces a feasible solution for the two parents more than the other crossover types tested. Since we are restricting our search to the feasible region of the solution space, two-position random crossover was the most suitable crossover operator for the proposed methodology. Unlike the one-point crossover chosen in [40] where they used a correction procedure after each crossover operation to transform the solution from infeasible to feasible solution, the two-position random crossover does not need such correction procedure since there is a high probability that the result of the crossover will be a feasible solution. Two-position random crossover operates very similarly to mutation, (see Section 4.4.2.5). Two examples of two-position random crossover are shown in Figure 4.5. One feasible pair of parents is crossovered twice to produce two feasible pairs of network designs. In Figure 4.5(a), the two children have the same number of links as their parents, while in Figure 4.5(b), the child *Network a2* has two more links than his parent *Network a* and the other child, *Network b2*, has two fewer links than his parent *Network b*. A good feature of two-position random crossover is its ability to modify (add, delete, or rearrange) the number of links in the backup network. As a result, the proposed methodology is robust to the input parameter (*delete*) of Stage I in finding the best solution. The two-position random crossover was chosen for the crossover operation of Stage II of the proposed methodology. All applications throughout this dissertation were solved by the proposed methodology that implements the above crossover operator.

Table 4.4 15-Node Network with Different Population Size

		Population size	Runs				
Working Capacity			464				
			1st Run	2nd Run	3rd Run	4th Run	5th Run
Spare Capacity	Stage I	60	258	240	250	260	240
	Stage II		242	234	238	236	240
			6th Run	7th Run	8th Run	9th Run	10th Run
Spare Capacity	Stage I	80	250	254	248	252	248
	Stage II		238	236	230	236	224
			11th Run	12th Run	13th Run	14th Run	15th Run
Spare Capacity	Stage I	100	248	256	254	248	248
	Stage II		236	218	236	232	220
			16th Run	17th Run	18th Run	19th Run	20th Run
Spare Capacity	Stage I	120	248	256	256	248	248
	Stage II		228	218	218	232	228
			21st Run	22nd Run	23rd Run	24th Run	25th Run
Spare Capacity	Stage I	140	246	244	246	248	240
	Stage II		236	238	228	236	236
			26th Run	27th Run	28th Run	29th Run	30th Run
Spare Capacity	Stage I	160	250	248	252	246	252
	Stage II		236	220	232	218	232

4.4.2.5 Mutation

Mutation is a way to add new genetic material to a population. It aims to help the GA to avoid the converging to a local optimum [51]. This is achieved by choosing a specific number of the population members (based on the *mutation rate*), and each of the chosen members is mutated by converting some if its alleles randomly (based on a *mutation probability*, usually very small). In our methodology, the *mutation rate* is taken to be 10% and the *mutation probability* is taken to be 0.05. Different values for the *mutation rate* and *mutation probability* were considered, but no obvious effects were noticed from either the quality of the solutions or the speed of the methodology. However, the mutation operator was included to help the population to have more diversity between its members and to have a complete implementation of typical GA.

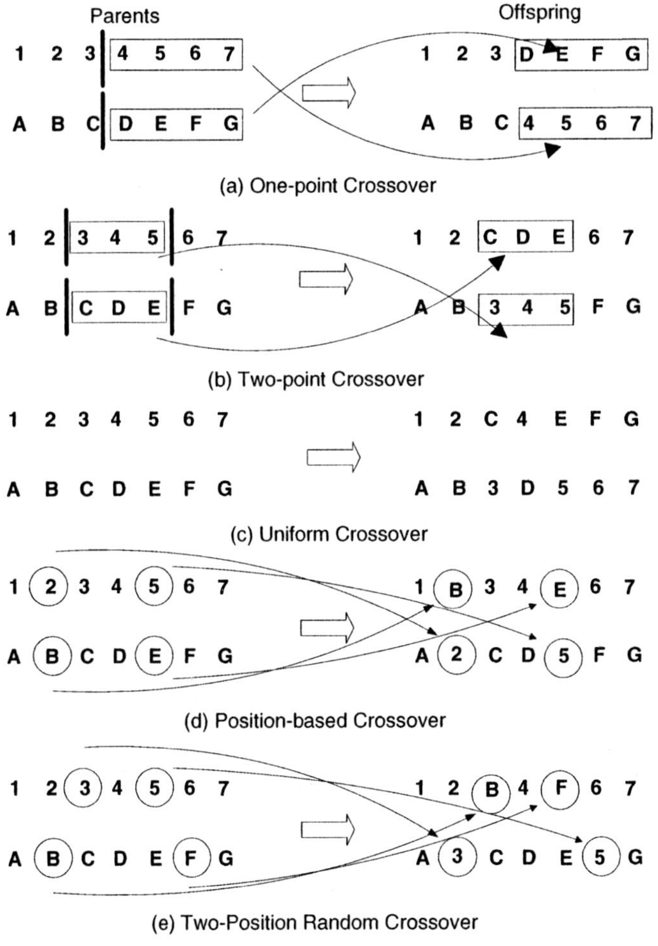

Figure 4.4 Some Crossover Operator Types

Table 4.5 Reproduction Rate with Different Population Size for 13-Node Network

		Population size	Reproduction Rate	Runs				
Working Capacity				324				
				1st Run	**2nd Run**	**3rd Run**	**4th Run**	**5th Run**
Spare Capacity	Stage I	20		**188**	**182**	**188**	**178**	**186**
	Stage II		20	178	170	184	166	174
			40	188	170	184	168	184
			60	188	172	178	170	180
			80	188	170	178	168	186
			100	188	172	184	170	180
				6th Run	**7th Run**	**8th Run**	**9th Run**	**10th Run**
Spare Capacity	Stage I	40		**180**	**186**	**180**	**186**	**184**
	Stage II		20	168	178	158	162	174
			40	172	172	162	174	174
			60	172	176	158	174	176
			80	172	174	162	178	178
			100	172	180	162	164	176
				11th Run	**12th Run**	**13th Run**	**14th Run**	**15th Run**
Spare Capacity	Stage I	60		**182**	**172**	**180**	**192**	**186**
	Stage II		20	158	160	168	176	168
			40	158	172	168	178	172
			60	162	158	168	176	168
			80	160	164	166	180	172
			100	162	166	168	176	172
				16th Run	**17th Run**	**18th Run**	**19th Run**	**20th Run**
Spare Capacity	Stage I	80		**170**	**180**	**190**	**186**	**180**
	Stage II		20	158	160	168	170	160
			40	160	166	168	178	176
			60	160	162	170	174	174
			80	158	160	170	178	176
			100	160	160	172	176	178
				21st Run	**22nd Run**	**23rd Run**	**24th Run**	**25th Run**
Spare Capacity	Stage I	100		**180**	**182**	**162**	**186**	**184**
	Stage II		20	160	170	162	168	170
			40	162	172	162	172	162
			60	162	170	162	174	172
			80	158	170	162	174	174
			100	162	178	162	170	168

Table 4.6 Reproduction Rate with Different Population Size for 15-Node Network

		Population size	Reproduction Rate	Runs				
Working Capacity				464				
				1st Run	**2nd Run**	**3rd Run**	**4th Run**	**5th Run**
Spare Capacity	Stage I	20		**254**	**256**	**258**	**264**	**258**
	Stage II		20	250	248	244	242	236
			40	248	250	238	248	238
			60	234	242	252	252	238
			80	246	246	238	242	238
			100	234	240	248	236	242
				6th Run	**7th Run**	**8th Run**	**9th Run**	**10th Run**
Spare Capacity	Stage I	40		**264**	**252**	**250**	**252**	**250**
	Stage II		20	244	234	242	250	250
			40	246	234	242	246	246
			60	240	234	244	246	250
			80	224	238	236	246	244
			100	250	240	244	246	248
				11th Run	**12th Run**	**13th Run**	**14th Run**	**15th Run**
Spare Capacity	Stage I	60		**250**	**248**	**250**	**254**	**254**
	Stage II		20	250	244	236	244	224
			40	248	232	240	236	224
			60	234	232	240	236	224
			80	250	236	242	246	224
			100	234	220	240	248	224
				16th Run	**17th Run**	**18th Run**	**19th Run**	**20th Run**
Spare Capacity	Stage I	80		**246**	**240**	**258**	**250**	**246**
	Stage II		20	220	220	236	232	240
			40	228	220	236	232	220
			60	220	220	240	232	236
			80	220	220	240	232	238
			100	220	232	250	232	242
				21st Run	**22nd Run**	**23rd Run**	**24th Run**	**25th Run**
Spare Capacity	Stage I	100		**256**	**248**	**242**	**256**	**248**
	Stage II		20	218	220	236	232	238
			40	218	220	236	234	228
			60	218	220	236	220	236
			80	218	220	236	220	230
			100	218	220	236	234	248

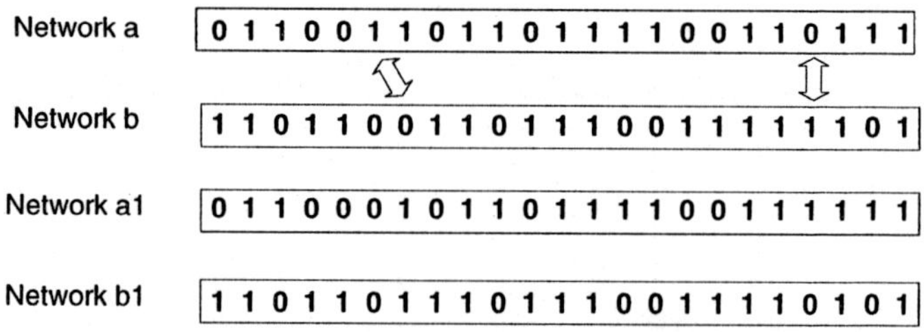

(a) First Example of Two-Position Random Crossover

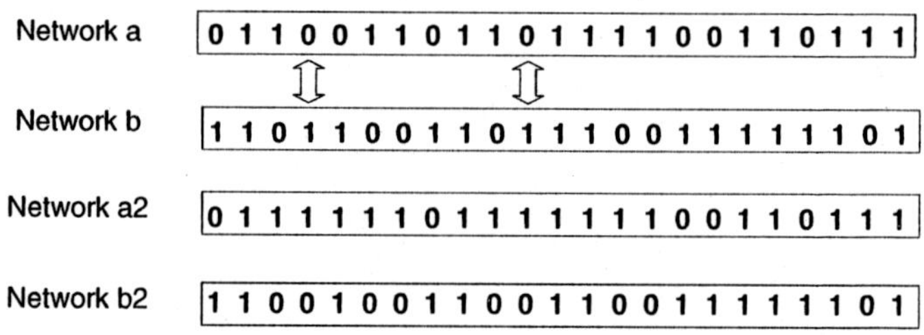

(b) Second Example of Two-Position Random Crossover

Figure 4.5 Two Examples of Two-Position Random Crossover That Produce Two Feasible Offspring with Different Numbers of Links

4.4.3 Memory Usage and Time Complexity of Stage II

The memory usage of Stage II is the same as the memory usage of Stage I, in addition to some matrices for intermediate network calculations. Stage II needs a matrix of twice the size of GTop ((2*NPop)*NL) to evaluate different network designs between each successive generation.

For the time complexity of Stage II, the most execution-intensive part of Stage II is testing the feasibility of the network design. In other words, testing if there is a disjoint backup path for each working path. This is achieved by removing all the links (or nodes in case of node-failure level) of the working path between node i and node j temporarily from the generated network design, and testing if a path exists from node i to node j. Since finding a path between two nodes is done by applying the shortest path algorithm, the testing of the existence of two disjoint paths between each node-pair takes the time complexity of the shortest path O(n log n) multiplied by the number of node-pairs. The time complexity is shown in the following equation:

$$\frac{n(n-1)}{2} * O(n \ \log \ n)$$

Note that the above equation is what it takes to find the backup paths between each node-pair. The working paths are calculated once and stored in the H matrix.

Since the testing is done for each node-pair chosen for the crossover operation, the time it takes to generate each network design depends on the average number of link-pair tested to find a feasible solution. The time it takes to find each network design can be written as:

$$(Average\ number\ of\ link\ \ pairs\ \ tested) * \frac{n(n-1)}{2} * O(n\ \ \log\ \ n)$$

And since Stage II generates NPop network designs in each generation, the time complexity of Stage II is

$$(number\ of\ \ generations) * (Average\ number\ of\ link\ \ pairs\ \ tested) * \frac{n(n-1)}{2} * O(n\ \ \log\ \ n)$$

In Section 6.5, the time complexity of both stages of the proposed methodology will be analyzed using the empirical execution time of the methodology implementation.

In the next chapter, a performance analysis of the proposed methodology is presented in comparison with other approaches proposed in the literature, with numerical results showing the advantage of the proposed methodology.

Chapter 5

Methodology Performance in Comparison with Previous Approaches

In this chapter, two previous approaches proposed in the literature for this problem are described. The Spare Link Placement Algorithm (SLPA) is described in Section 5.1. The IP approach that generates optimal solution based on link restoration is described in Section 5.2. The two previous approaches (SLPA and IP) along with the proposed methodology were applied to solve four networks. The four networks 1,2,3,4 are shown in Figure 4.1(a), Figure 4.2, Figure 5.1, and Figure 5.2, respectively. The comparison between the results of the three approaches is shown in Section 5.3. Finally, the discussion of the results is presented in Section 5.4.

5.1 The Spare Link Placement Algorithm (SLPA)

The Spare Link Placement Algorithm (SLPA) is a heuristic that uses a synthesis-based approach to design survivable networks. It is based on a link-restoration approach. A synthesis-based heuristic builds a feasible solution through successive network design improvements. It first starts with a design that is easy to generate and suitable with the heuristic mechanism.

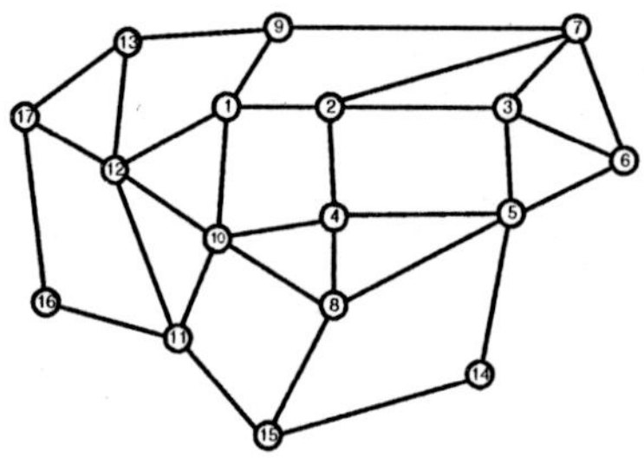

Figure 5.1 17-Node Network (Network 3)

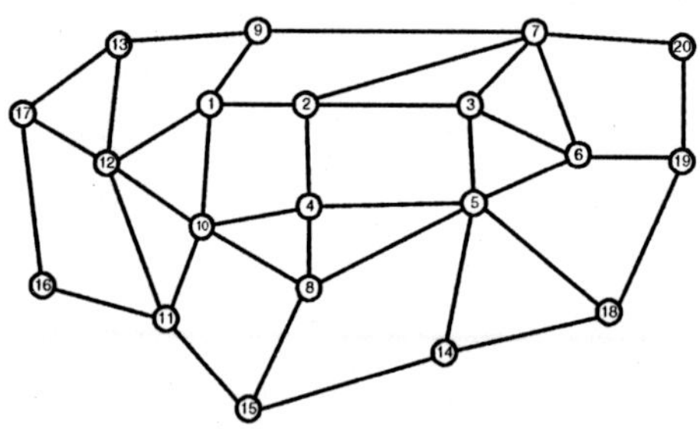

Figure 5.2 20-Node Network (Network 4)

SLPA starts with an initial design that is far below the restorability objective. Then, it improves the initial design by applying successive operations of addition, subtraction, or redistribution of the spare capacity. SLPA has two phases. The first phase is called Forward Synthesis (FS), and the second phase is called Design Tightening (DT). The first phase of SLPA aims to improve the initial design to satisfy the restorability constraints. It performs only operations that add spare capacity to increase network restorability. The second phase of SLPA performs only operations that reduce spare capacity while maintaining the restorability at the target level.

Each phase of SLPA is a "greedy" algorithm since each phase has the following operating characteristics:

- The same operation is performed at each step of a phase (adding spare capacity in phase one, and deleting spare capacity in phase two)
- The choice of spare capacity at each step is based on a maximum benefit to the objective (local optimum)
- Each phase follow the hill climbing approach where the restorability is increased in each step of phase one, and the spare capacity is reduced in each step of phase two.

In the following three subsections, more details of SLPA will be presented including: the initialization step, the two phases of SLPA, and the implementation optimization.

5.1.1 Initialization Step

The input to SLPA is a network topology with working capacity for each link. Before applying SLPA, a small amount of spare capacity (one spare capacity unit) is evenly distributed on all links. The reason for that is to bootstrap the optimization process. Without distributing the initial spare capacity evenly, SLPA would add two spare capacity units to one of the short restoration paths (since the shortest restoration path is two hops), and keep adding to that path and neglect the rest of the restoration paths. In addition, distributing the spare capacity evenly may avoid a bias during link selection in the early steps of phase I. The restoration paths for each link are calculated using the k-shortest path algorithm (see section 1.2.2.2, page 17 for more details). These paths are stored in a path table for easy reference by both phases I and II.

5.1.2 Phase I of SLPA (Forward Synthesis)

Phase I of SLPA (FS) is shown in the flowchart in Figure 5.3. It starts by temporarily adding one spare capacity unit to a link *l*. Then, the network restorability level (*RL*) is calculated. Each link is analyzed and the one that contributed the maximum increase in *RL* is selected. SLPA permanently adds a spare capacity unit to the selected link. This process is repeated until no more single link capacity unit can increase *RL*. This may occur by either one of the following situations: *RL* has reached the objective restorability level, or FS has reached a local optimum. If *RL* reached the target restorability objective, then FS is complete. Otherwise, FS adds a spare capacity unit to two links. In this case, FS analyzes all the possible combination of two links (on a path) and selects the two links that result in a maximum increase in RL. Then, FS will add one capacity unit permanently to the two links selected. Then, FS returns to the case of trying to add one spare capacity unit at a time. If FS could not find two links that result in an increase to RL, then it adds one spare capacity unit to a restoration path of an unrestored link. The above process is repeated until the network design meets the target restorability level. After FS is complete, DT is applied.

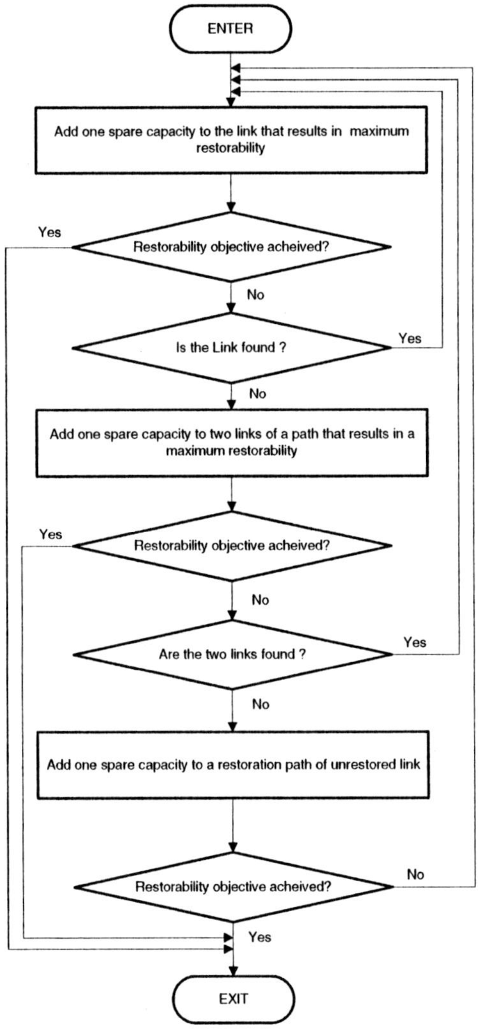

Figure 5.3 SLPA – Phase I (Forward Synthesis)

5.1.3 Phase II of SLPA (Design Tightening)

Phase II of SLPA is called Design Tightening (DT). The objective of DT is to reduce the amount of spare capacity while maintaining the restorability level objective. Figure 5.4 shows the flowchart of this phase. First, DT tries to remove a spare capacity from a link without violating the restorability level objective. This is step is called (Add0-Remove1). If it doesn't find any spare capacity to remove without affecting the target restorability level, then it tries to find three links where it adds one spare capacity to one link and removes a spare capacity from the other two links (Add1-Remove2). If it finds the three links, then it will rearrange the spare capacity and return to the Add0-Remove1 step. Otherwise, it tries to find five links where it adds one spare capacity to two links and removes one spare capacity from three of them (Add2-Remove3). If it finds the five links, then it will return to the Add0-Remove1 step. Otherwise, this stage is complete. By the completion of DT, SLPA is complete.

5.1.4 Implementation of SLPA

The most time consuming part of SLPA is the calculation of the Add2-Remove3 step, and the restorability calculation which occurs at each step in both phases. This step (Add2-Remove3) requires $O(NL^n)$ evaluations of restorability (where n in Add2-Remove3 step is 5, and NL is the number of links). In our implementation of SLPA, all the optimization tweaks which were proposed in [11] for SLPA were implemented. These optimization tweaks include a specialized path table to store all restoration paths.

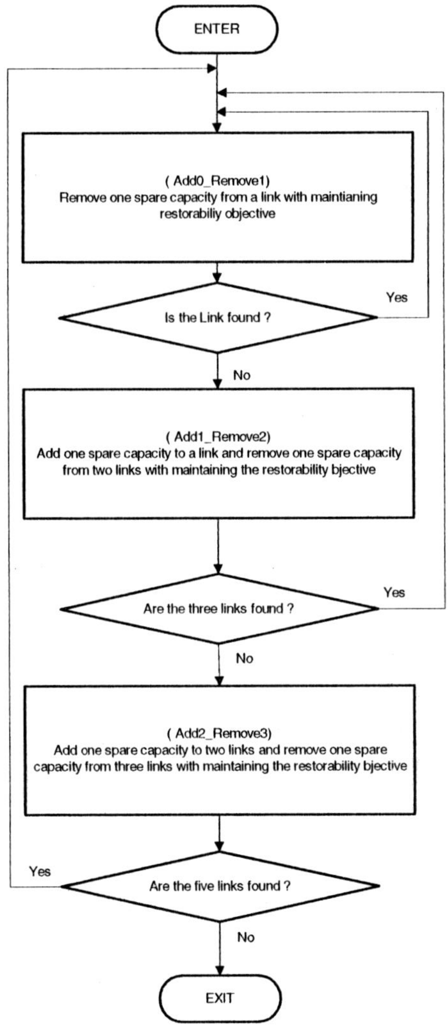

Figure 5.4 SLPA – Phase II (Design Tightening)

Use of the path table avoids repeated calculations of the explicit k-shortest path algorithm. In addition, the use of the path table expedites the calculation of the network restorability, which is performed at each step of both phases. Also, in the second step of FS, only a pair of links within a common family of potential paths is considered to reduce the search space.

5.2 Integer Programming Approach (IP)

Integer Programming (IP) has been used in many fields as an optimization technique. One of these fields is the telecommunication networks. IP is concerned with a linear programming (LP) model in which all the decision variables must take only integer values. IP models are much more difficult to solve than LP models. Where it is possible to solve linear programs with thousands of variables, it is often impossible to solve integer programs with hundreds of variables [55]. But before we apply IP to solve our problem, some preparatory steps are required (e.g. finding a path-set for each failure scenario). These steps will be illustrated first, then the IP model will be presented. The main advantage of the IP approach is its ability to find the optimal solution based on the link-restoration technique.

5.2.1 Calculating the Path-Sets

The restoration path-set for each link has to be calculated before the IP model is formulated. Since the number of possible restoration paths is huge for each link, a hop-limit constraint is usually used to limit the size of the path-set. The hop-limit constraint was always used in previous research in the IP approach [13, 20, 21]. In this section, an algorithm for finding the restoration path-set is presented. This algorithm was developed by the author.

5.2.1.1 Restoration Path-Set Algorithm

Before the steps of the algorithm are presented, some variables should be defined. Table 5.1 shows the variables used in the restoration path-set algorithm

Table 5.1 Variables Used in Restoration Path-Set Algorithm

Variable	Description
Top	Network topology
s	Source node
d	Destination node
l[s,d]	The link from node *s* to node *d*
h	Hop limit (maximum hop-length of a restoration path)
LS[s,d]	The set of all links that can be in a path of length h hops from node *s* or *d*
PS[s,d]	The set of all restoration paths of *l*[s,d]

To find PS[s,d], *l*[s,d] is deleted temporarily, and the following steps are applied:

STEP 1: the k-shortest path algorithm is applied to find new restoration paths for *l*[s,d] that satisfy the hop-limit constraint and not in PS[s,d].

STEP 2: for each *l* (where $l \in$ LS[s,d]), *l* is deleted temporarily, and *STEP 1* is applied.

STEP 3: for each combination of *n* links in LS[s,d] , the combination is deleted temporarily, then STEP 1 is applied (where n=2,3,..,|*ls*|), where *ls* is the number of links in LS[s,d].

In step 3, n is equal to 2, then 3, then 4, and so on. The above algorithm finds the restoration path-set for *l*[s,d] in the network.

By applying the above algorithm for each link, all the restoration path-sets for each link-failure scenario can be found. In [20], it was shown empirically that a hop-limit of 6 (h=6) was enough to find the optimal solution of moderate size network. The hop-limit used in all our IP applications is taken to 6 (h=6, the maximum hop-length of any restoration path).

After the above algorithm is applied to find the path-set for each link-failure, the k-shortest path algorithm is applied to include all the link-disjoint k-shortest paths in the path-set. For example, the restoration path-set of the link 2-3 (between node 2 and node 3) of the 13-node network (shown in Figure 4.1(a), page 62) is shown in Table 5.2. The first three restoration paths in Table 5.2 are the result of the k-shortest path algorithm, while the other 18 paths are the results of the restoration path-set algorithm. After all the path-sets are calculated, the IP model can be formulated

Table 5.2 Restoration Path-Set for Link 2-3 of the 13-node Network

Generated by	Path Number	Restoration Path
K-Shortest Path Algorithm	1	2 7 3
	2	2 4 5 3
	3	2 1 9 7 6 3
Restoration Path-Set Algorithm	4	2 1 10 4 5 3
	5	2 1 9 7 3
	6	2 1 12 10 4 5 3
	7	2 4 5 6 3
	8	2 1 10 4 5 6 3
	9	2 1 12 13 9 7 3
	10	2 4 5 6 7 3
	11	2 7 6 3
	12	2 7 6 5 3
	13	2 1 9 7 6 5 3
	14	2 4 8 5 3
	15	2 1 10 4 8 5 3
	16	2 1 12 11 8 5 3
	17	2 4 8 5 6 3
	18	2 4 8 5 6 7 3
	19	2 4 10 11 8 5 3
	20	2 1 10 11 8 5 3
	21	2 4 10 1 9 7 3

5.2.2 IP Formulation

The IP formulation for minimizing the spare capacity of survivable networks is shown in Figure 5.5. It is similar to the IP formulation model proposed in [10, 20]. The objective function is to minimize the spare capacity required for full restoration. The first set of constraints ensures that each link is fully restorable. The second set of constraints is derived from the flow definition, where each link should have sufficient spare capacity to carry the traffic load of the backup paths that pass through it for each link-failure scenario. The IP model has NL^2 constraints (where NL is the number of links in the network) and NL+P variables (where $P=\sum_{i=1}^{NL} P_i$, which represents the total number of restoration paths for all path-sets). For a network of size 100 nodes, average node degree (Deg) equals 4, and a hop-limit of 7, the number of constraints of the IP model = $NL^2 \cong 400^2 = 160{,}000$. The number of paths (P) in the network is of $O[N(Deg-1)^h] = 100(4-1)^7 \cong 220{,}000$. So, the number of variables NL+P = 220,400 [20]. It is clear that the size of the IP model is very large that it is very difficult to solve it in a reasonable time.

$$\text{Min} \left\{ \sum_{j=1}^{L} C_j \right\}$$

Subject to

$$\sum_{p=1}^{P_i} b_{i,p} \geq d_i \bullet W_i \qquad i=1,\ldots,L$$

$$C_j - \sum_{p=1}^{P_i} \lambda_{i,p}^{j} \bullet b_{i,p} \geq 0$$

$$b_{i,p} \geq 0 \qquad i=1,\ldots,L \quad p=1,\ldots,P_i$$

$$\lambda_{i,p}^{j} = 0 \; or \; 1 \quad \forall \; i,p$$

C_j Maximum restored capacity through link *j* following any single link failure in the network.

$b_{i,p}$ The restored capacity through the p*th* restoration route of link *i*, $i=1,\ldots,L$ $p=1,\ldots,P_i$.

d_i The restoration level required for link i, $0 \leq d_i \leq 1$ i=1,..,L.

W_i Amount of working capacity through link *i*, $i=1,\ldots,L$.

$\lambda_{i,p}^{j}$ Equals "1" if the p*th* restoration route of the failed link I uses the link *j*, "0" otherwise.

Figure 5.5 IP Formulation Model for Minimizing Spare Capacity

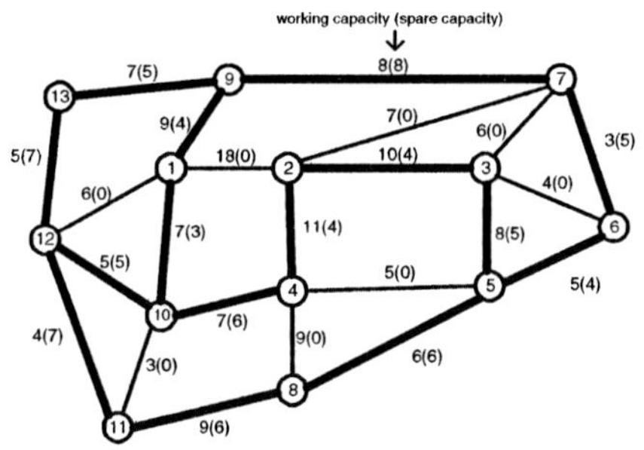

Figure 5.6 13-Node Network (Network 1) with Link-Failure Tolerance

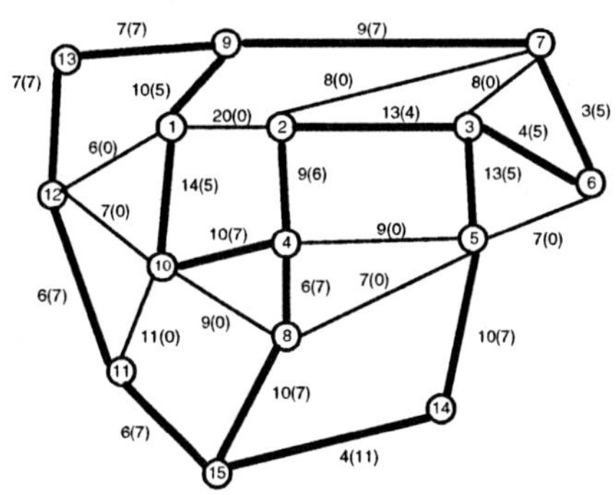

Figure 5.7 15-Node Network (Network 2) with Link-Failure Tolerance

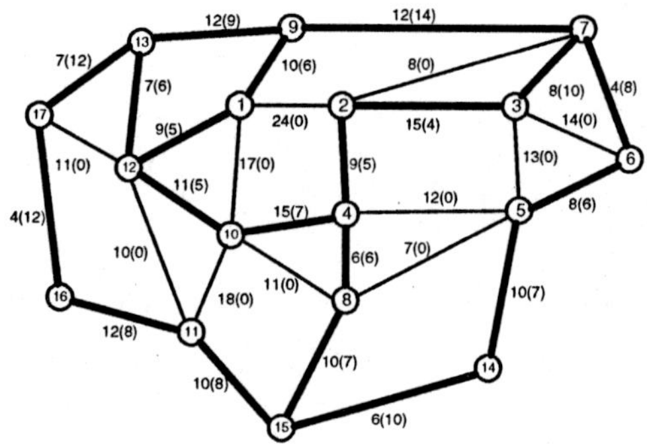

Figure 5.8 17-Node Network (Network 3) with Link-Failure Tolerance

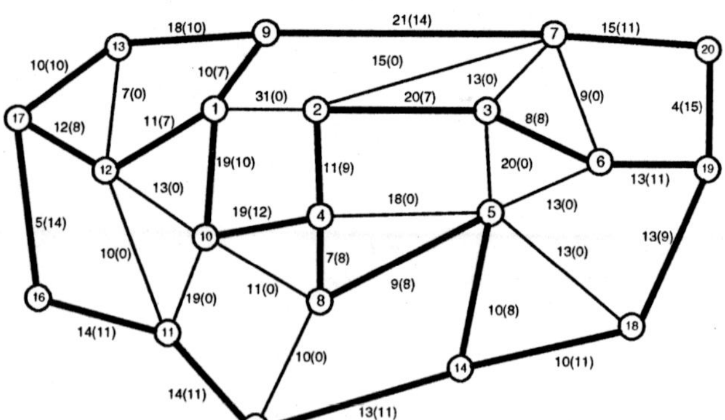

Figure 5.9 20-Node Network (Network 4) with Link-Failure Tolerance

5.3 Performance Comparison of Three Approaches

In order to compare the performance of the proposed methodology with previous heuristic and IP approaches, the Spare Link Placement Algorithm (SLPA) discussed in Section 5.1 was implemented, along with an IP formulation discussed in Section 5.2 and both were applied to the four networks studied (Network 1,2,3, and 4). Table 5.3 shows a summary of the four networks. SLPA is a heuristic based on link-restoration. The path-set for each link failure scenario was generated using the k-shortest path algorithm as specified in Section 5.1. The IP model used is shown in Figure 5.5. The path-sets for each link include all backup routes up to a given hop-limit (hop-limit is taken to 7), as well as the set of the k-shortest link-disjoint routes. Table 5.4 shows the number of eligible routes used and the size of the IP formulation. The IP models were solved by a commercial package known as CPLEX [56]. The above IP model was tested to verify its accuracy. It was applied on the 11-node network investigated in [7, 10, 20]. Our IP implementation achieved identical results (total spare capacity of 625) to the results presented in [7, 10, 20] with identical spare capacity distribution on each link.

The results of the proposed methodology on Networks 1,2,3, and 4 are shown in Figure 5.6, Figure 5.7, Figure 5.8, and Figure 5.9, respectively. These results are the best solutions of 5 runs of the proposed methodology on each network. The total network capacity for the linear link cost, single link fault tolerance case, as determined by the SLPA, IP, and the proposed methodology (GA) is given in Figure 5.10 and Table 5.5. The spare capacity for each link is shown in Table 5.5 and is the same in both directions except in the IP solution where both directions are shown (separated by a slash) when they are different.

Table 5.3 Summary of the Four Networks

Network	No. of nodes	No. of links	Avg. network degree	No. of Pt-to-pt demands	Total Amount of demand
1	13	23	3.54	78	156
2	15	27	3.60	105	210
3	17	31	3.65	136	272
4	20	37	3.70	190	380

Table 5.4 IP Formulation Details

Network	No. of eligible routes	No. of constraints	No. of variables
1	776	2116	822
2	1082	2916	1136
3	1084	3844	1146
4	1438	5476	1512

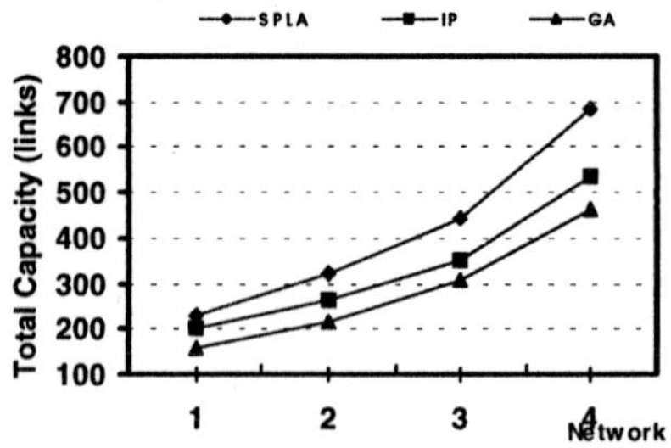

Figure 5.10 Total Spare Capacity of SLPA, IP, and GA

Table 5.5 Comparison between Link Capacities of IP, SLPA, and the Proposed Methodology (GA)

Link	Network # 1				Network # 2				Network # 3				Network # 4			
	Working	Spare			Working	Spare			Working	Spare			Working	Spare		
		GA	SLPA	IP		GA	SLPA	IP		GA	SLPA	IP		GA	SLPA	IP
1-2	18	0	6	1	20	0	5	0	24	0	8	1/2	31	0	13	10
1-9	9	4	7	7	10	5	7	7	10	6	7	10/9	10	7	13	16/17
1-10	7	3	7	8/7	14	5	8	6	17	0	12	8/9	19	10	11	7/6
1-12	6	0	7	3/4	6	0	7	7	9	5	6	6	11	7	10	8
2-3	10	4	4	5/6	13	4	5	4/5	15	4	5	6	20	7	8	6
2-4	11	4	7	7/6	9	6	8	7/9	9	5	12	13	11	9	11	10
2-7	7	0	7	6	8	0	7	9/6	8	0	7	5	15	0	13	15
3-5	8	5	4	5/6	13	5	5	4	13	0	5	6	20	0	7	6
3-6	4	0	2	3/2	4	5	4	6/4	4	0	4	6/4	8	8	6	10/9
3-7	6	0	4	2	8	0	5	3/5	8	10	6	3/5	13	0	8	4/5
4-5	5	0	4	1/0	9	0	5	3	12	0	5	1	18	0	7	4/3
4-8	9	0	5	3	6	7	0	4	6	6	2	6	7	8	4	6
4-10	7	6	7	8	10	7	8	6	15	7	12	7/8	19	12	11	6/7
5-6	5	4	1	2/1	7	0	3	3	8	6	3	3	13	0	7	2
5-8	6	6	4	6	7	0	10	3	7	0	10	3	9	8	7	4/3
5-14	-	-	-	-	10	7	5	4	10	7	6	6	10	8	7	7/8
5-18	-	-	-	-	-	-	-	-	-	-	-	-	13	0	7	4/3
6-7	3	5	3	3/2	3	5	3	3/1	4	8	4	4/2	9	0	15	2/1
6-19	-	-	-	-	-	-	-	-	-	-	-	-	13	11	15	6
7-9	8	8	7	7	9	7	7	7	12	14	7	8/7	21	14	13	15
7-20	-	-	-	-	-	-	-	-	-	-	-	-	15	11	6	4
8-10	-	-	-	-	9	0	5	3	11	0	5	3	11	0	7	5/4
8-11	9	6	5	7/4	-	-	-	-	-	-	-	-	-	-	-	-
8-15	-	-	-	-	10	7	10	4	10	7	10	6	10	0	7	9
9-13	7	5	5	5	7	7	7	7	12	9	5	3	18	10	8	4/5
10-11	3	0	5	6/5	10	0	5	3/2	18	0	5	5/4	19	0	7	5/6
10-12	5	5	2	0	7	0	5	3/4	11	5	8	1/3	13	0	8	5/4
11-12	4	7	4	4/3	6	7	5	4/3	10	0	12	8/6	10	0	14	5/6
11-15	-	-	-	-	6	7	5	6/7	10	8	5	6/8	14	11	6	6/5
11-16	-	-	-	-	-	-	-	-	12	8	5	4	14	11	5	8
12-13	5	7	7	7	7	7	7	7	7	6	6	4/5	7	0	10	7
12-17	-	-	-	-	-	-	-	-	11	0	12	5/4	12	8	14	3
13-17	-	-	-	-	-	-	-	-	7	12	6	7/8	10	10	8	11
14-15	-	-	-	-	4	11	10	10	6	10	10	10	13	11	7	5
14-18	-	-	-	-	-	-	-	-	-	-	-	-	10	11	6	5/6
16-17	-	-	-	-	-	-	-	-	4	12	12	12	5	14	14	14
18-19	-	-	-	-	-	-	-	-	-	-	-	-	8	9	7	9
19-20	-	-	-	-	-	-	-	-	-	-	-	-	4	15	15	15
Total	324	158	230	199	464	218	322	264	640	310	444	353	966	460	684	535
Redundancy %	-	**48.77**	**70.8**	**61.42**	-	**46.98**	**69.4**	**56.9**	-	**48.4**	**69.38**	**55.16**	-	**47.62**	**70.8**	**55.38**

The total network cost for each network is shown in Figure 5.11. The link cost of combined working and spare capacity based on the non-linear capacity cost function discussed earlier was considered. Since the IP and SLPA approaches can not accommodate a non-linear capacity cost function, the algorithms were solved first, based on optimizing the spare capacity, then the non-linear link capacity cost function for both working and spare was calculated to find the total network cost.

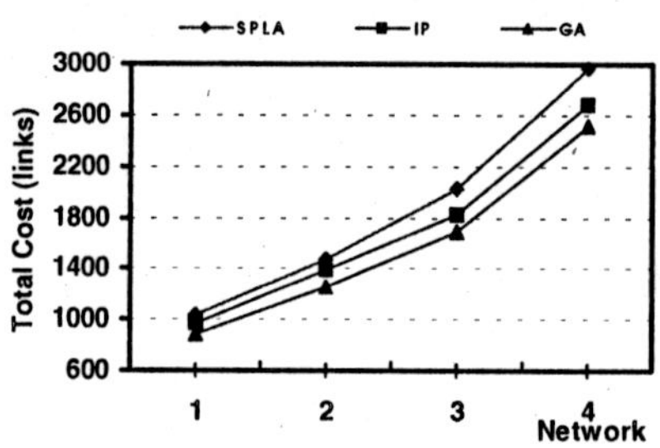

Figure 5.11 Total Network Cost of SLPA, IP, GA

Table 5.6 Total Network Cost for Network 1,2,3, and 4

	Network 1	Network 2	Network 3	Network 4
SLPA	1033	1467	2024	2960
IP	970	1387	1829	2687
GA	883	1262	1698	2516

5.4 Discussion of the Results

In analyzing the numerical results above, one can see that in the proposed methodology (GA) approach, Stage I finds a solution which is reasonably good, then Stage II improves it on average by 6.6% in redundancy (spare/working capacity). The redundancy of the final solution of the proposed methodology is better than the optimal solution of IP design by 9.29% on the average, and it is better than SLPA solution by 22.15 % on the average, based on the four tested networks (Networks 1, 2, 3, and 4).

The total network cost (with combined working and spare capacity) of the proposed methodology is better than the IP design by 7.9 % on the average, and it is better than the SLPA solution by 14.9 %, on the average. As shown in Figure 5.10 and Table 5.6, the proposed methodology achieved better results than both the IP optimal design (which was based on link-restoration), and SLPA heuristic. It also achieved a better solution with the combined working and spare capacity based on a non-linear link capacity cost function, as shown in Figure 5.11.

SLPA and the proposed methodology were implemented on a Pentium II 400 MHz PC with 128 MB RAM running Windows NT 4.0. The execution times of SLPA to solve Network 1,2,3, and 4 were 2, 4, 7, 16 minutes respectively. The execution times of the proposed methodology to solve Network 1,2,3, and 4 were 0.48, 0.65, 0.73, 1.38 minutes respectively. The IP formulation was solved using a commercial package called CPLEX running on a Sun Enterprise 4000 (with 10 UltraSPARC-II 250 MHz CPUs and 2.6 GB RAM). The execution times of the IP formulation to solve Network 1,2,3, and 4 were 1, 3, 8, 20 minutes respectively.

Chapter 6

Scalability of the Methodology and QoS Incorporation

This chapter presents the other capabilities of the proposed methodology that have not been covered so far in the previous chapters. In the first section, the proposed methodology is applied to solve different reliability levels such as node-failure tolerance and link-and-node failure tolerance. In the second section, the proposed methodology is applied to solve the four networks studied earlier based on minimum network cost criteria. In the third section, the proposed methodology is applied to solve networks with non-symmetrical traffic loads. In the fourth section, the capability of the proposed methodology to design networks that satisfy QoS constraints is shown. The last section presents the scalability of the proposed methodology to solve large-size telecommunication networks.

6.1 Different Levels of Reliability

Modern telecommunication networks are very large distributed systems. They depend on many components to function correctly. These components include software, hardware, human operators and maintainers. Any failure in one of these components can disturb or bring down the entire system.

Designing a survivable network that tolerates different failures is a very important goal in modern network design [2]. Network failures can be classified into link-failures, node-failures, and link-or-node failures. Link-failures can occur due to one of the following reasons: cable cut, unplugging one of the line interfaces (to the switch) by a human operator, intentional breaking of a cable to carry out some maintenance operation (e.g. rearrangement of equipment), etc. [1, 2, 5]. Node-failure may occur due to switch hardware malfunction, software error, or human error. Switch failure may disturb or bring down the entire system. In node-failure, all the traffic that passes through the failed switch is affected. As a result, congestion may occur not only on the adjacent nodes, but also on other parts of the network based on the routing procedure used for the working traffic in the network. Link-or-node failure is the occurrence of either link-failure or node-failure, as described above, in the network.

The proposed methodology can be used to determine the spare capacity requirements to tolerate all the three levels of failures. The three reliability levels are:

- Case I, link-failure with spare capacity optimization criteria
- Case II, node-failure with spare capacity optimization criteria
- Case III, link-or-node failure with spare capacity optimization criteria

The proposed methodology was applied on the four networks investigated in the previous chapters: the 13-node network shown in Figure 4.1(a) (on page 62) (*Network 1*), the 15-node network shown in Figure 4.2 (on page 67) (*Network 2*), the 17-node network shown in Figure 5.1 (on page 87) (*Network 3*), and the 20-node network shown in Figure 5.2 (on page 87) (*Network 4*). Table 5.3 shows a summary of the four networks. Each of the four networks is solved for each one of the three reliability cases. The input of the methodology is considered to be the following[11]:

delete = 7,8,9,11 (for Network 1, 2, 3, and 4 respectively)
population size (NPop) = 100
rot = 10
$\xi = 0.0001$
traffic rate = 1 traffic demand between each node-pair
Optimization: minimizing spare capacity

The results of the methodology for all four networks and the three reliability cases is shown in Table 6.1.

Table 6.1 Total Spare Capacity for Network 1, 2, 3, and 4

		Network 1			Network 2			Network 3			Network 4		
		Link	Node	Link+ Node	Link	Node	Link+ Node	Link	Node	Link+ Node	Link	Node	Link+ Node
Working		324			464			640			966		
Stage I	Capacity	182	160	184	256	254	270	346	362	394	518	550	602
	Redundancy %	56.17	49.38	56.79	55.17	54.74	58.19	54.06	56.56	61.56	53.62	56.94	62.32
Stage II	Capacity	158	154	174	218	228	246	310	328	354	460	506	534
	Redundancy %	48.77	47.53	53.70	46.98	49.14	53.02	48.44	51.25	55.31	47.62	52.38	55.28

[11] The shortest path algorithm is used for generating the working paths in all the applications presented in the dissertation.

The 13-node network design for reliability Case I with the distribution of working and spare capacity is shown in Figure 5.6. The working paths between each node-pair are shown in Table 8.1. The backup paths of Network 1 for Case I are shown in Table 8.2.

The 13-node network design for reliability Case II with the distribution of working and spare capacity is shown in Figure 6.1. The working paths between each node-pair are shown in Table 8.1. The backup paths of Network 2 for Case II are shown in Table 9.1.

The 13-node network design for reliability Case III with the distribution of working and spare capacity is shown in Figure 6.2. The working paths between each node-pair are shown in Table 8.1. The backup paths of Network 2 for Case II are shown in Table 9.2.

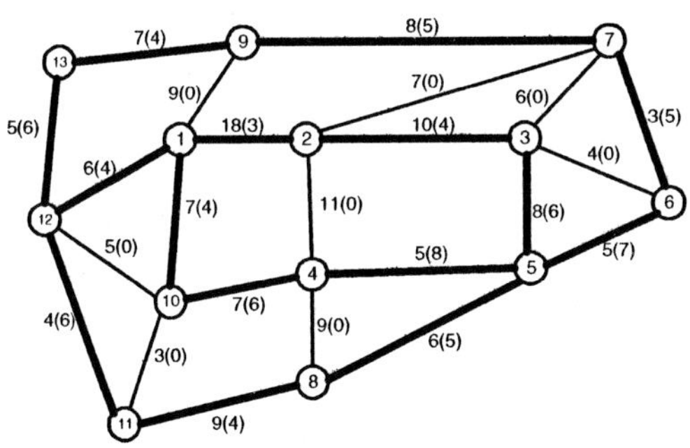

Figure 6.1 13-Node Network (Network 1) with Node-Failure Tolerance (Case II)

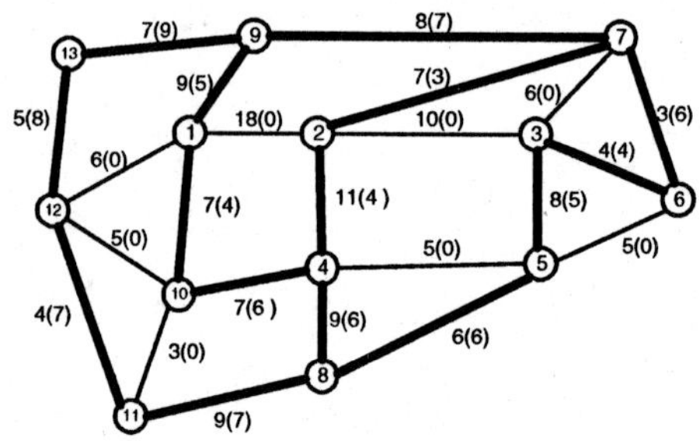

Figure 6.2 13-Node Network (Network 1) with Link-and-Node-Failure Tolerance (Case III)

The 15-node network design for reliability Case I with the distribution of working and spare capacity is shown in Figure 5.7. The working paths between each node-pair are shown in Table 8.3. The backup paths of Network 2 for Case I are shown in Table 8.4.

The 15-node network design for reliability Case II and Case III with the distribution of working and spare capacity are shown in Figure 9.1, and Figure 9.2 respectively. The backup paths of Network 2 for Case II and Case III are shown in Table 9.3, and Table 9.4, respectively.

The 17-node network design for reliability Case I with the distribution of working and spare capacity is shown in Figure 5.8. The working paths between each node-pair are shown in Table 8.5. The backup paths of Network 3 for Case I are shown in Table 8.6.

The 17-node network design for reliability Case II and Case III with the distribution of working and spare capacity are shown in Figure 9.3, and Figure 9.4

respectively. The backup paths of Network 3 for Case II and Case III are shown in Table 9.5 , and Table 9.6, respectively.

The 20-node network design for reliability Case I with the distribution of working and spare capacity is shown in Figure 5.9. The working paths between each node-pair are shown in Table 8.7. The backup paths of Network 4 for Case I are shown in Table 8.8.

The 20-node network design for reliability Case II and Case III with the distribution of working and spare capacity are shown in Figure 9.5, and Figure 9.6, respectively. The backup paths of Network 4 for Case II and Case III are shown in Table 9.7, and Table 9.8, respectively.

Table 6.2 Average Path Length for Network 1, 2, 3, and 4

	Network 1			Network 2			Network 3			Network 4		
	Link Case I	Node Case II	Link+ Node Case III	Link Case I	Node Case II	Link+ Node Case III	Link Case I	Node Case II	Link+ Node Case III	Link Case I	Node Case II	Link+ Node Case III
Average Working Path Length	2.08			2.21			2.35			2.54		
Average Backup Path Length	4.50	4.35	4.45	4.93	4.32	5.68	5.01	5.07	4.93	5.79	4.46	5.33

From Table 6.1, the average redundancy of node-failure design (Case II) was higher than the average link-failure design (Case I) by 2.1%. In case of *Network 1*, the total spare capacity of Case II was less than the total spare capacity of Case I. The reason for that is the elimination of the traffic load from/to the failed node in a small-size network has a large impact on the total traffic of the whole network which may result in a design that has less spare capacity for Case II than Case I. The average redundancy of link-and-node-failure design (Case III) was higher than the average link-failure design (Case II) by only 6.4%. The average path length of Case II was shorter than Case I by 0.51 hops, while the average path length of Case III was longer than Case I by 0.04 hops. The average path length of each case depends on the network design (the final topology of the solution) generated by the methodology.

In the next section, the proposed methodology was applied on the four networks based on minimum network criteria instead of minimum spare capacity.

6.2 Minimum Network Cost Optimization

Minimum network cost optimization is the second criteria that the proposed methodology is capable of optimizing. Since the cost of link capacity is in general not linear with link capacity [40, 41, 57], a more accurate optimization criteria is to evaluate each network based on its cost using a non-linear cost function. The cost of link capacity is a step function where each level of capacity has a specific cost associated with it. The cost of capacity is considered to be 3.7, 5.8, 19.6, and 64.4 for 1-, 3-, 12-, and 45-Mbps line rates, respectively. These cost values were taken from [57]. The non-linear capacity cost calculation is based on the combination of both working and spare capacity for each link. The exact equations for calculating the non-linear capacity cost are shown in Section 4.1.

The proposed methodology can tolerate all three levels of failures. The three reliability levels are:

- Case IV, link-failure with minimum network cost optimization criteria
- Case V, node-failure with minimum network cost optimization criteria
- Case VI, link-or-node failure with minimum network cost optimization criteria

The proposed methodology was applied on the four networks (Network 1 shown in Figure 4.1(a), Network 2 shown in Figure 4.2, Network 3 shown in Figure 5.1, and Network 4 shown in Figure 5.2) based on minimum cost optimization criteria. The input of the methodology is taken to be:

delete = 7,8,9,11 (for Network 1, 2, 3, and 4 respectively)
population size (NPop) = 100
rot = 10
$\xi = 0.0001$
traffic rate = 1 traffic demand between each node-pair
Optimization: minimizing network cost

The 13-node network design for reliability Case IV with the distribution of working and spare capacity is shown in Figure 6.3. On each link in the figure, the working capacity, spare capacity, and link cost are shown in this order. The working paths between each node-pair are shown in Table 8.1. The backup paths of Network 1 for Case IV are shown in Table 9.9.

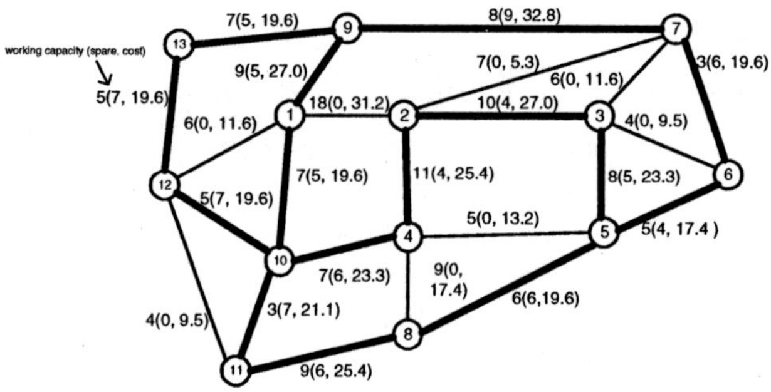

Figure 6.3 13-Node Network (Network 1) with Link-Failure and Minimum Network Cost Optimization (Case IV)

Table 6.3 Total Network Cost of Network 1,2,3, and 4

	Network 1			Network 2			Network 3			Network 4		
	Link Case IV	Node Case V	Link+ Node Case VI	Link Case IV	Node Case V	Link+ Node Case VI	Link Case IV	Node Case V	Link+ Node Case VI	Link Case IV	Node Case V	Link+ Node Case VI
Stage I	894.8	888.6	929.8	1304.6	1319.2	1359.6	1757.6	1796.0	1883.6	2636.6	2712.8	2748.2
Stage II	883.2	858.2	907.8	1262.0	1257.8	1297.0	1698.0	1727.0	1763.0	2516.2	2587.8	2610.4

Table 6.4 Average Path Length for Network 1, 2, 3, and 4

	Network 1			Network 2			Network 3			Network 4		
	Link Case IV	Node Case V	Link+ Node Case VI	Link Case IV	Node Case V	Link+ Node Case VI	Link Case IV	Node Case V	Link+ Node Case VI	Link Case IV	Node Case V	Link+ Node Case VI
Average Working Path Length	2.08			2.21			2.35			2.54		
Average Backup Path Length	4.50	4.35	4.04	3.85	4.32	4.29	4.67	4.53	5.01	4.93	4.77	4.62

The 13-node network design for reliability Case V and Case VI with the distribution of working and spare capacity are shown in Figure 9.7, and Figure 9.8, respectively. The backup paths of Network 2 for Case V and Case VI are shown in Table 9.10, and Table 9.11, respectively.

The 15-node network design for reliability Case IV, Case V, and Case VI with the distribution of working and spare capacity are shown in Figure 9.12, Figure 9.13, and Figure 9.14, respectively. The backup paths of Network 2 for Case IV, Case V, and Case VI are shown in Table 9.12, Table 9.13, and Table 9.14, respectively.

The 17-node network design for reliability Case IV, Case V, and Case VI with the distribution of working and spare capacity are shown in Figure 9.12, Figure 9.11, and Figure 9.14, respectively. The backup paths of Network 3 for Case IV, Case V, and Case VI are shown in Table 9.15, Table 9.13, and Table 9.17, respectively.

The 20-node network design for reliability Case IV, Case V, and Case VI with the distribution of working and spare capacity are shown in Figure 9.15, Figure 9.16, and Figure 9.17, respectively. The backup paths of Network 4 for Case IV, Case V, and Case VI are shown in Table 9.18, Table 9.19, and Table 9.20, respectively.

From Table 6.3, the average network cost (for both working and backup capacity) of node-failure design (Case V) was higher than the average link-failure design (Case IV) by 0.35%. In case of *Network 1 and 2*, the total network cost of Case V was less than the total network cost of Case IV. The reason for that is the elimination of the traffic load from/to the failed node in a small-size network has a large impact on the total traffic of the whole network which may result in a design that has less total network cost for Case V than Case IV. The average network cost of link-and-node-failure design (Case VI) was higher than the average of link-failure design (Case IV) by only 3.3%. The average path length of Case V was shorter than Case IV by 0.245 hops, while the average path length of Case VI was longer than Case V by 0.2525 hops. The average path length of each case depends on the network design (the final topology of the solution) generated by the methodology.

As a comparison between the total cost of the network (for both working and spare capacity) of spare capacity optimization and network cost optimization, the four networks were solved based on spare capacity optimization criteria, then the cost of the final solution for each network was calculated using the non-linear capacity cost function. The total network cost of Case I for *Network 1,2,3, and 4* were 909.2, 1305.8, 1762.4, and 2581.6, respectively. The total network cost of the solutions of spare capacity optimization were higher than the solutions of network cost optimization by 2.9%, 3.5 %, 3.8%. and 2.6 %, for Network 1,2,3, and 4, respectively.

6.3 Non-Symmetrical Traffic Load

So far in all the applications of the proposed methodology, the traffic load is considered to be symmetric. In other words, the traffic demand between node 1 and node 7 (in the 13-node network shown in Figure 4.1(a)) is considered to 1 MB, the same as the traffic demand between node 7 and node 1. In a more general case, these traffic loads need not be the same, in which case it is called a non-symmetrical traffic load. In this section, the proposed methodology was applied on the 13-node network (shown in Figure 4.1(a)) with different non-symmetrical traffic loads. The traffic load between each node-pair is considered to be a discrete uniformly distributed random number between 1 and 3. The traffic loads between each node-pair are shown in Table 6.5.

The output network design of the proposed methodology for the non-symmetrical traffic rate and link-failure tolerance is shown in Figure 6.4 with the distribution of working and spare capacity of each link. The backup paths of the network design are shown in Table 10.1. The total spare capacity of the network design is 358, while the working capacity is 662.

Table 6.5 Non-Symmetrical Traffic Rate for Each Node-pair for Network 1

From / To	1	2	3	4	5	6	7	8	9	10	11	12	13
1	0	2	3	3	1	1	2	3	1	1	2	1	3
2	2	0	1	1	3	2	3	3	3	2	3	1	2
3	1	3	0	2	1	3	3	2	2	2	3	2	3
4	2	2	2	0	2	1	3	3	2	3	3	2	3
5	3	3	2	3	0	1	3	3	2	1	1	3	2
6	3	3	2	3	3	0	1	1	2	2	1	2	3
7	2	2	2	3	2	3	0	1	2	3	3	3	1
8	2	3	3	1	1	3	3	0	1	1	2	1	1
9	2	2	3	2	1	2	2	2	0	3	3	3	1
10	2	2	2	2	2	1	1	2	1	0	1	3	1
11	3	1	2	2	2	2	1	2	2	1	0	2	1
12	3	1	3	1	2	1	3	2	1	3	2	0	1
13	2	1	3	2	1	1	3	1	2	3	2	3	0

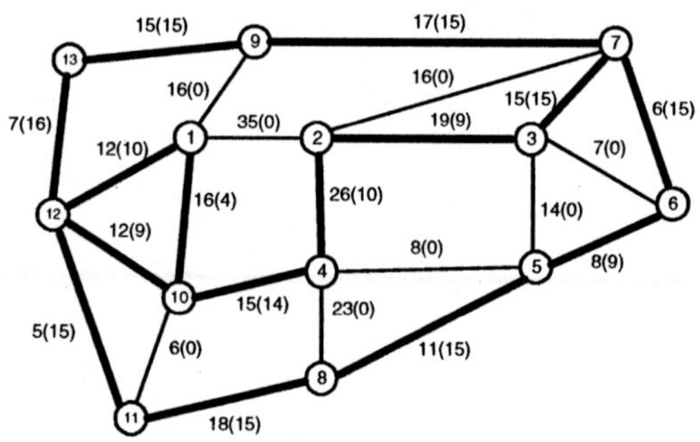

Figure 6.4 13-Node Network with Non-Symmetrical Traffic Rate

The proposed methodology was applied on the 13-node network using different non-symmetrical traffic loads. Five cases of different traffic loads were considered. The traffic rate was taken as a random number between 1 and 2 for each node-pair for the first case. For the second case, the traffic rate was taken as a random number between 1 and 3 for each node-pair. For the third case, the traffic rate was taken as a random number between 1 and 4 for each node-pair. For the fourth case, the traffic rate was taken as a random number between 1 and 5 for each node-pair. And for the fifth case, the traffic rate was taken as a random number between 1 and 6 for each node-pair. All the traffic rates were considered to be discrete random numbers with uniform distribution. Table 6.6 shows a summary of the network design generated by the proposed methodology for each of the five cases mentioned above. The working capacity, spare capacity, and network redundancy for each case are shown in the table.

Table 6.6 13-Node Network with Non-Symmetrical Traffic Rate

Non-Symmetrical Traffic Rate	1-2	1-3	1-4	1-5	1-6
Working Capacity	482	662	868	946	1129
Spare Capacity	295	358	495	553	664
Redundancy %	61.29	54.08	57.03	58.46	58.81

The 13-node network with non-symmetrical traffic load shown in Table 6.5 was solved using the IP approach (discussed in Section 5.2). This is to show how good the proposed methodology is in comparison to the optimal solution based on link restoration. The spare capacity of IP solution was 439 (which is 66.31% network redundancy), while the spare capacity of the solution of the proposed methodology was 358 (which is 54.08% network redundancy). The total network cost (for both working and backup capacity) of the IP solution is 7.6% (cost of 1927.5) higher than the total network cost of the proposed methodology (cost of 1791.3). This shows that the proposed methodology performs even much better than the IP approach with respect to non-symmetrical traffic rate.

6.4 Network Design Satisfying QoS Constraints

The two main design objectives in our methodology (as shown in Figure 3.1) are satisfying reliability constraints and QoS constraints. Satisfying the reliability constraints is what we have dealt with so far in the dissertation. Designing a survivable network that satisfies QoS constraints is presented in this section. The QoS constraints deal with many non-linear variables which makes designing a survivable network that satisfies QoS variables by the IP approach impossible. QoS variables considered in this section include a number of delay variables. The delay variables are extremely important in designing packet switch networks (e.g. the Internet) [19]. These delay variables include:

- Delay due to link congestion (queuing delay)
- Delay due to routing path length (propagation delay)
- Delay due to the capacity of the link (transmission delay)

The delay constraints include maximum path delay and overall network delay. Each path delay in the network design should satisfy the maximum path delay. In addition, the delay in the network as whole should satisfy the overall network delay constraint. The delay in each link is calculated using the following equation:

Link Delay = Queuing delay + Transmission delay + Propagation delay

Path Delay = Σ link delay (for each link in the path)

The exact equations for calculating link delay, path delay, and overall network delay are shown in Table 3.3, assuming an M/M/1 queuing model for each link. The capacity assignments for both the working and spare capacity are shown in Figure 3.5.

The proposed methodology was applied on the 13-node network shown in Figure 4.1(a), with the following QoS input parameters:

- Maximum path delay = 25 msec.
- Overall network delay = 20 msec.
- Traffic rate = 100 message/sec between each node-pair
- Average Message Length = 10 Kbits[12]

In addition to the other input variables:

- *delete* = 7
- population size (NPop) = 100
- rot = 10
- $\xi = 0.0001$
- traffic rate = 1 traffic demand between each node-pair
- Optimization: minimizing spare capacity

The output network design that satisfies the QoS variables is shown in Figure 6.5. Each link in Figure 6.5 has four numbers. These four numbers are working capacity, spare capacity, link length in kilometers, and delay of the link in milliseconds, respectively. The working capacity of the network design of Figure 6.5 is 408 and the spare capacity is 204. The network redundancy is 50.0%. The network design of Figure 6.5 satisfies the QoS constraints in both the normal condition and in case of any link failure. Note that in this case, the working capacity that satisfies the QoS constraint is

408, while it was 324 without considering the QoS constraints. The backup paths of the network design are shown in Table 10.2. The path delay of the working paths is shown in Table 6.7. The average path delay of the working paths is 9.92 msec. The path delay of the backup paths is shown in Table 6.8. The average path delay of the backup paths is 14.85 msec.

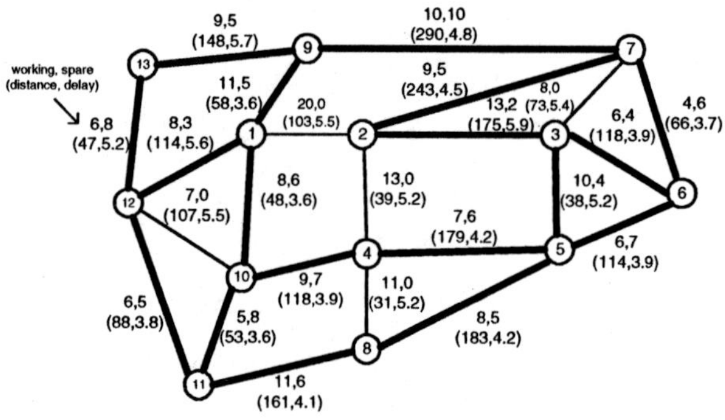

Figure 6.5 The 13-Node Network with Link-Failure Tolerance that Satisfy QoS Constraints

[12] The message size in TCP (the Internet) can range in size from 556 bytes to 64Kbytes [19]. The average message length in this example is taken to be 10 Kbits which is equal to 1250 bytes.

Table 6.7 Path Delay of Working Paths Between Each Node-Pair

From / To	1	2	3	4	5	6	7	8	9	10	11	12	13
1	0.0	5.5	11.4	10.7	16.6	15.3	10.1	15.9	3.6	3.6	7.2	5.6	9.4
2	5.5	0.0	5.9	5.2	11.1	9.8	4.5	10.4	9.1	9.1	14.5	11.1	14.9
3	11.4	5.9	0.0	11.1	5.2	3.9	5.4	9.4	10.1	15.0	13.6	17.0	15.9
4	10.7	5.2	11.1	0.0	4.2	8.1	9.7	5.2	14.3	3.9	9.3	9.5	14.7
5	16.6	11.1	5.2	4.2	0.0	3.9	10.6	4.2	15.3	8.2	8.4	13.7	21.1
6	15.3	9.8	3.9	8.1	3.9	0.0	3.7	8.2	8.4	12.1	12.3	20.9	14.2
7	10.1	4.5	5.4	9.7	10.6	3.7	0.0	14.9	4.8	13.6	19.0	15.6	10.5
8	15.9	10.4	9.4	5.2	4.2	8.2	14.9	0.0	19.5	9.1	4.1	7.9	13.1
9	3.6	9.1	10.1	14.3	15.3	8.4	4.8	19.5	0.0	7.2	10.8	9.2	5.7
10	3.6	9.1	15.0	3.9	8.2	12.1	13.6	9.1	7.2	0.0	3.6	5.5	10.8
11	7.2	14.5	13.6	9.3	8.4	12.3	19.0	4.1	10.8	3.6	0.0	3.8	9.0
12	5.6	11.1	17.0	9.5	13.7	20.9	15.6	7.9	9.2	5.5	3.8	0.0	5.2
13	9.4	14.9	15.9	14.7	21.1	14.2	10.5	13.1	5.7	10.8	9.0	5.2	0.0

Table 6.8 Path Delay of Backup Paths Between Each Node-Pair

From / To	1	2	3	4	5	6	7	8	9	10	11	12	13
1	0.0	13.0	16.9	7.5	11.7	12.1	8.4	11.3	16.5	12.9	9.3	10.9	10.8
2	13.0	0.0	12.1	15.3	12.1	8.2	13.5	15.3	9.3	19.2	20.1	20.3	23.8
3	16.9	12.1	0.0	9.4	7.8	9.1	10.4	23.7	20.5	13.3	19.6	17.4	22.6
4	7.5	15.3	9.4	0.0	15.9	19.6	11.8	8.5	16.6	16.2	7.5	16.4	22.3
5	11.7	12.1	7.8	15.9	0.0	9.1	7.6	15.9	15.3	12.0	11.8	12.2	17.4
6	12.1	8.2	9.1	19.6	9.1	0.0	14.3	23.4	19.3	15.6	19.2	16.1	21.3
7	8.4	13.5	10.4	11.8	7.6	14.3	0.0	11.8	22.9	15.7	15.6	15.8	25.0
8	11.3	15.3	23.7	8.5	15.9	23.4	11.8	0.0	16.6	7.7	16.0	21.5	22.3
9	16.5	9.3	20.5	16.6	15.3	19.3	22.9	16.6	0.0	18.3	14.7	11.0	14.4
10	12.9	19.2	13.3	16.2	12.0	15.6	15.7	7.7	18.3	0.0	12.9	9.1	12.9
11	9.3	20.1	19.6	7.5	11.7	19.2	15.6	16.0	14.7	12.9	0.0	12.7	16.5
12	10.9	20.3	17.4	16.4	12.2	16.1	15.8	21.5	11.0	9.1	12.7	0.0	14.9
13	10.8	23.8	22.6	22.3	17.4	21.3	25.0	22.3	14.4	12.9	16.5	14.9	0.0

The proposed methodology was applied in the 13-node network with different values for maximum path delay and overall network delay. Table 6.9 shows nine cases of the network design with different maximum path delay and overall network delay. The table shows the working and spare capacity for each case in addition to the network redundancy of the network design.

In this section, the methodology was applied to design survivable networks that satisfy QoS constraints, unlike the previous IP approach which is not capable of incorporating non-linear variables (such as QoS variables). The delay variables are very essential in designing packet switching networks.

Table 6.9 13-Node Network with QoS Constraints

Case	1	2	3	4	5	6	7	8
Max Path Delay(ms)	20	25	30	35	40	45	50	50
Overall Network Delay (ms)	15	20	20	20	25	20	35	40
Working Capacity	426	408	394	384	378	370	370	370
Spare Capacity	214	204	202	192	180	186	180	176
Redundancy %	50.23	50.0	51.27	50.0	47.62	50.27	48.65	47.57

6.5 Scalability of the Proposed Methodology

The proposed methodology was applied to a number of networks ranging from a 13-node network to a 70-node network to show its scalability. Table 6.10 shows a summary of nine networks with different sizes. The network topologies for Network 1, 2,

3, 4, 5, 6, 7, 8, and 9 are shown in Figure 4.1(a), Figure 4.2, Figure 5.1, Figure 5.2, Figure 11.1, Figure 11.2, Figure 11.3, Figure 11.4, and Figure 11.5, respectively. Table 6.10 shows the results of the methodology, for link-failure tolerance and spare capacity optimization, on each of the nine networks. It shows the working and spare capacity for both Stage I and Stage II. In addition, the time it takes to solve each network is shown.

Figure 6.6 shows the curve-fitting of the execution time for the proposed methodology. The application of the methodology is conducted using a Pentium II 400 MHz PC with 128 MB RAM running Windows NT 4.0.

Table 6.10 Summary of the Large-Size Networks Used for Scalability

Network	1	2	3	4	5	6	7	8	9
No. of Nodes	13	15	17	20	30	40	50	60	70
No. of Links	23	27	31	37	52	66	80	96	112
Avg. Network Degree	3.54	3.60	3.65	3.70	3.47	3.3	3.2	3.2	3.2
No. of Pt-to-Pt demands	78	105	136	190	435	780	1225	1770	2415
Total Amount of Demands	156	210	272	380	870	1560	2450	3540	4830
delete	7	8	9	11	13	14	18	21	25
Working Capacity	324	464	640	966	2806	6074	10912	17336	25610
Spare Capacity (Stage I)	176	256	346	498	1570	3074	6188	9194	12481
Spare Capacity	158	218	310	460	1410	2968	6074	8966	12134
Stage I Time (sec)	2	2	2	4	15	32	96	198	463
Stage II Time (sec)	28	36	42	89	236	458	882	1862	3050
Total Time (min)	0.48	0.65	0.73	1.383	4.15	8.167	16.3	34.3	58.72

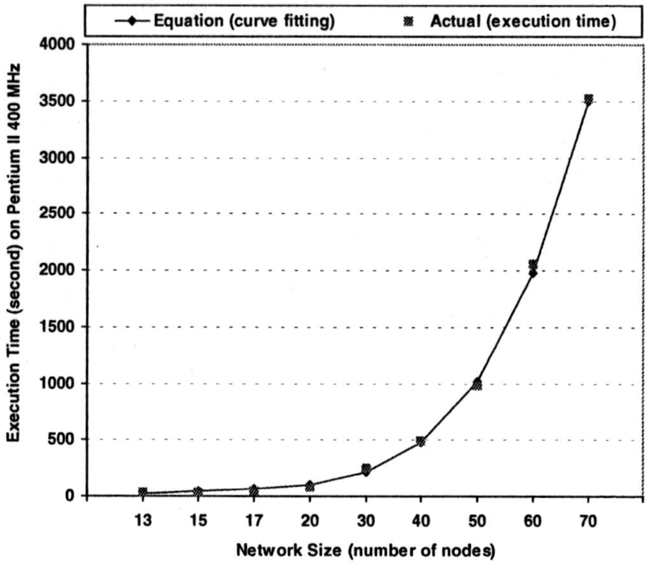

Figure 6.6 Curve-fitting of the Execution Time of the Proposed Methodology

The curve-fitting equation of the empirical execution time is found to be:

$$y = 0.023x^3 - 1.358x^2 + 36.056x - 263.728$$

where x: number of nodes
y: execution time of the proposed methodology using Pentium II 400 MHz

And it has a correlation equal to

$$R^2 : \frac{\sum(fit(x) - mean(y))^2}{\sum(y - mean(y))^2} = 0.999$$

This means that the fitted equation explains 99.9% of the variation between the measured time and the time calculated by the equation.

The curve-fitting equation was found using software called MathCad [58]. The type of curve-fitting used is the least-squares fit. From Figure 6.6, it is obvious that the implementation of the proposed methodology is very fast, that it solves a very large-scale network of 70 nodes in less than one hour. In other words, the proposed methodology is scalable to solve large-size mesh telecommunication networks.

Chapter 7

Conclusions and Future Work

In this dissertation, a new spare capacity planning methodology is proposed based on a shared spare capacity idea which is determined by the application of genetic algorithms. It is based on path-restoration and capable of determining the spare capacity requirements of tolerating not only single-link failures, but also single-link and single-node failure, unlike previous approaches which are usually based on link-restoration and limited to single-link failure tolerance. It is also capable of incorporating non-linear variables such as non-linear cost function and QoS variables, unlike the Integer Programming (IP) approaches which are limited to linear variables. In addition, the proposed methodology is capable of designing survivable networks with non-symmetrical traffic loads. Moreover, it is scalable to large-size mesh networks.

In Chapter One, a background of survivable network techniques is presented. Then, various survivable network architectures are discussed to provide the required level of survivability. Next, the traffic flow management used in survivable network such as k-shortest path (KSP) and maximum flow (MF) are presented.

In Chapter Two, a survey of the spare capacity planning approaches are reviewed and discussed. This includes a literature review of the previous work conducted to solve the spare capacity problem and the two main approaches used (integer programming and heuristic approaches). In addition, the problem considered in this dissertation is identified with the research objectives.

In Chapter Three, the proposed research which includes a new methodology for economical spare capacity planning with link, node, and both link and node failure tolerances is illustrated. Flowcharts and tables are given to illustrate the proposed methodology with its two stages, and the algorithms used are discussed.

In Chapter Four, the implementation details of the proposed methodology and its sensitivity are presented. The performance measures used to evaluate survivable networks are presented and the data structure used by the proposed methodology is described. The analysis of Stage I of the proposed methodology is presented with respect to its time complexity and memory usage in addition to its sensitivity to input variables. Next, the genetic algorithm implementation details are described including: seeding, reproduction, selection of parents, crossover, and mutation. Followed by the analysis of Stage II with respect to time complexity and memory usage in addition to its sensitivity to input variables.

In Chapter Five, the performance of the proposed methodology with comparison to the two previous approaches is presented and discussed. The Spare Link Placement Algorithm (SLPA) is described in detail with its various implementation techniques. An Integer Programming (IP) model to solve the spare capacity problem based on link restoration is presented in detail. The two previous approaches are implemented along with the proposed methodology and all are applied to four sample networks. The results of the proposed methodology and two previous approaches are shown with a discussion. The numerical results show the advantage of the proposed method over the previous approaches.

In Chapter Six, the proposed methodology was applied on many different design criteria to show its flexibility. The proposed methodology was applied on the four sample networks with different reliability levels: node-failure, and link-and-node failures. Next, the proposed methodology was applied on the four networks based on minimum network cost criteria with a non-linear capacity cost function. The result of each network with respect to each reliability level is presented. After that, the proposed methodology was applied on a sample network with non-symmetrical traffic loads. A comparison between the results of the proposed methodology for the non-symmetrical case and the IP solution is presented showing the advantage of the proposed methodology solution. Next, the incorporation of QoS variables in both the objective and constraints was shown. The proposed methodology was applied to a sample network with the two different delay requirements: maximum path delay, and overall network delay. Incorporating QoS variables is one of the features of the proposed methodology that is not possible in the IP approach (because of its linearity limitation). Needless to say, delay variables are essential for designing packet switching networks. Finally, the scalability of the proposed methodology is presented showing it ability to solve large size networks in a short time. The proposed methodology was able to solve very large size mesh networks (with 70 nodes) in less than one hour on a Pentium II 400 PC. The curve-fitting of the empirical execution time is found to be a polynomial of $O(n^3)$.

The main contribution of the proposed methodology can be summarized as follows:

- The proposed methodology is capable of optimizing spare capacity with link, node, and both link and node failure tolerances (which none of the available heuristics in the literature can).

- It scales to large-size survivable networks with very low computational time requirements.

- Unlike the previous approaches which do not consider the QoS constraints in the formulation, the proposed methodology incorporates the QoS constraints in the optimization process (QoS constraints that are considered, such as maximum path delay and average network delay, were not considered before in the current literature of spare capacity assignment problem). As a result, the proposed methodology is suitable to design not only circuit-switching networks, but also packet-switching networks.

- It incorporates a non-linear capacity cost function to optimize according to either minimum network cost criteria, or minimum spare capacity criteria (which was not considered in previous studies of spare capacity optimization)

- It was found in this dissertation, based on the 4 different-size networks studied, that the proposed methodology achieved solutions that are on the average 9.3% better than the optimal solution of the IP design that are based on link-restoration. It also achieved solutions that are on the average 22.2%

better than the previous heuristic, SLPA. Furthermore, the computation time of the approach is quite fast.

It is worth mentioning that the failure level considered in the dissertation for the network component (whether it is a link or node) is either 0% or 100%, where 0% means that the network component is not functioning at all, and 100% means that the network component is operational. In practice, it is possible to have the network component to be partially operational. In addition, it is worth mentioning that the methodology presented in this dissertation is based on the heuristic approach which does not guarantee finding the global optimal solution.

The work presented in this dissertation is very useful for professionals, researchers, and students. The professionals in the network design field can use the proposed methodology to design telecommunication networks that tolerate wide range of failure scenarios while satisfying QoS constraints. Students can use the proposed methodology with its implementation as an educational tool in the study of the network survivability field. Researches can extend the proposed work in many different ways. The work presented in this dissertation opens the way for various future work. The suggested future work includes the following:

- Extending the search space: in both stages of the proposed methodology, the search space is restricted to the feasible region (solutions). The search space can be extended to include the infeasible region (in addition to the feasible region). Adding the infeasible region to the search space requires using some penalty function in evaluating the cost of the network. The goal of the penalty function is to insure that the final solution is feasible. By extending the search space, the methodology may achieve a better final solution at the expense of an increase in the execution time.

- Improving the crossover operator: by investigating different crossover operators than the ones studied in this dissertation, the proposed methodology may achieve a better final solution. The investigation of different crossover operators can be mixed with extending the search space (describe above) to improve the final solution of the methodology.

- Improving the mutation operator: by investigating different mutation rate and mutation probability with and without the crossover operator, the proposed methodology may achieve a better final solution.

- Joint working and backup paths optimization: in the proposed methodology, the working paths are optimized first based on shortest path criteria, then the backup paths are optimized based on minimizing the spare capacity (or the total network cost). These two steps can be joined together in the optimization process in the hope that a better final solution can be achieved.

- Adding links to the network topology: one possible way to improve the design of survivable networks is to add more links to the network topology. Modifying the network topology may result in a solution with less spare capacity (total network cost). This step can be embedded in Stage I of the proposed methodology to increase the diversity in the network set (population). As a result, it may lead to a better final solution.

- More reliability levels: the proposed methodology is capable to tolerate link-failures, node-failures, and link-and-node failures. The proposed methodology can be extended to tolerate more failure scenarios such as: two link-failures, two-node failures, three link-failures, three node-failures, and more. While it is very rare to have a failure of more than one link or node in the network at the same time, it is useful in case of the occurrence of a disaster such as earthquakes or hurricanes. Of course, designing a network with a higher level of reliability will result in a higher cost for the final solution in both spare capacity and total network cost.

Appendix A

List of Symbols

Symbol	Description
ξ	Least improvement acceptable between two successive generations
ABPL	Average backup path length
AD	Average message delay at the network overall level (sec.)
AH	Average hop count of paths
BC	Total Backup Capacity of all links
BC[k]	Backup Capacity of link [k] (bits/sec.)
BL[i,j]	= 1, if the link used in backup routes
	= 0, if link was not used in backup routes
BP[i,j]	Backup Path of Traffic Stream from node i to node j
C	Total Working Capacity of all links
C[k]	Capacity of link [k] (bits/sec.)
c[k]	Working capacity of link k
CL	Total Cost of Links
CL[k]	Cost of link [k]
CLC[i]	Cost per 1 km for link capacity of CM[i]
CM[i]	Different line rates (e.g. CM[1,2,3,4,5,6] = 622-, 150-, 45-, 12-,3-, 1-Mbps
Connected	= 1 ,if the topology is connected and it contains two disjoint paths between every pair of nodes
	= 0 , otherwise
CPGETop	Cost of all topologies of the population in a generation
CPGETop[z]	Cost of topology z of the population
CTG	Cost of all the generated topology
CTG[i]	Cost of the generated topology$_i$ $1 \le i \le NPop$ of Stage I

d	Destination node
D[i,j]	Distance between node i and node j (meters)
D[k]	The length of link k (km)
Deg	Average node degree
delete	Number of links to be deleted in Stage I
DelStr	Delete strategy (e.g. randomly, or any other criterion)
DF[k]	Data flow through link [k] (bps)
F[k]	Message flow through link [k] (message/sec.)
G[i]	Angular distance north or south of the Equator for node i [radian]
GETop[x,i,j]	= 1 , if there is a link from node i to node j = 0 , otherwise
GETop[x]	Topology matrix n**X**n of the generated population (living) $1 \le x \le$ NPop
GETopP	Set of pairs of topologies of a generation of GA
GETopP[m,n]	The nth element of the mth pair in GETopP $1 \le n \le 2$, $1 \le m \le$ NPop
GTop	matrix of all generated topologies of Stage I
Gtop[x,i,j]	= 1 , if there is a link from node i to node j in the network x = 0 , otherwise
GTop[x]	Matrix n**X**n of the generated topologies of Stage I
h	Hop limit (maximum hop-length of a restoration path)
H[i,j]	Path of Traffic Stream from node i to node j
L[i]	Angular distance east or west of Greenwich for node i [radian]
l[s,d]	The link from node *s* to node *d*
LD[k]	Delay through link [k] (sec.)
LL[i,j]	Length of link from node i to node j

LOC[k,m[i]]	Number of channels of line rate CM[i] in link k.
LS[s,d]	The set of all links that can be in a path of length h hops from node *s* or *d*
M[i,j]	Average message length for the stream of traffic from node i to node j (bits)
m[i]	Number of lines of capacity CM[i]
M[k]	Average message length through link [k] (bits)
Mdelete	Average number of link deletion attempts (both successful and unsuccessful) of Stage I
N	Number of sites where nodes are placed
ND	Maximum acceptable message average path delay through the network (sec)
NH[i,j]	Number of Hops in the Path from node i to node j
NL	Number of Links in the network
NPop	Number of topologies (population size)
NS	Number of Traffic Streams
PD	Maximum acceptable message delay through a path (sec)
PD[i,j]	Delay through the path from node i to node j (sec.)
PGETop	All topologies of one generation of the genetic algorithm (GA)
$PGETop_y$	Topology y of the population $1 \leq y \leq 2$ NPop (GA)
P[i,j]	Path from node i to node j
PS[s,d]	The set of all restoration paths of l_{sd}
r[k]	Restored working capacity of link k
Reliable	Reliability level (link-failure, node-failure, link-and-node failure)
rot	Number of successive generations with improvement less than ξ
Routing	Routing strategy (e.g. shortest path)

RR	Restored ratio of backup traffic to working traffic
s	Source node
S[i,j]	Traffic rate from node i to node j (messages/sec)
SL	Chosen link to be deleted
TC	Topology cost
TCR	Total capacity reserved
TD	Total distances between all node-pairs
TL	Total length of all links
Top[i,j]	Network Topology, Top[i,j] = 1 (link exists, 0 link does not exists)
WP[i,j]	Working Path of Traffic Stream from node i to node j

Appendix B

Tables and Figures for Case I

This appendix includes tables for Networks 1,2,3, and 4. It includes the working paths for Networks 1,2,3, and 4. It also includes the backup paths for Case I (link-failure tolerance) for Networks 1,2,3, and 4.

The six optimization cases mentioned in the appendices are:

- Case I: link-failure with spare capacity optimization criteria
- Case II: node-failure with spare capacity optimization criteria
- Case III: link-or-node failure with spare capacity optimization criteria
- Case IV: link-failure with minimum network cost optimization criteria
- Case V: node-failure with minimum network cost optimization criteria
- Case VI: link-or-node failure with minimum network cost optimization criteria

Node	1	2	3	4	5	6	7	8	9	10	11	12	13
1	---	1 2	1 2 3	1 2 4	1 2 3 5	1 2 3 6	1 2 7	1 2 4 8	1 9	1 10	1 10 11	1 12	1 9 13
2	2 1	---	2 3	2 4	2 3 5	2 3 6	2 7	2 4 8	2 1 9	2 1 10	2 4 8 11	2 1 12	2 1 9 13
3	3 2 1	3 2	---	3 2 4	3 5	3 6	3 7	3 5 8	3 7 9	3 2 1 10	3 5 8 11	3 2 1 12	3 7 9 13
4	4 2 1	4 2	4 2 3	---	4 5	4 5 6	4 2 7	4 8	4 2 1 9	4 10	4 8 11	4 10 12	4 10 12 13
5	5 3 2 1	5 3 2	5 3	5 4	---	5 6	5 3 7	5 8	5 3 7 9	5 4 10	5 8 11	5 4 10 12	5 3 7 9 13
6	6 3 2 1	6 3 2	6 3	6 5 4	6 5	---	6 7	6 5 8	6 7 9	6 5 4 10	6 5 8 11	6 3 2 1 12	6 7 9 13
7	7 2 1	7 2	7 3	7 2 4	7 3 5	7 6	---	7 2 4 8	7 9	7 2 1 10	7 2 4 8 11	7 2 1 12	7 9 13
8	8 4 2 1	8 4 2	8 5 3	8 4	8 5	8 5 6	8 4 2 7	---	8 4 2 1 9	8 4 10	8 11	8 11 12	8 11 12 13
9	9 1	9 1 2	9 7 3	9 1 2 4	9 7 3 5	9 7 6	9 7	9 1 2 4 8	---	9 1 10	9 1 10 11	9 1 12	9 13
10	10 1	10 1 2	10 1 2 3	10 4	10 4 5	10 4 5 6	10 1 2 7	10 4 8	10 1 9	---	10 11	10 12	10 12 13
11	11 10 1	11 8 4 2	11 8 5 3	11 8 4	11 8 5	11 8 5 6	11 8 4 2 7	11 8	11 10 1 9	11 10	---	11 12	11 12 13
12	12 1	12 1 2	12 1 2 3	12 10 4	12 10 4 5	12 1 2 3 6	12 1 2 7	12 11 8	12 1 9	12 10	12 11	---	12 13
13	13 9 1	13 9 1 2	13 9 7 3	13 12 10 4	13 9 7 3 5	13 9 7 6	13 9 7	13 12 11 8	13 9	13 12 10	13 12 11	13 12	---

Working Paths of The 13-Node Network

Table 8.1 The Working Paths of The 13-Node Network (Network 1)

Node	1	2	3	4	5	6	7	8	9	10	11	12	13
1	—	1 10 4 2	1 9 7 6 5 3	1 10 4	1 9 7 6 5	1 9 7 6	1 9 7	1 10 12 11 8	1 10 12 13 9	1 9 13 12 10	1 9 13 12 11	1 10 12	1 10 12 13
2	2 4 10 1	—	2 4 10 12 11 8 5 3	2 3 5 8 11 12 10 4	2 4 10 12 11 8 5	2 4 10 1 9 7 6	2 3 5 6 7	2 3 5 8	2 3 5 6 7 9	2 4 10	2 3 5 6 7 9 13 12 11	2 4 10 12	2 4 10 12 13
3	3 5 6 7 9 1	3 5 8 11 12 10 4 2	—	3 5 8 11 12 10 4	3 2 4 10 12 11 8 5	3 5 6	3 5 6 7	3 2 4 10 12 11 8	3 2 4 10 1 9	3 5 8 11 12 10	3 2 4 10 12 11	3 5 8 11 12	3 2 4 10 12 13
4	4 10 1	4 10 12 11 8 5 3 2	4 10 12 11 8 5 3	—	4 2 3 5	4 10 1 9 7 6	4 10 1 9 7	4 2 3 5 8	4 10 12 13 9	4 2 3 5 8 11 12 10	4 10 12 11	4 2 3 5 8 11 12	4 2 3 5 6 7 9 13
5	5 6 7 9 1	5 8 11 12 10 4 2	5 8 11 12 10 4 2 3	5 3 2 4	—	5 8 11 12 13 9 7 6	5 6 7	5 3 2 4 10 12 11 8	5 8 11 12 13 9	5 8 11 12 10	5 3 2 4 10 12 11	5 8 11 12	5 8 11 12 13
6	6 7 9 1	6 7 9 1 10 4 2	6 5 3	6 7 9 1 10 4	6 7 9 13 12 11 8 5	—	6 5 8 11 12 13 9 7	6 7 9 13 12 11 8	6 5 8 11 12 13 9	6 7 9 1 10	6 7 9 13 12 11	6 5 8 11 12	6 5 8 11 12 13
7	7 9 1	7 6 5 3 2	7 6 5 3	7 9 1 10 4	7 6 5	7 9 13 12 11 8 5 6	—	7 6 5 8	7 6 5 8 11 12 13 9	7 9 13 12 10	7 9 13 12 11	7 9 13 12	7 6 5 8 11 12 13
8	8 11 12 10 1	8 5 3 2	8 11 12 10 4 2 3	8 5 3 2 4	8 11 12 10 4 2 3 5	8 11 12 13 9 7 6	8 5 6 7	—	8 5 6 7 9	8 11 12 10	8 5 3 2 4 10 12 11	8 5 3 2 4 10 12	8 5 6 7 9 13
9	9 13 12 10 1	9 7 6 5 3 2	9 1 10 4 2 3	9 13 12 10 4	9 13 12 11 8 5	9 13 12 11 8 5 6	9 13 12 11 8 5 6 7	9 7 6 5 8	—	9 13 12 10	9 13 12 11	9 13 12	9 1 10 12 13
10	10 12 13 9 1	10 4 2	10 12 11 8 5 3	10 12 11 8 5 3 2 4	10 12 11 8 5	10 1 9 7 6	10 12 13 9 7	10 12 11 8	10 12 13 9	—	10 12 11	10 1 9 13 12	10 1 9 13
11	11 12 13 9 1	11 12 13 9 7 6 5 3 2	11 12 10 4 2 3	11 12 10 4	11 12 10 4 2 3 5	11 12 13 9 7 6	11 12 13 9 7	11 12 10 4 2 3 5 8	11 12 13 9	11 12 10	—	11 8 5 3 2 4 10 12	11 8 5 6 7 9 13
12	12 10 1	12 10 4 2	12 11 8 5 3	12 11 8 5 3 2 4	12 11 8 5	12 11 8 5 6	12 13 9 7	12 10 4 2 3 5 8	12 13 9	12 13 9 1 10	12 10 4 2 3 5 8 11	—	12 10 1 9 13
13	13 12 10 1	13 12 10 4 2	13 12 10 4 2 3	13 9 7 6 5 3 2 4	13 12 11 8 5	13 12 11 8 5 6	13 12 11 8 5 6 7	13 9 7 6 5 8	13 12 10 1 9	13 9 1 10	13 9 7 6 5 8 11	13 9 1 10 12	—

Backup Paths of The 13-Node - Case I

Table 8.2 Backup Paths of The 13-Node Network with Link-Failure Tolerance (Case I)

Node	1	2	3	4	5	6	7	8	9	10	11	12	13	14	15
1	---	1 2	1 2 3	1 2 4	1 2 3 5	1 2 3 6	1 2 7	1 10 8	1 9	1 10	1 10 11	1 12	1 9 13	1 2 3 5 14	1 10 8 15
2	2 1	---	2 3	2 4	2 3 5	2 3 6	2 7	2 4 8	2 1 9	2 1 10	2 1 10 11	2 1 12	2 1 9 13	2 3 5 14	2 4 8 15
3	3 2 1	3 2	---	3 2 4	3 5	3 6	3 7	3 5 8	3 7 9	3 2 1 10	3 2 1 10 11	3 2 1 12	3 7 9 13	3 5 14	3 5 8 15
4	4 2 1	4 2	4 2 3	---	4 5	4 5 6	4 2 7	4 8	4 2 1 9	4 10	4 10 11	4 10 12	4 10 12 13	4 5 14	4 8 15
5	5 3 2 1	5 3 2	5 3	5 4	---	5 6	5 3 7	5 8	5 3 7 9	5 4 10	5 4 10 11	5 4 10 12	5 3 7 9 13	5 14	5 8 15
6	6 3 2 1	6 3 2	6 3	6 5 4	6 5	---	6 7	6 5 8	6 7 9	6 5 4 10	6 5 4 10 11	6 3 2 1 12	6 7 9 13	6 5 14	6 5 8 15
7	7 2 1	7 2	7 3	7 2 4	7 3 5	7 6	---	7 2 4 8	7 9	7 2 1 10	7 2 1 10 11	7 2 1 12	7 9 13	7 3 5 14	7 2 4 8 15
8	8 10 1	8 4 2	8 5 3	8 4	8 5	8 5 6	8 4 2 7	---	8 10 1 9	8 10	8 10 11	8 10 12	8 10 12 13	8 5 14	8 15
9	9 1	9 1 2	9 7 3	9 1 2 4	9 7 3 5	9 7 6	9 7	9 1 10 8	---	9 1 10	9 1 10 11	9 1 12	9 13	9 7 3 5 14	9 1 10 8 15
10	10 1	10 1 2	10 1 2 3	10 4	10 4 5	10 4 5 6	10 1 2 7	10 8	10 1 9	---	10 11	10 12	10 12 13	10 4 5 14	10 8 15
11	11 10 1	11 10 1 2	11 10 1 2 3	11 10 4	11 10 4 5	11 10 4 5 6	11 10 1 2 7	11 10 8	11 10 1 9	11 10	---	11 12	11 12 13	11 15 14	11 15
12	12 1	12 1 2	12 1 2 3	12 10 4	12 10 4 5	12 1 2 3 6	12 1 2 7	12 10 8	12 1 9	12 10	12 11	---	12 13	12 11 15 14	12 11 15
13	13 9 1	13 9 1 2	13 9 7 3	13 12 10 4	13 9 7 3 5	13 9 7 6	13 9 7	13 12 10 8	13 9	13 12 10	13 12 11	13 12	---	13 12 11 15 14	13 12 11 15
14	14 5 3 2 1	14 5 3 2	14 5 3	14 5 4	14 5	14 5 6	14 5 3 7	14 5 8	14 5 3 7 9	14 5 4 10	14 15 11	14 15 11 12	14 15 11 12 13	---	14 15
15	15 8 10 1	15 8 4 2	15 8 5 3	15 8 4	15 8 5	15 8 5 6	15 8 4 2 7	15 8	15 8 10 1 9	15 8 10	15 11	15 11 12	15 11 12 13	15 14	---

Working Paths of The 15-Node Network

Table 8.3 The Working Paths of The 15-Node Network (Network 2)

Backup Paths of The 15 Node Network - Case I

Node	1	2	3	4	5	6	7	8	9	10	11	12	13	14	15
1	---	1 10 4 2	1 9 7 6 3	1 10 4	1 10 4 8 15 14 5	1 9 7 6	1 9 7	1 9 13 12 11 15 8	1 10 4 2 3 6 7 9	1 9 7 6 3 2 4 10	1 9 13 12 11	1 9 13 12	1 10 4 8 15 11 12 13	1 10 4 8 15 14	1 9 13 12 11 15
2	2 4 10 1	---	2 4 8 15 14 5 3	2 3 5 14 15 8 4	2 4 8 15 14 5	2 4 10 1 9 7 6	2 3 6 7	2 3 5 14 15 8	2 3 6 7 9	2 4 10	2 4 8 15 11	2 4 8 15 11 12	2 4 8 15 11 12 13	2 4 8 15 14	2 3 5 14 15
3	3 6 7 9 1	3 5 14 15 8 4 2	---	3 5 14 15 8 4	3 2 4 8 15 14 5	3 2 4 10 1 9 7 6	3 6 7	3 2 4 8	3 2 4 10 1 9	3 5 14 15 8 4 10	3 5 14 15 11	3 5 14 15 11 12	3 5 14 15 11 12 13	3 2 4 8 15 14	3 6 7 9 13 12 11 15
4	4 10 1	4 8 15 14 5 3 2	4 8 15 14 5 3	---	4 2 3 5	4 2 3 6	4 10 1 9 7	4 2 3 5 14 15 8	4 8 15 11 12 13 9	4 2 3 6 7 9 1 10	4 8 15 11	4 8 15 11 12	4 2 3 6 7 9 13	4 8 15 14	4 2 3 5 14 15
5	5 14 15 8 4 10 1	5 14 15 8 4 2	5 14 15 8 4 2 3	5 3 2 4	---	5 3 6	5 14 15 11 12 13 9 7	5 14 15 8	5 14 15 11 12 13 9	5 3 6 7 9 1 10	5 14 15 11	5 14 15 11 12	5 14 15 11 12 13	5 3 2 4 8 15 14	5 14 15
6	6 7 9 1	6 7 9 1 10 4 2	6 7 9 1 10 4 2 3	6 3 2 4	6 3 5	---	6 3 2 4 10 1 9 7	6 3 2 4 8	6 3 2 4 10 1 9	6 7 9 1 10	6 7 9 13 12 11	6 7 9 13 12	6 3 5 14 15 11 12 13	6 3 2 4 8 15 14	6 3 5 14 15
7	7 9 1	7 6 3 2	7 6 3	7 9 1 10 4	7 9 13 12 11 15 14 5	7 9 1 10 4 2 3 6	---	7 9 13 12 11 15 8	7 6 3 2 4 10 1 9	7 6 3 2 4 10	7 9 13 12 11	7 9 13 12	7 6 3 5 14 15 11 12 13	7 9 13 12 11 15 14	7 9 13 12 11 15
8	8 15 11 12 13 9 1	8 15 14 5 3 2	8 4 2 3	8 15 14 5 3 2 4	8 15 14 5	8 4 2 3 6	8 15 11 12 13 9 7	---	8 15 11 12 13 9	8 4 10	8 15 11	8 15 11 12	8 4 10 1 9 13	8 15 14	8 4 2 3 5 14 15
9	9 7 6 3 2 4 10 1	9 7 6 3 2	9 1 10 4 2 3	9 13 12 11 15 8 4	9 13 12 11 15 14 5	9 1 10 4 2 3 6	9 1 10 4 2 3 6 7	9 13 12 11 15 8	---	9 7 6 3 2 4 10	9 13 12 11	9 13 12	9 1 10 4 8 15 11 12 13	9 13 12 11 15 14	9 13 12 11 15
10	10 4 2 3 6 7 9 1	10 4 2	10 4 8 15 14 5 3	10 1 9 7 6 3 2 4	10 1 9 7 6 3 5	10 1 9 7 6	10 4 2 3 6 7	10 4 8	10 4 2 3 6 7 9	---	10 4 8 15 11	10 1 9 13 12	10 1 9 13	10 1 9 13 12 11 15 14	10 1 9 13 12 11 15
11	11 12 13 9 1	11 15 8 4 2	11 15 14 5 3	11 15 8 4	11 15 14 5	11 12 13 9 7 6	11 12 13 9 7	11 15 8	11 12 13 9	11 15 8 4 10	---	11 15 8 4 10 1 9 13 12	11 15 8 4 10 1 9 13	11 12 13 9 7 6 3 5 14	11 12 13 9 1 10 4 8 15
12	12 13 9 1	12 11 15 8 4 2	12 11 15 14 5 3	12 11 15 8 4	12 11 15 14 5	12 13 9 7 6	12 13 9 7	12 11 15 8	12 13 9	12 13 9 1 10	12 13 9 1 10 4 8 15 11	---	12 11 15 8 4 10 1 9 13	12 13 9 7 6 3 5 14	12 13 9 1 10 4 8 15
13	13 12 11 15 8 4 10 1	13 12 11 15 8 4 2	13 12 11 15 14 5 3	13 9 7 6 3 2 4	13 12 11 15 14 5	13 12 11 15 14 5 3 6	13 12 11 15 14 5 3 6 7	13 9 1 10 4 8	13 12 11 15 8 4 10 1 9	13 9 1 10	13 9 1 10 4 8 15 11	13 9 1 10 4 8 15 11 12	---	13 9 7 6 3 5 14	13 9 1 10 4 8 15
14	14 15 8 4 10 1	14 15 8 4 2	14 15 8 4 2 3	14 15 8 4	14 15 8 4 2 3 5	14 15 8 4 2 3 6	14 15 11 12 13 9 7	14 15 8	14 15 11 12 13 9	14 15 11 12 13 9 1 10	14 5 3 6 7 9 13 12 11	14 5 3 6 7 9 13 12	14 5 3 6 7 9 13	---	14 5 3 2 4 8 15
15	15 11 12 13 9 1	15 14 5 3 2	15 11 12 13 9 7 6 3	15 14 5 3 2 4	15 14 5	15 14 5 3 6	15 11 12 13 9 7	15 14 5 3 2 4 8	15 11 12 13 9	15 11 12 13 9 1 10	15 8 4 10 1 9 13 12 11	15 8 4 10 1 9 13 12	15 8 4 10 1 9 13	15 8 4 2 3 5 14	---

Table 8.4 Backup Paths of the 15-Node Network with Link-Failure Tolerance (Case I)

Node	1	2	3	4	5	6	7	8	9	10	11	12	13	14	15	16	17
1	---	1 2	1 2 3	1 2 4	1 2 3 5	1 2 3 6	1 2 7	1 10 8	1 9	1 10	1 10 11	1 12	1 9 13	1 2 3 5 14	1 10 8 15	1 10 11 16	1 12 17
2	2 1	---	2 3	2 4	2 3 5	2 3 6	2 7	2 4 8	2 1 9	2 1 10	2 1 10 11	2 1 12	2 1 9 13	2 3 5 14	2 4 8 15	2 1 10 11 16	2 1 12 17
3	3 2 1	3 2	---	3 2 4	3 5	3 6	3 7	3 5 8	3 7 9	3 2 1 10	3 2 1 10 11	3 2 1 12	3 7 9 13	3 5 14	3 5 8 15	3 2 1 10 11 16	3 2 1 12 17
4	4 2 1	4 2	4 2 3	---	4 5	4 5 6	4 2 7	4 8	4 2 1 9	4 10	4 10 11	4 10 12	4 10 12 13	4 5 14	4 8 15	4 10 11 16	4 10 12 17
5	5 3 2 1	5 3 2	5 3	5 4	---	5 6	5 3 7	5 8	5 3 7 9	5 4 10	5 4 10 11	5 4 10 12	5 3 7 9 13	5 14	5 8 15	5 4 10 11 16	5 4 10 12 17
6	6 3 2 1	6 3 2	6 3	6 5 4	6 5	---	6 7	6 5 8	6 7 9	6 5 4 10	6 5 4 10 11	6 3 2 1 12	6 7 9 13	6 5 14	6 5 8 15	6 5 4 10 11 16	6 7 9 13 17
7	7 2 1	7 2	7 3	7 2 4	7 3 5	7 6	---	7 2 4 8	7 9	7 2 1 10	7 2 1 10 11	7 2 1 12	7 9 13	7 3 5 14	7 2 4 8 15	7 9 13 17 16	7 9 13 17
8	8 10 1	8 4 2	8 5 3	8 4	8 5	8 5 6	8 4 2 7	---	8 10 1 9	8 10	8 10 11	8 10 12	8 10 12 13	8 5 14	8 15	8 10 11 16	8 10 12 17
9	9 1	9 1 2	9 7 3	9 1 2 4	9 7 3 5	9 7 6	9 7	9 1 10 8	---	9 1 10	9 1 10 11	9 1 12	9 13	9 7 3 5 14	9 1 10 8 15	9 13 17 16	9 13 17
10	10 1	10 1 2	10 1 2 3	10 4	10 4 5	10 4 5 6	10 1 2 7	10 8	10 1 9	---	10 11	10 12	10 12 13	10 4 5 14	10 8 15	10 11 16	10 12 17
11	11 10 1	11 10 1 2	11 10 1 2 3	11 10 4	11 10 4 5	11 10 4 5 6	11 10 1 2 7	11 10 8	11 10 1 9	11 10	---	11 12	11 12 13	11 15 14	11 15	11 16	11 12 17
12	12 1	12 1 2	12 1 2 3	12 10 4	12 10 4 5	12 1 2 3 6	12 1 2 7	12 10 8	12 1 9	12 10	12 11	---	12 13	12 11 15 14	12 11 15	12 11 16	12 17
13	13 9 1	13 9 1 2	13 9 7 3	13 12 10 4	13 9 7 3 5	13 9 7 6	13 9 7	13 12 10 8	13 9	13 12 10	13 12 11	13 12	---	13 12 11 15 14	13 12 11 15	13 17 16	13 17
14	14 5 3 2 1	14 5 3 2	14 5 3	14 5 4	14 5	14 5 6	14 5 3 7	14 5 8	14 5 3 7 9	14 5 4 10	14 15 11	14 15 11 12	14 15 11 12 13	---	14 15	14 15 11 16	14 15 11 12 17
15	15 8 10 1	15 8 4 2	15 8 5 3	15 8 4	15 8 5	15 8 5 6	15 8 4 2 7	15 8	15 8 10 1 9	15 8 10	15 11	15 11 12	15 11 12 13	15 14	---	15 11 16	15 11 12 17
16	16 11 10 1	16 11 10 1 2	16 11 10 1 2 3	16 11 10 4	16 11 10 4 5	16 11 10 4 5 6	16 17 13 9 7	16 11 10 8	16 17 13 9	16 11 10	16 11	16 11 12	16 17 13	16 11 15 14	16 11 15	---	16 17
17	17 12 1	17 12 1 2	17 12 1 2 3	17 12 10 4	17 12 10 4 5	17 13 9 7 6	17 13 9 7	17 12 10 8	17 13 9	17 12 10	17 12 11	17 12	17 13	17 12 11 15 14	17 12 11 15	17 16	---

Working Paths of The 17-Node Network

Table 8.5 Working Paths of The 17-Node Network (Network 3)

Node	1	2	3	4	5	6	7	8	9	10	11	12	13	14	15	16	17
1	---	1 9 7 3 2	1 9 7 3	1 12 10 4	1 9 7 6 5	1 9 7 6	1 9 7	1 12 10 4 8	1 12 13 9	1 12 10	1 9 13 17 16 11	1 9 13 12	1 12 13	1 12 10 4 8 15 14	1 9 13 17 16 11 15	1 9 13 17 16	1 9 13 17
2	2 3 7 9 1	---	2 4 10 12 1 9 7 3	2 3 7 9 1 12 10 4	2 4 8 15 14 5	2 4 8 15 14 5 6	2 3 7	2 3 7 6 5 14 15 8	2 3 7 9	2 4 10	2 4 8 15 11	2 4 10 12	2 4 10 12 13	2 4 8 15 14	2 3 7 6 5 14 15	2 3 7 9 13 17 16	2 3 7 9 13 17
3	3 7 9 1	3 7 9 1 12 10 4 2	---	3 7 9 1 12 10 4	3 7 6 5	3 7 6	3 2 4 10 12 1 9 7	3 2 4 8	3 2 4 10 12 1 9	3 7 9 1 12 10	3 7 6 5 14 15 11	3 7 9 13 12	3 2 4 10 12 13	3 2 4 8 15 14	3 7 6 5 14 15	3 7 9 13 17 16	3 7 9 13 17
4	4 10 12 1	4 10 12 1 9 7 3 2	4 10 12 1 9 7 3	---	4 8 15 14 5	4 2 3 7 6	4 10 12 1 9 7	4 10 12 13 17 16 11 15 8	4 10 12 13 9	4 2 3 7 9 1 12 10	4 8 15 11	4 2 3 7 9 1 12	4 2 3 7 9 13	4 8 15 14	4 10 12 13 17 16 11 15	4 2 3 7 9 13 17 16	4 8 15 11 16 17
5	5 6 7 9 1	5 14 15 8 4 2	5 6 7 3	5 14 15 8 4	---	5 14 15 8 4 2 3 7 6	5 6 7	5 14 15 8	5 14 15 11 16 17 13 9	5 6 7 9 1 12 10	5 14 15 11	5 6 7 9 1 12	5 14 15 11 16 17 13	5 6 7 3 2 4 8 15 14	5 14 15	5 6 7 9 13 17 16	5 6 7 9 13 17
6	6 7 9 1	6 5 14 15 8 4 2	6 7 3	6 7 3 2 4	6 7 3 2 4 8 15 14 5	---	6 5 14 15 8 4 2 3 7	6 7 3 2 4 8	6 5 14 15 11 16 17 13 9	6 7 9 1 12 10	6 7 9 13 17 16 11	6 7 9 13 12	6 5 14 15 11 16 17 13	6 7 3 2 4 8 15 14	6 7 9 13 17 16 11 15	6 7 9 13 17 16	6 5 14 15 11 16 17
7	7 9 1	7 3 2	7 9 1 12 10 4 2 3	7 9 1 12 10 4	7 6 5	7 3 2 4 8 15 14 5 6	---	7 6 5 14 15 8	7 3 2 4 10 12 1 9	7 3 2 4 10	7 6 5 14 15 11	7 9 13 12	7 3 2 4 10 12 13	7 9 13 17 16 11 15 14	7 6 5 14 15	7 6 5 14 15 11 16	7 6 5 14 15 11 16 17
8	8 4 10 12 1	8 15 14 5 6 7 3 2	8 4 2 3	8 15 11 16 17 13 12 10 4	8 15 14 5	8 4 2 3 7 6	8 15 14 5 6 7	---	8 4 2 3 7 9	8 4 10	8 15 11	8 15 11 16 17 13 12	8 15 11 16 17 13	8 15 14	8 4 10 12 13 17 16 11 15	8 4 10 12 13 17 16	8 15 11 16 17
9	9 13 12 1	9 7 3 2	9 1 12 10 4 2 3	9 13 12 10 4	9 13 17 16 11 15 14 5	9 13 17 16 11 15 14 5 6	9 1 12 10 4 2 3 7	9 7 3 2 4 8	---	9 13 12 10	9 13 17 16 11	9 13 12	9 1 12 13	9 13 17 16 11 15 14	9 13 17 16 11 15	9 7 6 5 14 15 11 16	9 7 6 5 14 15 11 16 17
10	10 12 1	10 4 2	10 12 1 9 7 3	10 12 1 9 7 3 2 4	10 12 1 9 7 6 5	10 12 1 9 7 6	10 4 2 3 7	10 4 8	10 12 13 9	---	10 4 8 15 11	10 4 2 3 7 9 1 12	10 4 2 3 7 9 13	10 12 13 17 16 11 15 14	10 12 13 17 16 11 15	10 12 13 17 16	10 4 8 15 11 16 17
11	11 16 17 13 9 1	11 15 8 4 2	11 15 14 5 6 7 3	11 15 8 4	11 15 14 5	11 16 17 13 9 7 6	11 15 14 5 6 7	11 15 8	11 16 17 13 9	11 15 8 4 10	---	11 16 17 13 12	11 16 17 13	11 16 17 13 9 7 6 5 14	11 16 17 13 12 10 4 8 15	11 15 8 4 10 12 13 17 16	11 16 17
12	12 13 9 1	12 10 4 2	12 13 9 7 3	12 1 9 7 3 2 4	12 1 9 7 6 5	12 13 9 7 6	12 13 9 7	12 13 17 16 11 15 8	12 13 9	12 1 9 7 3 2 4 10	12 13 17 16 11	---	12 1 9 13	12 1 9 7 6 5 14	12 10 4 8 15	12 13 17 16	12 13 17
13	13 12 1	13 12 10 4 2	13 12 10 4 2 3	13 9 7 3 2 4	13 17 16 11 15 14 5	13 17 16 11 15 14 5 6	13 12 10 4 2 3 7	13 17 16 11 15 8	13 12 1 9	13 9 7 3 2 4 10	13 17 16 11	13 9 1 12	---	13 9 7 6 5 14	13 9 7 6 5 14 15	13 12 10 4 8 15 11 16	13 12 10 4 8 15 11 16 17
14	14 15 8 4 10 12 1	14 15 8 4 2	14 15 8 4 2 3	14 15 8 4	14 15 8 4 2 3 7 6 5	14 15 8 4 2 3 7 6	14 15 11 16 17 13 9 7	14 15 8	14 15 11 16 17 13 9	14 15 11 16 17 13 12 10	14 5 6 7 9 13 17 16 11	14 5 6 7 9 1 12	14 5 6 7 9 13	---	14 5 6 7 3 2 4 8 15	14 5 6 7 9 13 17 16	14 5 6 7 9 13 17
15	15 11 16 17 13 9 1	15 14 5 6 7 3 2	15 14 5 6 7 3	15 11 16 17 13 12 10 4	15 14 5	15 11 16 17 13 9 7 6	15 14 5 6 7	15 11 16 17 13 12 10 4 8	15 11 16 17 13 9	15 11 16 17 13 12 10	15 8 4 10 12 13 17 16 11	15 8 4 10 12	15 14 5 6 7 9 13	15 8 4 2 3 7 6 5 14	---	15 8 4 10 12 13 17 16	15 8 4 10 12 13 17
16	16 17 13 9 1	16 17 13 9 7 3 2	16 17 13 9 7 3	16 17 13 9 7 3 2 4	16 17 13 9 7 6 5	16 17 13 9 7 6	16 11 15 14 5 6 7	16 17 13 12 10 4 8	16 11 15 14 5 6 7 9	16 17 13 12 10	16 17 13 12 10 4 8 15 11	16 17 13 12	16 11 15 8 4 10 12 13	16 17 13 9 7 6 5 14	16 17 13 12 10 4 8 15	---	16 11 15 8 4 10 12 13 17
17	17 13 9 1	17 13 9 7 3 2	17 13 9 7 3	17 16 11 15 8 4	17 13 9 7 6 5	17 16 11 15 14 5 6	17 16 11 15 14 5 6 7	17 16 11 15 8	17 16 11 15 14 5 6 7 9	17 16 11 15 8 4 10	17 16 11	17 13 12	17 16 11 15 8 4 10 12 13	17 13 9 7 6 5 14	17 13 12 10 4 8 15	17 13 12 10 4 8 15 11 16	---

Backup Paths of The 17-Node - Case I

Table 8.6 Backup Paths of The 17-Node Network with Link-Failure Tolerance (Case I)

Node	1	2	3	4	5	6	7	8	9	10	11	12	13	14	15	16	17	18	19	20
1	---	1 2	1 2 3	1 2 4	1 2 3 5	1 2 3 6	1 2 7	1 10 8	1 9	1 10	1 10 11	1 12	1 9 13	1 2 3 5 14	1 10 8 15	1 10 11 16	1 12 17	1 2 3 5 18	1 2 3 6 19	1 2 7 20
2	2 1	---	2 3	2 4	2 3 5	2 3 6	2 7	2 4 8	2 1 9	2 1 10	2 1 10 11	2 1 12	2 1 9 13	2 3 5 14	2 4 8 15	2 1 10 11 16	2 1 12 17	2 3 5 18	2 3 6 19	2 7 20
3	3 2 1	3 2	---	3 2 4	3 5	3 6	3 7	3 5 8	3 7 9	3 2 1 10	3 2 1 10 11	3 2 1 12	3 7 9 13	3 5 14	3 5 8 15	3 2 1 10 11 16	3 2 1 12 17	3 5 18	3 6 19	3 7 20
4	4 2 1	4 2	4 2 3	---	4 5	4 5 6	4 2 7	4 8	4 2 1 9	4 10	4 10 11	4 10 12	4 10 12 13	4 5 14	4 8 15	4 10 11 16	4 10 12 17	4 5 18	4 5 6 19	4 2 7 20
5	5 3 2 1	5 3 2	5 3	5 4	---	5 6	5 3 7	5 8	5 3 7 9	5 4 10	5 4 10 11	5 4 10 12	5 3 7 9 13	5 14	5 8 15	5 4 10 11 16	5 4 10 12 17	5 18	5 6 19	5 3 7 20
6	6 3 2 1	6 3 2	6 3	6 5 4	6 5	---	6 7	6 5 8	6 7 9	6 5 4 10	6 5 4 10 11	6 3 2 1 12	6 7 9 13	6 5 14	6 5 8 15	6 5 4 10 11 16	6 7 9 13 17	6 5 18	6 19	6 7 20
7	7 2 1	7 2	7 3	7 2 4	7 3 5	7 6	---	7 2 4 8	7 9	7 2 1 10	7 2 1 10 11	7 2 1 12	7 9 13	7 3 5 14	7 2 4 8 15	7 9 13 17 16	7 9 13 17	7 3 5 18	7 6 19	7 20
8	8 10 1	8 4 2	8 5 3	8 4	8 5	8 5 6	8 4 2 7	---	8 10 1 9	8 10	8 10 11	8 10 12	8 10 12 13	8 5 14	8 15	8 10 11 16	8 10 12 17	8 5 18	8 5 6 19	8 4 2 7 20
9	9 1	9 1 2	9 7 3	9 1 2 4	9 7 3 5	9 7 6	9 7	9 1 10 8	---	9 1 10	9 1 10 11	9 1 12	9 13	9 7 3 5 14	9 1 10 8 15	9 13 17 16	9 13 17	9 7 3 5 18	9 7 6 19	9 7 20
10	10 1	10 1 2	10 1 2 3	10 4	10 4 5	10 4 5 6	10 1 2 7	10 8	10 1 9	---	10 11	10 12	10 12 13	10 4 5 14	10 8 15	10 11 16	10 12 17	10 4 5 18	10 4 5 6 19	10 1 2 7 20
11	11 10 1	11 10 1 2	11 10 1 2 3	11 10 4	11 10 4 5	11 10 4 5 6	11 10 1 2 7	11 10 8	11 10 1 9	11 10	---	11 12	11 12 13	11 15 14	11 15	11 16	11 12 17	11 15 14 18	11 15 14 18 19	11 10 1 2 7 20
12	12 1	12 1 2	12 1 2 3	12 10 4	12 10 4 5	12 1 2 3 6	12 1 2 7	12 10 8	12 1 9	12 10	12 11	---	12 13	12 11 15 14	12 11 15	12 11 16	12 17	12 10 4 5 18	12 1 2 3 6 19	12 1 2 7 20
13	13 9 1	13 9 1 2	13 9 7 3	13 12 10 4	13 9 7 3 5	13 9 7 6	13 9 7	13 12 10 8	13 9	13 12 10	13 12 11	13 12	---	13 12 11 15 14	13 12 11 15	13 17 16	13 17	13 9 7 3 5 18	13 9 7 6 19	13 9 7 20
14	14 5 3 2 1	14 5 3 2	14 5 3	14 5 4	14 5	14 5 6	14 5 3 7	14 5 8	14 5 3 7 9	14 5 4 10	14 15 11	14 15 11 12	14 15 11 12 13	---	14 15	14 15 11 16	14 15 11 12 17	14 18	14 18 19	14 18 19 20
15	15 8 10 1	15 8 4 2	15 8 5 3	15 8 4	15 8 5	15 8 5 6	15 8 4 2 7	15 8	15 8 10 1 9	15 8 10	15 11	15 11 12	15 11 12 13	15 14	---	15 11 16	15 11 12 17	15 14 18	15 14 18 19	15 14 18 19 20
16	16 11 10 1	16 11 10 1 2	16 11 10 1 2 3	16 11 10 4	16 11 10 4 5	16 11 10 4 5 6	16 17 13 9 7	16 11 10 8	16 17 13 9	16 11 10	16 11	16 11 12	16 17 13	16 11 15 14	16 11 15	---	16 17	16 11 15 14 18	16 11 15 14 18 19	16 17 13 9 7 20
17	17 12 1	17 12 1 2	17 12 1 2 3	17 12 10 4	17 12 10 4 5	17 13 9 7 6	17 13 9 7	17 12 10 8	17 13 9	17 12 10	17 12 11	17 12	17 13	17 12 11 15 14	17 12 11 15	17 16	---	17 12 10 4 5 18	17 13 9 7 6 19	17 13 9 7 20
18	18 5 3 2 1	18 5 3 2	18 5 3	18 5 4	18 5	18 5 6	18 5 3 7	18 5 8	18 5 3 7 9	18 5 4 10	18 14 15 11	18 5 4 10 12	18 5 3 7 9 13	18 14	18 14 15	18 14 15 11 16	18 5 4 10 12 17	---	18 19	18 19 20
19	19 6 3 2 1	19 6 3 2	19 6 3	19 6 5 4	19 6 5	19 6	19 6 7	19 6 5 8	19 6 7 9	19 6 5 4 10	19 18 14 15 11	19 6 3 2 1 12	19 6 7 9 13	19 18 14	19 18 14 15	19 18 14 15 11 16	19 6 7 9 13 17	19 18	---	19 20
20	20 7 2 1	20 7 2	20 7 3	20 7 2 4	20 7 3 5	20 7 6	20 7	20 7 2 4 8	20 7 9	20 7 2 1 10	20 7 2 1 10 11	20 7 2 1 12	20 7 9 13	20 19 18 14	20 19 18 14 15	20 7 9 13 17 16	20 7 9 13 17	20 19 18	20 19	---

Working Paths of The 20-Node Network

Table 8.7 Working Paths of The 20-Node Network (Network 4)

Backup Paths of The 20-Node Network - Case I

From / To	1	2	3	4	5	6	7	8	9	10	11	12	13	14	15	16	17	18	19	20
1	—	1 10 4 2	1 9 7 20 19 6 3	1 10 4	1 10 4 8 5	1 9 7 20 19 6	1 9 7	1 12 17 16 11 15 14 5 8	1 12 17 13 9	1 9 7 20 19 6 3 2 4 10	1 12 17 16 11	1 9 13 17 12	1 12 17 13	1 12 17 16 11 15 14	1 12 17 16 11 15	1 12 17 16	1 9 13 17	1 9 7 20 19 18	1 9 7 20 19	1 10 4 2 3 6 19 20
2	2 4 10 1	—	2 4 8 5 14 18 19 6 3	2 3 6 19 18 14 5 8 4	2 4 8 5	2 4 8 5 14 18 19 6	2 4 10 1 9 7	2 3 6 19 18 14 5 8	2 3 6 19 20 7 9	2 4 10	2 4 8 5 14 15 11	2 4 10 1 9 13 17 12	2 4 10 1 12 17 13	2 4 10 1 12 17 16 11 15 14	2 3 6 19 18 14 15	2 3 6 19 20 7 9 13 17 16	2 4 10 1 9 13 17	2 4 8 5 14 18	2 4 8 5 14 18 19	2 3 6 19 20
3	3 6 19 20 7 9 1	3 6 19 18 14 5 8 4 2	—	3 6 19 18 14 5 8 4	3 2 4 8 5	3 2 4 8 5 14 18 19 6	3 6 19 20 7	3 2 4 8	3 2 4 10 1 9	3 6 19 18 14 5 8 4 10	3 6 19 18 14 15 11	3 6 19 20 7 9 13 17 12	3 2 4 10 1 12 17 13	3 6 19 18 14	3 6 19 18 14 15	3 6 19 20 7 9 13 17 16	3 6 19 20 7 9 13 17	3 6 19 18	3 2 4 8 5 14 18 19	3 6 19 20
4	4 10 1	4 8 5 14 18 19 6 3 2	4 8 5 14 18 19 6 3	—	4 8 5	4 2 3 6	4 10 1 9 7	4 2 3 6 19 18 14 5 8	4 10 1 12 17 13 9	4 2 3 6 19 20 7 9 1 10	4 8 5 14 15 11	4 8 5 14 15 11 16 17 12	4 2 3 6 19 20 7 9 13	4 2 3 6 19 18 14	4 10 1 12 17 16 11 15	4 2 3 6 19 20 7 9 13 17 16	4 8 5 14 15 11 16 17	4 8 5 14 18	4 8 5 14 18 19	4 8 5 14 18 19 20
5	5 8 4 10 1	5 8 4 2	5 8 4 2 3	5 8 4	—	5 14 18 19 6	5 14 18 19 20 7	5 14 18 19 6 3 2 4 8	5 8 4 10 1 9	5 14 18 19 20 7 9 1 10	5 14 15 11	5 14 15 11 16 17 12	5 14 15 11 16 17 13	5 8 4 2 3 6 19 18 14	5 14 15	5 14 18 19 20 7 9 13 17 16	5 14 15 11 16 17	5 14 18	5 14 18 19	5 14 18 19 20
6	6 19 20 7 9 1	6 19 18 14 5 8 4 2	6 19 18 14 5 8 4 2 3	6 3 2 4	6 19 18 14 5	—	6 19 20 7	6 3 2 4 8	6 3 2 4 10 1 9	6 19 20 7 9 1 10	6 19 18 14 15 11	6 19 20 7 9 13 17 12	6 3 2 4 10 1 12 17 13	6 19 18 14	6 19 18 14 15	6 19 20 7 9 13 17 16	6 3 2 4 10 1 12 17	6 19 18	6 3 2 4 8 5 14 18 19	6 19 20
7	7 9 1	7 9 1 10 4 2	7 20 19 6 3	7 9 1 10 4	7 20 19 18 14 5	7 20 19 6	—	7 20 19 18 14 5 8	7 20 19 6 3 2 4 10 1 9	7 20 19 6 3 2 4 10	7 9 13 17 16 11	7 9 13 17 12	7 20 19 18 14 15 11 16 17 13	7 20 19 18 14	7 20 19 18 14 15	7 20 19 18 14 15 11 16	7 20 19 18 14 15 11 16 17	7 20 19 18	7 20 19	7 9 1 10 4 2 3 6 19 20
8	8 5 14 15 11 16 17 12 1	8 5 14 18 19 6 3 2	8 4 2 3	8 5 14 18 19 6 3 2 4	8 4 2 3 6 19 18 14 5	8 4 2 3 6	8 5 14 18 19 20 7	—	8 5 14 18 19 20 7 9	8 4 10	8 5 14 15 11	8 4 10 1 12	8 4 10 1 9 13	8 4 2 3 6 19 18 14	8 5 14 15	8 4 10 1 12 17 16	8 4 10 1 9 13 17	8 4 2 3 6 19 18	8 4 10 1 9 7 20 19	8 5 14 18 19 20
9	9 13 17 12 1	9 7 20 19 6 3 2	9 1 10 4 2 3	9 13 17 12 1 10 4	9 1 10 4 8 5	9 1 10 4 2 3 6	9 1 10 4 2 3 6 19 20 7	9 7 20 19 18 14 5 8	—	9 7 20 19 6 3 2 4 10	9 13 17 16 11	9 13 17 12	9 1 12 17 13	9 13 17 16 11 15 14	9 13 17 16 11 15	9 7 20 19 18 14 15 11 16	9 1 12 17	9 1 10 4 8 5 14 18	9 1 10 4 8 5 14 18 19	9 1 10 4 2 3 6 19 20
10	10 4 2 3 6 19 20 7 9 1	10 4 2	10 4 8 5 14 18 19 6 3	10 1 9 7 20 19 6 3 2 4	10 1 9 7 20 19 18 14 5	10 1 9 7 20 19 6	10 4 2 3 6 19 20 7	10 4 8	10 4 2 3 6 19 20 7 9	—	10 1 12 17 16 11	10 1 12	10 1 9 13	10 1 12 17 16 11 15 14	10 4 8 5 14 15	10 1 12 17 16	10 1 9 13 17	10 1 9 7 20 19 18	10 1 9 7 20 19	10 4 2 3 6 19 20
11	11 16 17 12 1	11 15 14 5 8 4 2	11 15 14 18 19 6 3	11 15 14 5 8 4	11 15 14 5	11 15 14 18 19 6	11 16 17 13 9 7	11 15 14 5 8	11 16 17 13 9	11 16 17 12 1 10	—	11 16 17 12	11 16 17 13	11 16 17 12 1 10 4 8 5 14	11 16 17 12 1 10 4 8 5 14 15	11 15 14 5 8 4 10 1 12 17 16	11 16 17	11 16 17 13 9 7 20 19 18	11 16 17 13 9 7 20 19	11 15 14 18 19 20
12	12 17 13 9 1	12 17 13 9 1 10 4 2	12 17 13 9 7 20 19 6 3	12 17 16 11 15 14 5 8 4	12 17 16 11 15 14 5	12 17 13 9 7 20 19 6	12 17 13 9 7	12 1 10 4 8	12 17 13 9	12 1 10	12 17 16 11	—	12 17 13	12 1 10 4 8 5 14	12 1 10 4 8 5 14 15	12 17 16	12 1 9 13 17	12 17 16 11 15 14 18	12 17 13 9 7 20 19	12 17 16 11 15 14 18 19 20
13	13 17 12 1	13 17 12 1 10 4 2	13 17 12 1 10 4 2 3	13 9 7 20 19 6 3 2 4	13 17 16 11 15 14 5	13 17 12 1 10 4 2 3 6	13 17 16 11 15 14 18 19 20 7	13 9 1 10 4 8	13 17 12 1 9	13 9 1 10	13 17 16 11	13 17 12	—	13 9 7 20 19 18 14	13 9 7 20 19 18 14 15	13 9 7 20 19 18 14 15 11 16	13 9 1 12 17	13 17 16 11 15 14 18	13 17 16 11 15 14 18 19	13 17 16 11 15 14 18 19 20
14	14 15 11 16 17 12 1	14 15 11 16 17 12 1 10 4 2	14 18 19 6 3	14 18 19 6 3 2 4	14 18 19 6 3 2 4 8 5	14 18 19 6	14 18 19 20 7	14 18 19 6 3 2 4 8	14 15 11 16 17 13 9	14 15 11 16 17 12 1 10	14 5 8 4 10 1 12 17 16 11	14 5 8 4 10 1 12	14 18 19 20 7 9 13	—	14 5 8 4 10 1 12 17 16 11 15	14 5 8 4 10 1 12 17 16	14 18 19 20 7 9 13 17	14 5 8 4 2 3 6 19 18	14 5 8 4 2 3 6 19	14 5 8 4 10 1 9 7 20
15	15 11 16 17 12 1	15 14 18 19 6 3 2	15 14 18 19 6 3	15 11 16 17 12 1 10 4	15 14 5	15 14 18 19 6	15 14 18 19 20 7	15 14 5 8	15 11 16 17 13 9	15 14 5 8 4 10	15 14 5 8 4 10 1 12 17 16 11	15 14 5 8 4 10 1 12	15 14 18 19 20 7 9 13	15 11 16 17 12 1 10 4 8 5 14	—	15 14 5 8 4 10 1 12 17 16	15 14 18 19 20 7 9 13 17	15 11 16 17 13 9 7 20 19 18	15 11 16 17 13 9 7 20 19	15 11 16 17 13 9 7 20
16	16 17 12 1	16 17 13 9 7 20 19 6 3 2	16 17 13 9 7 20 19 6 3	16 17 13 9 7 20 19 6 3 2 4	16 17 13 9 7 20 19 18 14 5	16 17 13 9 7 20 19 6	16 11 15 14 18 19 20 7	16 17 12 1 10 4 8	16 11 15 14 18 19 20 7 9	16 17 12 1 10	16 17 12 1 10 4 8 5 14 15 11	16 17 12	16 11 15 14 18 19 20 7 9 13	16 17 12 1 10 4 8 5 14	16 17 12 1 10 4 8 5 14 15	—	16 11 15 14 5 8 4 10 1 12 17	16 17 13 9 7 20 19 18	16 17 13 9 7 20 19	16 11 15 14 18 19 20
17	17 13 9 1	17 13 9 1 10 4 2	17 13 9 7 20 19 6 3	17 16 11 15 14 5 8 4	17 16 11 15 14 5	17 12 1 10 4 2 3 6	17 16 11 15 14 18 19 20 7	17 13 9 1 10 4 8	17 12 1 9	17 13 9 1 10	17 16 11	17 13 9 1 12	17 12 1 9 13	17 13 9 7 20 19 18 14	17 13 9 7 20 19 18 14 15	17 12 1 10 4 8 5 14 15 11 16	—	17 16 11 15 14 18	17 16 11 15 14 18 19	17 16 11 15 14 18 19 20
18	18 19 20 7 9 1	18 14 5 8 4 2	18 19 6 3	18 14 5 8 4	18 14 5	18 19 6	18 19 20 7	18 19 6 3 2 4 8	18 14 5 8 4 10 1 9	18 19 20 7 9 1 10	18 19 20 7 9 13 17 16 11	18 14 15 11 16 17 12	18 14 15 11 16 17 13	18 19 6 3 2 4 8 5 14	18 19 20 7 9 13 17 16 11 15	18 19 20 7 9 13 17 16	18 14 15 11 16 17	—	18 14 5 8 4 2 3 6 19	18 14 5 8 4 10 1 9 7 20
19	19 20 7 9 1	19 18 14 5 8 4 2	19 18 14 5 8 4 2 3	19 18 14 5 8 4	19 18 14 5	19 18 14 5 8 4 2 3 6	19 20 7	19 20 7 9 1 10 4 8	19 18 14 5 8 4 10 1 9	19 20 7 9 1 10	19 20 7 9 13 17 16 11	19 20 7 9 13 17 12	19 18 14 15 11 16 17 13	19 6 3 2 4 8 5 14	19 20 7 9 13 17 16 11 15	19 20 7 9 13 17 16	19 18 14 15 11 16 17	19 6 3 2 4 8 5 14 18	—	19 6 3 2 4 10 1 9 7 20
20	20 19 6 3 2 4 10 1	20 19 6 3 2	20 19 6 3	20 19 18 14 5 8 4	20 19 18 14 5	20 19 6	20 19 6 3 2 4 10 1 9 7	20 19 18 14 5 8	20 19 6 3 2 4 10 1 9	20 19 6 3 2 4 10	20 19 18 14 15 11	20 19 18 14 15 11 16 17 12	20 19 18 14 15 11 16 17 13	20 7 9 1 10 4 8 5 14	20 7 9 13 17 16 11 15	20 19 18 14 15 11 16	20 19 18 14 15 11 16 17	20 7 9 1 10 4 8 5 14 18	20 7 9 1 10 4 2 3 6 19	—

Table 8.8 Backup Paths of The 20-Node Network with Link-Failure Tolerance (Case I)

Appendix C

Tables and Figures for Case II and III

This appendix includes tables and figures for Networks 1,2,3, and 4. It includes the backup paths and figures for Case II and Case III for Networks 1,2,3, and 4.

The six optimization cases mentioned in the appendices are:

- Case I: link-failure with spare capacity optimization criteria
- Case II: node-failure with spare capacity optimization criteria
- Case III: link-or-node failure with spare capacity optimization criteria
- Case IV: link-failure with minimum network cost optimization criteria
- Case V: node-failure with minimum network cost optimization criteria
- Case VI: link-or-node failure with minimum network cost optimization criteria

Node	1	2	3	4	5	6	7	8	9	10	11	12	13
1	---	1 10 4 5 3 2	1 10 4 5 3	1 10 4	1 10 4 5	1 10 4 5 6	1 12 13 9 7	1 12 11 8	1 12 13 9	1 2 3 5 4 10	1 12 11	1 2 3 5 8 11 12	1 12 13
2	2 3 5 4 10 1	---	2 1 10 4 5 3	2 3 5 4	2 1 10 4 5	2 1 10 4 5 6	2 3 5 6 7	2 3 5 8	2 3 5 6 7 9	2 3 5 4 10	2 1 12 11	2 3 5 8 11 12	2 3 5 8 11 12 13
3	3 5 4 10 1	3 5 4 10 1 2	---	3 5 4	3 2 1 10 4 5	3 5 6	3 5 6 7	3 2 1 12 11 8	3 2 1 12 13 9	3 5 4 10	3 2 1 12 11	3 5 8 11 12	3 2 1 12 13
4	4 10 1	4 5 3 2	4 5 3	---	4 10 1 2 3 5	4 10 1 12 13 9 7 6	4 5 6 7	4 5 8	4 5 6 7 9	4 5 3 2 1 10	4 10 1 12 11	4 5 8 11 12	4 5 6 7 9 13
5	5 4 10 1	5 4 10 1 2	5 4 10 1 2 3	5 3 2 1 10 4	---	5 8 11 12 13 9 7 6	5 6 7	5 3 2 1 12 11 8	5 8 11 12 13 9	5 3 2 1 10	5 3 2 1 12 11	5 8 11 12	5 8 11 12 13
6	6 5 4 10 1	6 5 4 10 1 2	6 5 3	6 7 9 13 12 1 10 4	6 7 9 13 12 11 8 5	---	6 5 8 11 12 13 9 7	6 7 9 13 12 11 8	6 5 8 11 12 13 9	6 7 9 13 12 1 10	6 7 9 13 12 11	6 5 8 11 12	6 5 8 11 12 13
7	7 9 13 12 1	7 6 5 3 2	7 6 5 3	7 6 5 4	7 6 5	7 9 13 12 11 8 5 6	---	7 6 5 8	7 6 5 8 11 12 13 9	7 6 5 4 10	7 9 13 12 11	7 9 13 12	7 6 5 8 11 12 13
8	8 11 12 1	8 5 3 2	8 11 12 1 2 3	8 5 4	8 11 12 1 2 3 5	8 11 12 13 9 7 6	8 5 6 7	---	8 5 6 7 9	8 11 12 1 10	8 5 3 2 1 12 11	8 5 3 2 1 12	8 5 6 7 9 13
9	9 13 12 1	9 7 6 5 3 2	9 13 12 1 2 3	9 7 6 5 4	9 13 12 11 8 5	9 13 12 11 8 5 6	9 13 12 11 8 5 6 7	9 7 6 5 8	---	9 7 6 5 4 10	9 13 12 11	9 13 12	9 7 6 5 8 11 12 13
10	10 4 5 3 2 1	10 4 5 3 2	10 4 5 3	10 1 2 3 5 4	10 1 2 3 5	10 1 12 13 9 7 6	10 4 5 6 7	10 1 12 11 8	10 4 5 6 7 9	---	10 1 12 11	10 1 12	10 4 5 6 7 9 13
11	11 12 1	11 12 1 2	11 12 1 2 3	11 12 1 10 4	11 12 1 2 3 5	11 12 13 9 7 6	11 12 13 9 7	11 12 1 2 3 5 8	11 12 13 9	11 12 1 10	---	11 8 5 3 2 1 12	11 8 5 6 7 9 13
12	12 11 8 5 3 2 1	12 11 8 5 3 2	12 11 8 5 3	12 11 8 5 4	12 11 8 5	12 11 8 5 6	12 13 9 7	12 1 2 3 5 8	12 13 9	12 1 10	12 1 2 3 5 8 11	---	12 11 8 5 6 7 9 13
13	13 12 1	13 12 11 8 5 3 2	13 12 1 2 3	13 9 7 6 5 4	13 12 11 8 5	13 12 11 8 5 6	13 12 11 8 5 6 7	13 9 7 6 5 8	13 12 11 8 5 6 7 9	13 9 7 6 5 4 10	13 9 7 6 5 8 11	13 9 7 6 5 8 11 12	---

Backup Paths of The 13-Node Network - Case II

Table 9.1 The Backup Paths of The 13-Node Network with Node-Failure Tolerance (Case II)

Backup Paths of The 13-Node Network - Case III

Node	1	2	3	4	5	6	7	8	9	10	11	12	13
1	---	1 10 4 2	1 9 7 6 3	1 10 4	1 10 4 8 5	1 9 7 6	1 9 7	1 9 13 12 11 8	1 10 4 2 7 9	1 9 7 2 4 10	1 9 13 12 11	1 9 13 12	1 10 4 8 11 12 13
2	2 4 10 1	---	2 7 6 3	2 7 9 1 10 4	2 4 8 5	2 7 6	2 4 10 1 9 7	2 7 6 3 5 8	2 7 9	2 4 10	2 7 9 13 12 11	2 4 8 11 12	2 4 8 11 12 13
3	3 6 7 9 1	3 6 7 2	---	3 5 8 4	3 6 7 2 4 8 5	3 5 8 4 2 7 6	3 6 7	3 6 7 2 4 8	3 5 8 4 10 1 9	3 5 8 4 10	3 6 7 9 13 12 11	3 5 8 11 12	3 5 8 11 12 13
4	4 10 1	4 10 1 9 7 2	4 8 5 3	---	4 8 5	4 2 7 6	4 10 1 9 7	4 2 7 6 3 5 8	4 8 11 12 13 9	4 2 7 9 1 10	4 10 1 9 13 12 11	4 8 11 12	4 2 7 9 13
5	5 8 4 10 1	5 8 4 2	5 8 4 2 7 6 3	5 8 4	---	5 3 6	5 8 4 2 7	5 3 6 7 2 4 8	5 8 4 10 1 9	5 3 6 7 9 1 10	5 3 6 7 9 13 12 11	5 8 11 12	5 8 11 12 13
6	6 7 9 1	6 7 2	6 7 2 4 8 5 3	6 7 2 4	6 3 5	---	6 3 5 8 4 2 7	6 7 2 4 8	6 3 5 8 4 10 1 9	6 7 9 1 10	6 7 9 13 12 11	6 7 9 13 12	6 3 5 8 11 12 13
7	7 9 1	7 9 1 10 4 2	7 6 3	7 9 1 10 4	7 2 4 8 5	7 2 4 8 5 3 6	---	7 6 3 5 8	7 2 4 10 1 9	7 6 3 5 8 4 10	7 9 13 12 11	7 9 13 12	7 2 4 8 11 12 13
8	8 11 12 13 9 1	8 5 3 6 7 2	8 4 2 7 6 3	8 5 3 6 7 2 4	8 4 2 7 6 3 5	8 4 2 7 6	8 5 3 6 7	---	8 11 12 13 9	8 11 12 13 9 1 10	8 4 10 1 9 13 12 11	8 4 10 1 9 13 12	8 4 10 1 9 13
9	9 7 2 4 10 1	9 7 2	9 1 10 4 8 5 3	9 13 12 11 8 4	9 1 10 4 8 5	9 1 10 4 8 5 3 6	9 1 10 4 2 7	9 13 12 11 8	---	9 7 2 4 10	9 13 12 11	9 13 12	9 7 2 4 8 11 12 13
10	10 4 2 7 9 1	10 4 2	10 4 8 5 3	10 1 9 7 2 4	10 1 9 7 6 3 5	10 1 9 7 6	10 4 8 5 3 6 7	10 1 9 13 12 11 8	10 4 2 7 9	---	10 4 8 11	10 4 8 11 12	10 1 9 13
11	11 12 13 9 1	11 12 13 9 7 2	11 12 13 9 7 6 3	11 12 13 9 1 10 4	11 12 13 9 7 6 3 5	11 12 13 9 7 6	11 12 13 9 7	11 12 13 9 1 10 4 8	11 12 13 9	11 8 4 10	---	11 8 4 10 1 9 13 12	11 8 4 10 1 9 13
12	12 13 9 1	12 11 8 4 2	12 11 8 5 3	12 11 8 4	12 11 8 5	12 13 9 7 6	12 13 9 7	12 13 9 1 10 4 8	12 13 9	12 11 8 4 10	12 13 9 1 10 4 8 11	---	12 11 8 4 10 1 9 13
13	13 12 11 8 4 10 1	13 12 11 8 4 2	13 12 11 8 5 3	13 9 7 2 4	13 12 11 8 5	13 12 11 8 5 3 6	13 12 11 8 4 2 7	13 9 1 10 4 8	13 12 11 8 4 2 7 9	13 9 1 10	13 9 1 10 4 8 11	13 9 1 10 4 8 11 12	---

Table 9.2 Backup Paths of The 13-Node Network with Node-and-Link Failure Tolerance (Case III)

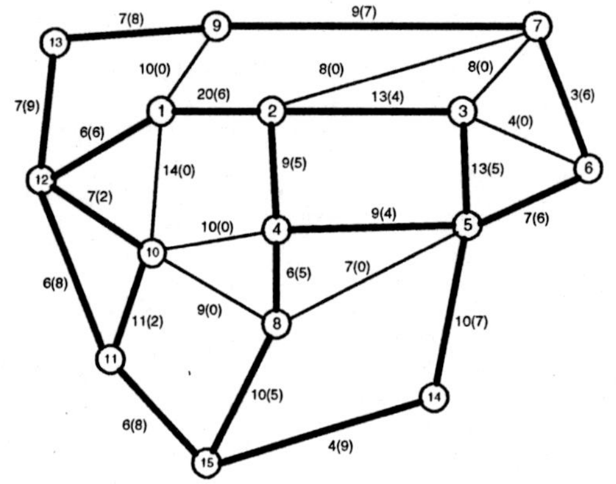

Figure 9.1 15-Node Network (Network 2) with Node-Failure Tolerance (Case II)

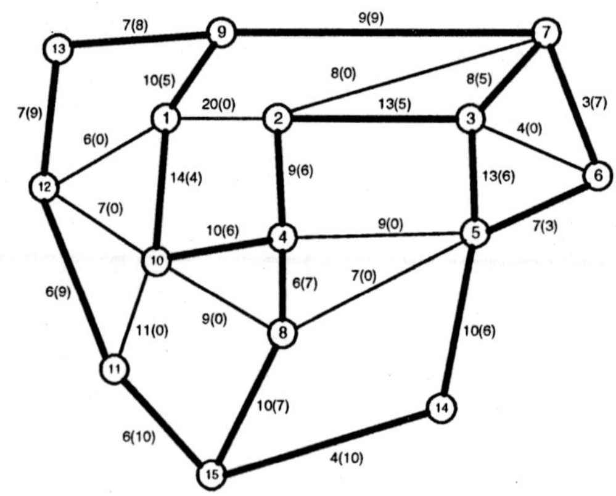

Figure 9.2 15-Node Network (Network 2) with Link-and-Node-Failure Tolerance (Case III)

Backup Paths of The 15-Node - Case II

Node	1	2	3	4	5	6	7	8	9	10	11	12	13	14	15
1	---	1 12 11 15 8 4 2	1 12 11 15 14 5 3	1 12 11 15 8 4	1 12 11 15 14 5	1 12 13 9 7 6	1 12 13 9 7	1 2 4 8	1 12 13 9	1 12 10	1 12 11	1 2 4 8 15 11 12	1 12 13	1 12 11 15 14	1 12 11 15
2	2 4 8 15 11 12 1	---	2 4 5 3	2 3 5 4	2 4 5	2 4 5 6	2 3 5 6 7	2 1 12 11 15 8	2 3 5 6 7 9	2 4 8 15 11 10	2 4 8 15 11	2 4 8 15 11 12	2 4 8 15 11 12 13	2 4 8 15 14	2 1 12 11 15
3	3 5 14 15 11 12 1	3 5 4 2	---	3 5 4	3 2 4 5	3 5 6	3 5 6 7	3 2 4 8	3 2 1 12 13 9	3 5 14 15 11 10	3 5 14 15 11	3 5 14 15 11 12	3 2 1 12 13	3 2 4 8 15 14	3 2 1 12 11 15
4	4 8 15 11 12 1	4 5 3 2	4 5 3	---	4 2 3 5	4 2 1 12 13 9 7 6	4 5 6 7	4 5 14 15 8	4 5 6 7 9	4 8 15 11 10	4 8 15 11	4 2 1 12	4 5 6 7 9 13	4 8 15 14	4 5 14 15
5	5 14 15 11 12 1	5 4 2	5 4 2 3	5 3 2 4	---	5 3 2 1 12 13 9 7 6	5 6 7	5 4 8	5 4 2 1 12 13 9	5 14 15 11 10	5 14 15 11	5 3 2 1 12	5 4 2 1 12 13	5 4 8 15 14	5 14 15
6	6 7 9 13 12 1	6 5 4 2	6 5 3	6 7 9 13 12 1 2 4	6 7 9 13 12 1 2 3 5	---	6 5 3 2 1 12 13 9 7	6 7 9 13 12 11 15 8	6 5 3 2 1 12 13 9	6 7 9 13 12 10	6 7 9 13 12 11	6 7 9 13 12	6 5 3 2 1 12 13	6 7 9 13 12 11 15 14	6 7 9 13 12 11 15
7	7 9 13 12 1	7 6 5 3 2	7 6 5 3	7 6 5 4	7 6 5	7 9 13 12 1 2 3 5 6	---	7 6 5 14 15 8	7 6 5 3 2 1 12 13 9	7 9 13 12 10	7 9 13 12 11	7 9 13 12	7 6 5 3 2 1 12 13	7 9 13 12 11 15 14	7 6 5 14 15
8	8 4 2 1	8 15 11 12 1 2	8 4 2 3	8 15 14 5 4	8 4 5	8 15 11 12 13 9 7 6	8 15 14 5 6 7	---	8 4 5 6 7 9	8 15 11 10	8 15 11	8 15 11 12	8 4 5 6 7 9 13	8 15 14	8 4 5 14 15
9	9 13 12 1	9 7 6 5 3 2	9 13 12 1 2 3	9 7 6 5 4	9 13 12 1 2 4 5	9 13 12 1 2 3 5 6	9 13 12 1 2 3 5 6 7	9 7 6 5 4 8	---	9 13 12 10	9 13 12 11	9 13 12	9 7 6 5 3 2 1 12 13	9 13 12 11 15 14	9 13 12 11 15
10	10 12 1	10 11 15 8 4 2	10 11 15 14 5 3	10 11 15 8 4	10 11 15 14 5	10 12 13 9 7 6	10 12 13 9 7	10 11 15 8	10 12 13 9	---	10 12 11	10 11 12	10 11 15 14 5 6 7 9 13	10 11 15 14	10 11 15
11	11 12 1	11 15 8 4 2	11 15 14 5 3	11 15 8 4	11 15 14 5	11 12 13 9 7 6	11 12 13 9 7	11 15 8	11 12 13 9	11 12 10	---	11 10 12	11 15 14 5 6 7 9 13	11 12 1 2 3 5 14	11 12 1 2 4 8 15
12	12 11 15 8 4 2 1	12 11 15 8 4 2	12 11 15 14 5 3	12 1 2 4	12 1 2 3 5	12 13 9 7 6	12 13 9 7	12 11 15 8	12 13 9	12 11 10	12 10 11	---	12 1 2 3 5 6 7 9 13	12 1 2 3 5 14	12 1 2 4 8 15
13	13 12 1	13 12 11 15 8 4 2	13 12 1 2 3	13 9 7 6 5 4	13 12 1 2 4 5	13 12 1 2 3 5 6	13 12 1 2 3 5 6 7	13 9 7 6 5 4 8	13 12 1 2 3 5 6 7 9	13 9 7 6 5 14 15 11 10	13 9 7 6 5 14 15 11	13 9 7 6 5 3 2 1 12	---	13 9 7 6 5 14	13 9 7 6 5 14 15
14	14 15 11 12 1	14 15 8 4 2	14 15 8 4 2 3	14 15 8 4	14 15 8 4 5	14 15 11 12 13 9 7 6	14 15 11 12 13 9 7	14 15 8	14 15 11 12 13 9	14 15 11 10	14 5 3 2 1 12 11	14 5 3 2 1 12	14 5 6 7 9 13	---	14 5 4 8 15
15	15 11 12 1	15 11 12 1 2	15 11 12 1 2 3	15 14 5 4	15 14 5	15 11 12 13 9 7 6	15 14 5 6 7	15 14 5 4 8	15 11 12 13 9	15 11 10	15 8 4 2 1 12 11	15 8 4 2 1 12	15 14 5 6 7 9 13	15 8 4 5 14	---

Table 9.3 Backup Paths of The 15-Node Network with Node-Failure Tolerance (Case II)

Node	1	2	3	4	5	6	7	8	9	10	11	12	13	14	15
1	---	1 10 4 2	1 9 7 3	1 10 4	1 9 7 6 5	1 9 7 6	1 9 7	1 9 7 3 2 4 8	1 10 4 2 3 7 9	1 9 7 3 2 4 10	1 9 13 12 11	1 9 13 12	1 10 4 8 15 11 12 13	1 10 4 8 15 14	1 9 13 12 11 15
2	2 4 10 1	---	2 4 8 15 14 5 3	2 3 5 14 15 8 4	2 4 8 15 14 5	2 4 8 15 14 5 6	2 3 7	2 3 5 14 15 8	2 3 7 9	2 4 10	2 4 8 15 11	2 4 8 15 11 12	2 4 8 15 11 12 13	2 4 8 15 14	2 3 5 14 15
3	3 7 9 1	3 5 14 15 8 4 2	---	3 5 14 15 8 4	3 7 6 5	3 5 6	3 5 6 7	3 2 4 8	3 2 4 10 1 9	3 5 14 15 8 4 10	3 5 14 15 11	3 7 9 13 12	3 5 14 15 11 12 13	3 2 4 8 15 14	3 7 9 13 12 11 15
4	4 10 1	4 8 15 14 5 3 2	4 8 15 14 5 3	---	4 2 3 5	4 2 3 7 6	4 10 1 9 7	4 2 3 5 14 15 8	4 8 15 11 12 13 9	4 2 3 7 9 1 10	4 8 15 11	4 8 15 11 12	4 2 3 7 9 13	4 8 15 14	4 2 3 5 14 15
5	5 6 7 9 1	5 14 15 8 4 2	5 6 7 3	5 3 2 4	---	5 3 7 6	5 6 7	5 14 15 8	5 14 15 11 12 13 9	5 3 7 9 1 10	5 14 15 11	5 14 15 11 12	5 14 15 11 12 13	5 3 2 4 8 15 14	5 14 15
6	6 7 9 1	6 5 14 15 8 4 2	6 5 3	6 7 3 2 4	6 7 3 5	---	6 5 3 7	6 7 3 2 4 8	6 5 3 2 4 10 1 9	6 7 9 1 10	6 7 9 13 12 11	6 7 9 13 12	6 5 14 15 11 12 13	6 7 3 2 4 8 15 14	6 7 9 13 12 11 15
7	7 9 1	7 3 2	7 6 5 3	7 9 1 10 4	7 6 5	7 3 5 6	---	7 3 5 14 15 8	7 3 2 4 10 1 9	7 3 5 14 15 8 4 10	7 9 13 12 11	7 9 13 12	7 3 5 14 15 11 12 13	7 9 13 12 11 15 14	7 3 5 14 15
8	8 4 2 3 7 9 1	8 15 14 5 3 2	8 4 2 3	8 15 14 5 3 2 4	8 15 14 5	8 4 2 3 7 6	8 15 14 5 3 7	---	8 4 2 3 7 9	8 4 10	8 15 11	8 15 11 12	8 4 2 3 7 9 13	8 15 14	8 4 2 3 5 14 15
9	9 7 3 2 4 10 1	9 7 3 2	9 1 10 4 2 3	9 13 12 11 15 8 4	9 13 12 11 15 14 5	9 1 10 4 2 3 5 6	9 1 10 4 2 3 7	9 7 3 2 4 8	---	9 7 3 2 4 10	9 13 12 11	9 13 12	9 1 10 4 8 15 11 12 13	9 13 12 11 15 14	9 13 12 11 15
10	10 4 2 3 7 9 1	10 4 2	10 4 8 15 14 5 3	10 1 9 7 3 2 4	10 1 9 7 3 5	10 1 9 7 6	10 4 8 15 14 5 3 7	10 4 8	10 4 2 3 7 9	---	10 4 8 15 11	10 1 9 13 12	10 1 9 13	10 1 9 13 12 11 15 14	10 1 9 13 12 11 15
11	11 12 13 9 1	11 15 8 4 2	11 15 14 5 3	11 15 8 4	11 15 14 5	11 12 13 9 7 6	11 12 13 9 7	11 15 8	11 12 13 9	11 15 8 4 10	---	11 15 8 4 10 1 9 13 12	11 15 8 4 10 1 9 13	11 12 13 9 7 3 5 14	11 12 13 9 1 10 4 8 15
12	12 13 9 1	12 11 15 8 4 2	12 13 9 7 3	12 11 15 8 4	12 11 15 14 5	12 13 9 7 6	12 13 9 7	12 11 15 8	12 13 9	12 13 9 1 10	12 13 9 1 10 4 8 15 11	---	12 11 15 8 4 10 1 9 13	12 13 9 7 3 5 14	12 13 9 1 10 4 8 15
13	13 12 11 15 8 4 10 1	13 12 11 15 8 4 2	13 12 11 15 14 5 3	13 9 7 3 2 4	13 12 11 15 14 5	13 12 11 15 14 5 6	13 12 11 15 14 5 3 7	13 9 7 3 2 4 8	13 12 11 15 8 4 10 1 9	13 9 1 10	13 9 1 10 4 8 15 11	13 9 1 10 4 8 15 11 12	---	13 9 7 3 5 14	13 9 1 10 4 8 15
14	14 15 8 4 10 1	14 15 8 4 2	14 15 8 4 2 3	14 15 8 4	14 15 8 4 2 3 5	14 15 8 4 2 3 7 6	14 15 11 12 13 9 7	14 15 8	14 15 11 12 13 9	14 15 11 12 13 9 1 10	14 5 3 7 9 13 12 11	14 5 3 7 9 13 12	14 5 3 7 9 13	---	14 5 3 2 4 8 15
15	15 11 12 13 9 1	15 14 5 3 2	15 11 12 13 9 7 3	15 14 5 3 2 4	15 14 5	15 11 12 13 9 7 6	15 14 5 3 7	15 14 5 3 2 4 8	15 11 12 13 9	15 11 12 13 9 1 10	15 8 4 10 1 9 13 12 11	15 8 4 10 1 9 13 12	15 8 4 10 1 9 13	15 8 4 2 3 5 14	---

Backup Paths of The 15 Node Network - Case III

Table 9.4 Backup Paths of The 15-Node Network with Node-and-Link Failure Tolerance (Case III)

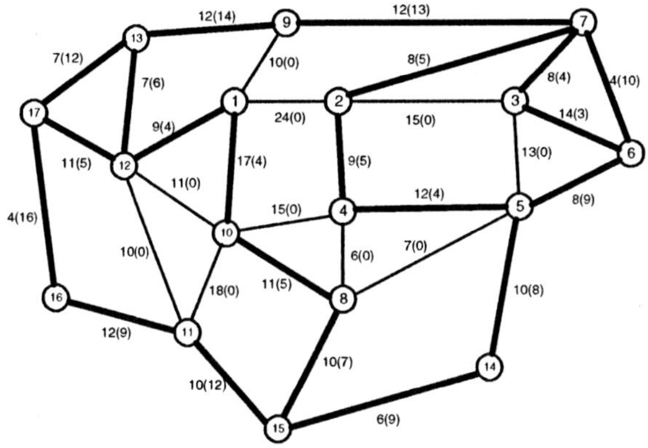

Figure 9.3 17-Node Network (Network 3) with Node-Failure Tolerance (Case II)

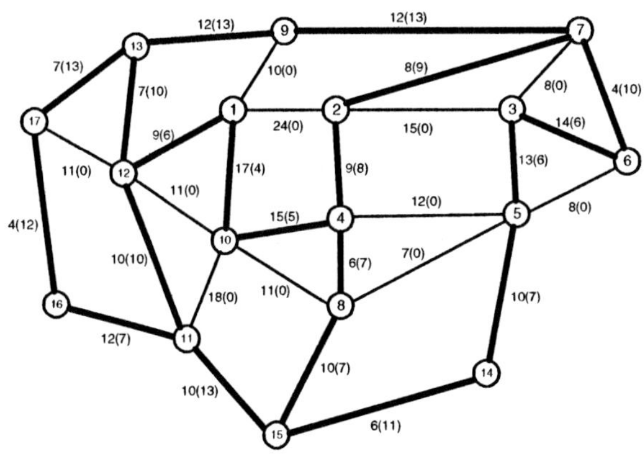

Figure 9.4 17-Node Network (Network 3) with Link-and-Node-Failure Tolerance (Case III)

To \ From	1	2	3	4	5	6	7	8	9	10	11	12	13	14	15	16	17
1	---	1 12 13 9 7 2	1 12 13 9 7 3	1 10 8 15 14 5 4	1 10 8 15 14 5	1 12 13 9 7 6	1 12 13 9 7	1 12 17 16 11 15 8	1 12 13 9	1 12 17 16 11 15 8 10	1 12 17 16 11	1 10 8 15 11 16 17 12	1 12 13	1 10 8 15 14	1 12 17 16 11 15	1 12 17 16	1 10 8 15 11 16 17
2	2 7 9 13 12 1	---	2 7 3	2 7 6 5 4	2 4 5	2 7 6	2 4 5 6 7	2 7 6 5 14 15 8	2 7 9	2 4 5 14 15 8 10	2 4 5 14 15 11	2 7 9 13 12	2 4 5 14 15 11 16 17 13	2 7 9 13 17 16 11 15 14	2 7 6 5 14 15	2 7 9 13 17 16	2 7 9 13 17
3	3 7 9 13 12 1	3 7 2	---	3 6 5 4	3 6 5	3 7 6	3 6 7	3 7 9 13 12 1 10 8	3 6 5 14 15 11 16 17 13 9	3 6 5 14 15 8 10	3 6 5 14 15 11	3 7 9 13 12	3 6 5 14 15 11 16 17 13	3 7 9 13 17 16 11 15 14	3 7 9 13 17 16 11 15	3 7 9 13 17 16	3 7 9 13 17
4	4 5 14 15 8 10 1	4 5 6 7 2	4 5 6 3	---	4 2 7 6 5	4 2 7 6	4 5 6 7	4 5 14 15 8	4 5 6 7 9	4 5 14 15 8 10	4 5 14 15 11	4 2 7 9 13 12	4 2 7 9 13	4 2 7 9 13 17 16 11 15 14	4 5 14 15	4 2 7 9 13 17 16	4 2 7 9 13 17
5	5 14 15 8 10 1	5 4 2	5 6 3	5 6 7 2 4	---	5 4 2 7 6	5 6 7	5 14 15 8	5 14 15 11 16 17 13 9	5 14 15 8 10	5 14 15 11	5 6 7 9 13 12	5 14 15 11 16 17 13	5 6 7 9 13 17 16 11 15 14	5 14 15	5 6 7 9 13 17 16	5 6 7 9 13 17
6	6 7 9 13 12 1	6 7 2	6 7 3	6 7 2 4	6 7 2 4 5	---	6 3 7	6 7 9 13 12 1 10 8	6 5 14 15 11 16 17 13 9	6 7 9 13 12 1 10	6 7 9 13 17 16 11	6 7 9 13 12	6 5 14 15 11 16 17 13	6 7 9 13 17 16 11 15 14	6 7 9 13 17 16 11 15	6 7 9 13 17 16	6 5 14 15 11 16 17
7	7 9 13 12 1	7 6 5 4 2	7 6 3	7 6 5 4	7 6 5	7 3 6	---	7 6 5 14 15 8	7 6 5 14 15 11 16 17 13 9	7 6 5 14 15 8 10	7 6 5 14 15 11	7 9 13 12	7 6 5 14 15 11 16 17 13	7 9 13 17 16 11 15 14	7 6 5 14 15	7 6 5 14 15 11 16	7 6 5 14 15 11 16 17
8	8 15 11 16 17 12 1	8 15 14 5 6 7 2	8 10 1 12 13 9 7 3	8 15 14 5 4	8 15 14 5	8 10 1 12 13 9 7 6	8 15 14 5 6 7	---	8 15 14 5 6 7 9	8 15 11 16 17 12 1 10	8 15 11	8 15 11 16 17 12	8 15 11 16 17 13	8 15 14	8 10 1 12 17 16 11 15	8 15 14 5 6 7 9 13 17 16	8 15 11 16 17
9	9 13 12 1	9 7 2	9 13 17 16 11 15 14 5 6 3	9 7 6 5 4	9 13 17 16 11 15 14 5	9 13 17 16 11 15 14 5 6	9 13 17 16 11 15 14 5 6 7	9 7 6 5 14 15 8	---	9 13 17 16 11 15 8 10	9 13 17 16 11	9 13 12	9 7 6 5 14 15 11 16 17 13	9 13 17 16 11 15 14	9 13 17 16 11 15	9 7 6 5 14 15 11 16	9 7 6 5 14 15 11 16 17
10	10 8 15 11 16 17 12 1	10 8 15 14 5 4 2	10 8 15 14 5 6 3	10 8 15 14 5 4	10 8 15 14 5	10 1 12 13 9 7 6	10 8 15 14 5 6 7	10 1 12 17 16 11 15 8	10 8 15 11 16 17 13 9	---	10 8 15 11	10 1 12	10 8 15 11 16 17 13	10 8 15 14	10 1 12 17 16 11 15	10 1 12 17 16	10 8 15 11 16 17
11	11 16 17 12 1	11 15 14 5 4 2	11 15 14 5 6 3	11 15 14 5 4	11 15 14 5	11 16 17 13 9 7 6	11 15 14 5 6 7	11 15 8	11 16 17 13 9	11 15 8 10	---	11 16 17 12	11 16 17 13	11 16 17 13 9 7 6 5 14	11 16 17 12 1 10 8 15	11 15 8 10 1 12 17 16	11 16 17
12	12 17 16 11 15 8 10 1	12 13 9 7 2	12 13 9 7 3	12 13 9 7 2 4	12 13 9 7 6 5	12 13 9 7 6	12 13 9 7	12 17 16 11 15 8	12 13 9	12 1 10	12 17 16 11	---	12 17 13	12 13 9 7 6 5 14	12 1 10 8 15	12 17 16	12 13 17
13	13 12 1	13 17 16 11 15 14 5 4 2	13 17 16 11 15 14 5 6 3	13 9 7 2 4	13 17 16 11 15 14 5	13 17 16 11 15 14 5 6	13 17 16 11 15 14 5 6 7	13 17 16 11 15 8	13 17 16 11 15 14 5 6 7 9	13 17 16 11 15 8 10	13 17 16 11	13 17 12	---	13 9 7 6 5 14	13 9 7 6 5 14 15	13 12 1 10 8 15 11 16	13 12 17
14	14 15 8 10 1	14 15 11 16 17 13 9 7 2	14 15 11 16 17 13 9 7 3	14 15 11 16 17 13 9 7 2 4	14 15 11 16 17 13 9 7 6 5	14 15 11 16 17 13 9 7 6	14 15 11 16 17 13 9 7	14 15 8	14 15 11 16 17 13 9	14 15 8 10	14 5 6 7 9 13 17 16 11	14 5 6 7 9 13 12	14 5 6 7 9 13	---	14 5 6 7 9 13 17 16 11 15	14 5 6 7 9 13 17 16	14 5 6 7 9 13 17
15	15 11 16 17 12 1	15 14 5 6 7 2	15 11 16 17 13 9 7 3	15 14 5 4	15 14 5	15 11 16 17 13 9 7 6	15 14 5 6 7	15 11 16 17 12 1 10 8	15 11 16 17 13 9	15 11 16 17 12 1 10	15 8 10 1 12 17 16 11	15 8 10 1 12	15 14 5 6 7 9 13	15 11 16 17 13 9 7 6 5 14	---	15 8 10 1 12 17 16	15 14 5 6 7 9 13 17
16	16 17 12 1	16 17 13 9 7 2	16 17 13 9 7 3	16 17 13 9 7 2 4	16 17 13 9 7 6 5	16 17 13 9 7 6	16 11 15 14 5 6 7	16 17 13 9 7 6 5 14 15 8	16 11 15 14 5 6 7 9	16 17 12 1 10	16 17 12 1 10 8 15 11	16 17 12	16 11 15 8 10 1 12 13	16 17 13 9 7 6 5 14	16 17 12 1 10 8 15	---	16 11 15 8 10 1 12 17
17	17 16 11 15 8 10 1	17 13 9 7 2	17 13 9 7 3	17 13 9 7 2 4	17 13 9 7 6 5	17 16 11 15 14 5 6	17 16 11 15 14 5 6 7	17 16 11 15 8	17 16 11 15 14 5 6 7 9	17 16 11 15 8 10	17 16 11	17 13 12	17 12 13	17 13 9 7 6 5 14	17 13 9 7 6 5 14 15	17 12 1 10 8 15 11 16	---

Backup Paths of The 17-Node Network - Case II

Table 9.5 The Backup Paths of The 17-Node Network with Node-Failure Tolerance (Case II)

Node	1	2	3	4	5	6	7	8	9	10	11	12	13	14	15	16	17
1	---	1 10 4 2	1 12 11 15 14 5 3	1 10 4	1 12 11 15 14 5	1 12 13 9 7 6	1 12 13 9 7	1 12 11 15 8	1 12 13 9	1 12 11 15 8 4 10	1 12 11	1 10 4 8 15 11 12	1 12 13	1 12 11 15 14	1 12 11 15	1 12 13 17 16	1 10 4 2 7 9 13 17
2	2 4 10 1	---	2 7 6 3	2 7 9 13 12 1 10 4	2 4 8 15 14 5	2 7 6	2 4 10 1 12 13 9 7	2 7 9 13 12 11 15 8	2 7 9	2 4 10	2 4 8 15 11	2 7 9 13 12	2 4 8 15 11 12 13	2 4 8 15 14	2 7 9 13 12 11 15	2 7 9 13 17 16	2 7 9 13 17
3	3 5 14 15 11 12 1	3 6 7 2	---	3 5 14 15 8 4	3 6 7 2 4 8 15 14 5	3 5 14 15 8 4 2 7 6	3 6 7	3 6 7 2 4 8	3 5 14 15 11 12 13 9	3 5 14 15 8 4 10	3 5 14 15 11	3 5 14 15 11 12	3 5 14 15 11 12 13	3 6 7 2 4 8 15 14	3 6 7 9 13 12 11 15	3 6 7 9 13 17 16	3 6 7 9 13 17
4	4 10 1	4 10 1 12 13 9 7 2	4 8 15 14 5 3	---	4 8 15 14 5	4 2 7 6	4 10 1 12 13 9 7	4 10 1 12 11 15 8	4 8 15 11 12 13 9	4 8 15 11 12 1 10	4 8 15 11	4 8 15 11 12	4 2 7 9 13	4 8 15 14	4 10 1 12 11 15	4 2 7 9 13 17 16	4 2 7 9 13 17
5	5 14 15 11 12 1	5 14 15 8 4 2	5 14 15 8 4 2 7 6 3	5 14 15 8 4	---	5 3 6	5 14 15 8 4 2 7	5 14 15 8	5 14 15 11 12 13 9	5 14 15 11 12 1 10	5 14 15 11	5 14 15 11 12	5 14 15 11 12 13	5 3 6 7 2 4 8 15 14	5 14 15	5 3 6 7 9 13 17 16	5 14 15 11 16 17
6	6 7 9 13 12 1	6 7 2	6 7 2 4 8 15 14 5 3	6 7 2 4	6 3 5	---	6 3 5 14 15 8 4 2 7	6 7 2 4 8	6 3 5 14 15 11 12 13 9	6 7 9 13 12 1 10	6 7 9 13 12 11	6 7 9 13 12	6 3 5 14 15 11 12 13	6 7 2 4 8 15 14	6 7 9 13 12 11 15	6 7 9 13 17 16	6 3 5 14 15 11 16 17
7	7 9 13 12 1	7 9 13 12 1 10 4 2	7 6 3	7 9 13 12 1 10 4	7 2 4 8 15 14 5	7 2 4 8 15 14 5 3 6	---	7 9 13 12 11 15 8	7 2 4 10 1 12 13 9	7 9 13 12 11 15 8 4 10	7 9 13 12 11	7 9 13 12	7 2 4 10 1 12 13	7 2 4 8 15 14	7 9 13 12 11 15	7 2 4 8 15 11 16	7 2 4 8 15 11 16 17
8	8 15 11 12 1	8 15 11 12 13 9 7 2	8 4 2 7 6 3	8 15 11 12 1 10 4	8 15 14 5	8 4 2 7 6	8 15 11 12 13 9 7	---	8 4 2 7 9	8 4 10	8 15 11	8 15 11 12	8 4 2 7 9 13	8 15 14	8 4 10 1 12 11 15	8 4 2 7 9 13 17 16	8 15 11 16 17
9	9 13 12 1	9 7 2	9 13 12 11 15 14 5 3	9 13 12 11 15 8 4	9 13 12 11 15 14 5	9 13 12 11 15 14 5 3 6	9 13 12 1 10 4 2 7	9 7 2 4 8	---	9 7 2 4 10	9 13 12 11	9 13 12	9 7 2 4 10 1 12 13	9 13 12 11 15 14	9 13 12 11 15	9 7 2 4 8 15 11 16	9 7 2 4 8 15 11 16 17
10	10 4 8 15 11 12 1	10 4 2	10 4 8 15 14 5 3	10 1 12 11 15 8 4	10 1 12 11 15 14 5	10 1 12 13 9 7 6	10 4 8 15 11 12 13 9 7	10 4 8	10 4 2 7 9	---	10 1 12 11	10 1 12	10 4 2 7 9 13	10 1 12 11 15 14	10 1 12 11 15	10 1 12 13 17 16	10 4 2 7 9 13 17
11	11 12 1	11 15 8 4 2	11 15 14 5 3	11 15 8 4	11 15 14 5	11 12 13 9 7 6	11 12 13 9 7	11 15 8	11 12 13 9	11 12 1 10	---	11 16 17 13 12	11 16 17 13	11 12 13 9 7 6 3 5 14	11 12 1 10 4 8 15	11 12 13 17 16	11 16 17
12	12 11 15 8 4 10 1	12 13 9 7 2	12 11 15 14 5 3	12 11 15 8 4	12 11 15 14 5	12 13 9 7 6	12 13 9 7	12 11 15 8	12 13 9	12 1 10	12 13 17 16 11	---	12 11 16 17 13	12 13 9 7 6 3 5 14	12 1 10 4 8 15	12 13 17 16	12 13 17
13	13 12 1	13 12 11 15 8 4 2	13 12 11 15 14 5 3	13 9 7 2 4	13 12 11 15 14 5	13 12 11 15 14 5 3 6	13 12 1 10 4 2 7	13 9 7 2 4 8	13 12 1 10 4 2 7 9	13 9 7 2 4 10	13 17 16 11	13 17 16 11 12	---	13 9 7 6 3 5 14	13 9 7 2 4 8 15	13 12 11 16	13 12 11 16 17
14	14 15 11 12 1	14 15 8 4 2	14 15 8 4 2 7 6 3	14 15 8 4	14 15 8 4 2 7 6 3 5	14 15 8 4 2 7 6	14 15 8 4 2 7	14 15 8	14 15 11 12 13 9	14 15 11 12 1 10	14 5 3 6 7 9 13 12 11	14 5 3 6 7 9 13 12	14 5 3 6 7 9 13	---	14 5 3 6 7 2 4 8 15	14 5 3 6 7 9 13 17 16	14 5 3 6 7 9 13 17
15	15 11 12 1	15 11 12 13 9 7 2	15 11 12 13 9 7 6 3	15 11 12 1 10 4	15 14 5	15 11 12 13 9 7 6	15 11 12 13 9 7	15 11 12 1 10 4 8	15 11 12 13 9	15 11 12 1 10	15 8 4 10 1 12 11	15 8 4 10 1 12	15 8 4 2 7 9 13	15 8 4 2 7 6 3 5 14	---	15 8 4 2 7 9 13 17 16	15 8 4 2 7 9 13 17
16	16 17 13 12 1	16 17 13 9 7 2	16 17 13 9 7 6 3	16 17 13 9 7 2 4	16 17 13 9 7 6 3 5	16 17 13 9 7 6	16 11 15 8 4 2 7	16 17 13 9 7 2 4 8	16 11 15 8 4 2 7 9	16 17 13 12 1 10	16 17 13 12 11	16 17 13 12	16 11 12 13	16 17 13 9 7 6 3 5 14	16 17 13 9 7 2 4 8 15	---	16 11 12 13 17
17	17 13 9 7 2 4 10 1	17 13 9 7 2	17 13 9 7 6 3	17 13 9 7 2 4	17 16 11 15 14 5	17 16 11 15 14 5 3 6	17 16 11 15 8 4 2 7	17 16 11 15 8	17 16 11 15 8 4 2 7 9	17 13 9 7 2 4 10	17 16 11	17 13 12	17 16 11 12 13	17 13 9 7 6 3 5 14	17 13 9 7 2 4 8 15	17 13 12 11 16	---

Backup Paths of The 17-Node - Case III

Table 9.6 Backup Paths of The 17-Node Network with Node-and-Link Failure Tolerance (Case III)

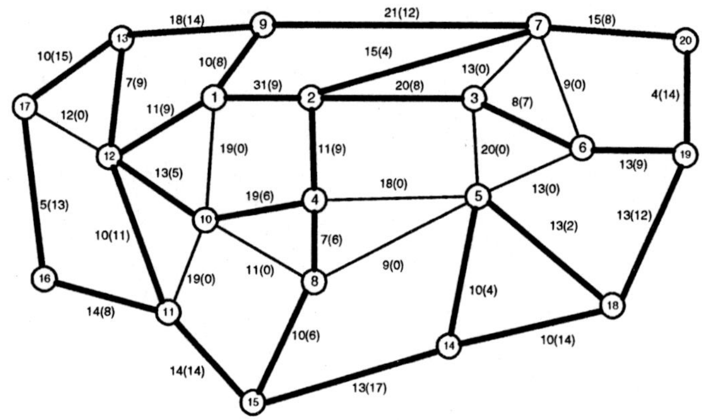

Figure 9.5 20-Node Network (Network 4) with Node-Failure Tolerance (Case II)

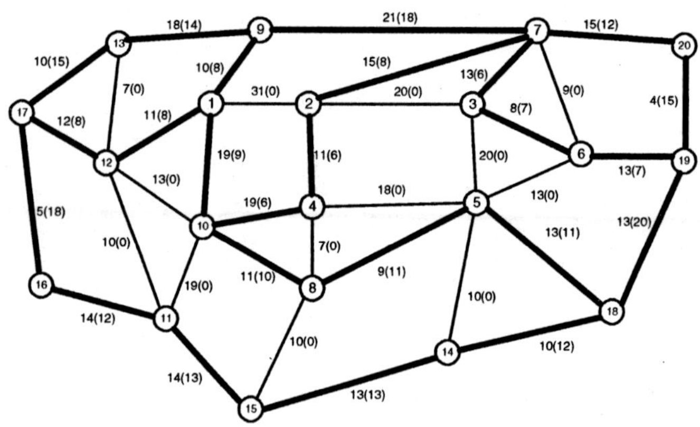

Figure 9.6 20-Node Network (Network 4) with Link-and-Node-Failure Tolerance (Case III)

From / To	1	2	3	4	5	6	7	8	9	10	11	12	13	14	15	16	17	18	19	20
1	---	1 9 7 2	1 9 7 20 19 6 3	1 12 10 4	1 12 11 15 14 5	1 9 7 20 19 6	1 9 7	1 2 4 8	1 2 7 9	1 12 10	1 12 11	1 9 13 12	1 12 13	1 12 11 15 14	1 12 11 15	1 9 13 17 16	1 9 13 17	1 12 11 15 14 18	1 9 7 20 19	1 12 11 15 14 18 19 20
2	2 7 9 1	---	2 7 20 19 6 3	2 1 12 10 4	2 4 8 15 14 5	2 7 20 19 6	2 1 9 7	2 1 12 11 15 8	2 7 9	2 4 10	2 4 8 15 11	2 4 10 12	2 4 10 12 13	2 4 8 15 14	2 1 12 11 15	2 7 9 13 17 16	2 7 9 13 17	2 7 20 19 18	2 7 20 19	2 3 6 19 20
3	3 6 19 20 7 9 1	3 6 19 20 7 2	---	3 6 19 18 14 15 8 4	3 6 19 18 5	3 2 7 20 19 6	3 2 7	3 2 4 8	3 2 1 9	3 6 19 18 14 15 8 4 10	3 6 19 18 14 15 11	3 6 19 18 14 15 11 12	3 2 1 12 13	3 6 19 18 14	3 2 1 12 11 15	3 6 19 20 7 9 13 17 16	3 6 19 20 7 9 13 17	3 6 19 18	3 2 7 20 19	3 6 19 20
4	4 10 12 1	4 10 12 1 2	4 8 15 14 18 19 6 3	---	4 8 15 14 5	4 2 3 6	4 10 12 1 9 7	4 10 12 11 15 8	4 10 12 13 9	4 2 1 12 10	4 8 15 11	4 2 1 12	4 2 1 9 13	4 8 15 14	4 10 12 11 15	4 2 1 9 13 17 16	4 2 1 9 13 17	4 8 15 14 18	4 2 7 20 19	4 8 15 14 18 19 20
5	5 14 15 11 12 1	5 14 15 8 4 2	5 18 19 6 3	5 14 15 8 4	---	5 18 19 6	5 18 19 20 7	5 14 15 8	5 14 15 11 12 1 9	5 14 15 11 12 10	5 14 15 11	5 14 15 11 12	5 14 15 11 12 13	5 18 14	5 14 15	5 18 19 20 7 9 13 17 16	5 14 15 11 16 17	5 14 18	5 18 19	5 18 19 20
6	6 19 20 7 9 1	6 19 20 7 2	6 19 20 7 2 3	6 3 2 4	6 19 18 5	---	6 3 2 7	6 3 2 4 8	6 3 2 1 9	6 3 2 1 12 10	6 3 2 1 12 11	6 19 18 14 15 11 12	6 3 2 1 12 13	6 19 18 14	6 19 18 14 15	6 3 2 1 9 13 17 16	6 3 2 1 12 11 16 17	6 19 18	6 3 2 7 20 19	6 19 20
7	7 9 1	7 9 1 2	7 2 3	7 9 1 12 10 4	7 20 19 18 5	7 2 3 6	---	7 9 1 12 11 15 8	7 2 1 9	7 9 13 12 10	7 9 13 12 11	7 9 13 12	7 2 1 12 13	7 20 19 18 14	7 9 1 12 11 15	7 2 1 12 11 16	7 2 1 12 11 16 17	7 20 19 18	7 20 19	7 2 3 6 19 20
8	8 4 2 1	8 15 11 12 1 2	8 4 2 3	8 15 11 12 10 4	8 15 14 5	8 4 2 3 6	8 15 11 12 1 9 7	---	8 4 2 7 9	8 4 10	8 15 11	8 15 11 12	8 4 2 1 9 13	8 15 14	8 4 10 12 11 15	8 4 2 1 9 13 17 16	8 15 11 16 17	8 15 14 18	8 15 14 18 19	8 15 14 18 19 20
9	9 7 2 1	9 7 2	9 1 2 3	9 13 12 10 4	9 1 12 11 15 14 5	9 1 2 3 6	9 1 2 7	9 7 2 4 8	---	9 13 12 10	9 13 12 11	9 13 12	9 1 12 13	9 1 12 11 15 14	9 13 12 11 15	9 1 12 11 16	9 1 12 11 16 17	9 1 12 11 15 14 18	9 1 12 11 15 14 18 19	9 1 2 3 6 19 20
10	10 12 1	10 4 2	10 4 8 15 14 18 19 6 3	10 12 1 2 4	10 12 11 15 14 5	10 12 1 2 3 6	10 12 13 9 7	10 4 8	10 12 13 9	---	10 12 11	10 4 2 1 12	10 4 2 1 9 13	10 12 11 15 14	10 12 11 15	10 12 13 17 16	10 4 2 1 9 13 17	10 12 11 15 14 18	10 12 11 15 14 18 19	10 4 8 15 14 18 19 20
11	11 12 1	11 15 8 4 2	11 15 14 18 19 6 3	11 15 8 4	11 15 14 5	11 12 1 2 3 6	11 12 13 9 7	11 15 8	11 12 13 9	11 12 10	---	11 16 17 13 12	11 16 17 13	11 12 1 2 3 6 19 18 14	11 12 10 4 8 15	11 12 13 17 16	11 16 17	11 12 1 2 3 6 19 18	11 12 1 2 3 6 19	11 15 14 18 19 20
12	12 13 9 1	12 10 4 2	12 11 15 14 18 19 6 3	12 1 2 4	12 11 15 14 5	12 11 15 14 18 19 6	12 13 9 7	12 11 15 8	12 13 9	12 1 2 4 10	12 13 17 16 11	---	12 1 9 13	12 1 2 3 6 19 18 14	12 10 4 8 15	12 13 17 16	12 13 17	12 11 15 14 18	12 11 15 14 18 19	12 11 15 14 18 19 20
13	13 12 1	13 12 10 4 2	13 12 1 2 3	13 9 1 2 4	13 12 11 15 14 5	13 12 1 2 3 6	13 12 1 2 7	13 9 1 2 4 8	13 12 1 9	13 9 1 2 4 10	13 17 16 11	13 9 1 12	---	13 9 7 20 19 18 14	13 9 1 2 4 8 15	13 12 11 16	13 12 11 16 17	13 12 11 15 14 18	13 12 11 15 14 18 19	13 12 1 2 3 6 19 20
14	14 15 11 12 1	14 15 8 4 2	14 18 19 6 3	14 15 8 4	14 18 5	14 18 19 6	14 18 19 20 7	14 15 8	14 15 11 12 1 9	14 15 11 12 10	14 18 19 6 3 2 1 12 11	14 18 19 6 3 2 1 12	14 18 19 20 7 9 13	---	14 18 19 6 3 2 4 8 15	14 18 19 20 7 9 13 17 16	14 18 19 20 7 9 13 17	14 5 18	14 15 8 4 2 3 6 19	14 15 8 4 2 7 20
15	15 11 12 1	15 11 12 1 2	15 11 12 1 2 3	15 11 12 10 4	15 14 5	15 14 18 19 6	15 11 12 1 9 7	15 11 12 10 4 8	15 11 12 13 9	15 11 12 10	15 8 4 10 12 11	15 8 4 10 12	15 8 4 2 1 9 13	15 8 4 2 3 6 19 18 14	---	15 8 4 10 12 13 17 16	15 8 4 2 1 9 13 17	15 8 4 2 3 6 19 18	15 8 4 2 3 6 19	15 8 4 2 7 20
16	16 17 13 9 1	16 17 13 9 7 2	16 17 13 9 7 20 19 6 3	16 17 13 9 1 2 4	16 17 13 9 7 20 19 18 5	16 17 13 9 1 2 3 6	16 11 12 1 2 7	16 17 13 9 1 2 4 8	16 11 12 1 9	16 17 13 12 10	16 17 13 12 11	16 17 13 12	16 11 12 13	16 17 13 9 7 20 19 18 14	16 17 13 12 10 4 8 15	---	16 11 12 13 17	16 17 13 9 7 20 19 18	16 17 13 9 7 20 19	16 11 15 14 18 19 20
17	17 13 9 1	17 13 9 7 2	17 13 9 7 20 19 6 3	17 13 9 1 2 4	17 16 11 15 14 5	17 16 11 12 1 2 3 6	17 16 11 12 1 2 7	17 16 11 15 8	17 16 11 12 1 9	17 13 9 1 2 4 10	17 16 11	17 13 12	17 16 11 12 13	17 13 9 7 20 19 18 14	17 13 9 1 2 4 8 15	17 13 12 11 16	---	17 16 11 15 14 18	17 16 11 15 14 18 19	17 16 11 15 14 18 19 20
18	18 14 15 11 12 1	18 19 20 7 2	18 19 6 3	18 14 15 8 4	18 14 5	18 19 6	18 19 20 7	18 14 15 8	18 14 15 11 12 1 9	18 14 15 11 12 10	18 19 6 3 2 1 12 11	18 14 15 11 12	18 14 15 11 12 13	18 5 14	18 19 6 3 2 4 8 15	18 19 20 7 9 13 17 16	18 14 15 11 16 17	---	18 14 15 8 4 2 3 6 19	18 14 15 8 4 2 7 20
19	19 20 7 9 1	19 20 7 2	19 20 7 2 3	19 20 7 2 4	19 18 5	19 20 7 2 3 6	19 20 7	19 18 14 15 8	19 18 14 15 11 12 1 9	19 18 14 15 11 12 10	19 6 3 2 1 12 11	19 18 14 15 11 12	19 18 14 15 11 12 13	19 6 3 2 4 8 15 14	19 6 3 2 4 8 15	19 20 7 9 13 17 16	19 18 14 15 11 16 17	19 6 3 2 4 8 15 14 18	---	19 6 3 2 7 20
20	20 19 18 14 15 11 12 1	20 19 6 3 2	20 19 6 3	20 19 18 14 15 8 4	20 19 18 5	20 19 6	20 19 6 3 2 7	20 19 18 14 15 8	20 19 6 3 2 1 9	20 19 18 14 15 8 4 10	20 19 18 14 15 11	20 19 18 14 15 11 12	20 19 6 3 2 1 12 13	20 7 2 4 8 15 14	20 7 2 4 8 15	20 19 18 14 15 11 16	20 19 18 14 15 11 16 17	20 7 2 4 8 15 14 18	20 7 2 3 6 19	---

Backup Paths of The 20-Node Network - Case II

Table 9.7 Backup Paths of The 20-Node Network with Node-Failure Tolerance (Case II)

From / To	1	2	3	4	5	6	7	8	9	10	11	12	13	14	15	16	17	18	19	20
1	—	1 10 4 2	1 9 7 3	1 10 4	1 10 8 5	1 9 7 20 19 6	1 9 7	1 9 7 20 19 18 5 8	1 12 17 13 9	1 9 7 2 4 10	1 12 17 16 11	1 9 13 17 12	1 12 17 13	1 12 17 16 11 15 14	1 12 17 16 11 15	1 12 17 16	1 9 13 17	1 9 7 20 19 18	1 9 7 20 19	1 10 8 5 18 19 20
2	2 4 10 1	—	2 7 3	2 7 9 1 10 4	2 4 10 8 5	2 7 20 19 6	2 4 10 1 9 7	2 7 9 1 10 8	2 7 9	2 4 10	2 7 9 13 17 16 11	2 7 9 13 17 12	2 7 20 19 18 14 15 11 16 17 13	2 7 20 19 18 14	2 7 20 19 18 14 15	2 7 9 13 17 16	2 7 9 13 17	2 7 20 19 18	2 7 20 19	2 4 10 8 5 18 19 20
3	3 7 9 1	3 7 2	—	3 7 9 1 10 4	3 6 19 18 5	3 7 20 19 6	3 6 19 20 7	3 7 9 1 10 8	3 6 19 18 5 8 10 1 9	3 6 19 18 5 8 10	3 6 19 18 14 15 11	3 7 9 13 17 12	3 6 19 18 14 15 11 16 17 13	3 6 19 18 14	3 6 19 18 14 15	3 7 9 13 17 16	3 7 9 13 17	3 6 19 18	3 7 20 19	3 6 19 20
4	4 10 1	4 10 1 9 7 2	4 10 1 9 7 3	—	4 10 8 5	4 2 7 3 6	4 10 1 9 7	4 10 8	4 10 8 5 18 19 20 7 9	4 2 7 9 1 10	4 2 7 9 13 17 16 11	4 2 7 9 1 12	4 2 7 9 13	4 2 7 20 19 18 14	4 10 1 12 17 16 11 15	4 2 7 9 13 17 16	4 2 7 9 13 17	4 2 7 20 19 18	4 2 7 20 19	4 10 8 5 18 19 20
5	5 8 10 1	5 8 10 4 2	5 18 19 6 3	5 8 10 4	—	5 18 19 6	5 18 19 20 7	5 18 19 20 7 9 1 10 8	5 8 10 1 9	5 8 10	5 18 14 15 11	5 18 19 20 7 9 1 12	5 8 10 1 12 17 13	5 18 14	5 18 14 15	5 18 19 20 7 9 13 17 16	5 18 14 15 11 16 17	5 8 10 4 2 7 20 19 18	5 18 19	5 18 19 20
6	6 19 20 7 9 1	6 19 20 7 2	6 19 20 7 3	6 3 7 2 4	6 19 18 5	—	6 3 7	6 3 7 9 1 10 8	6 19 18 5 8 10 1 9	6 3 7 9 1 10	6 19 18 14 15 11	6 19 20 7 9 13 17 12	6 19 18 14 15 11 16 17 13	6 19 18 14	6 19 18 14 15	6 3 7 9 13 17 16	6 19 18 14 15 11 16 17	6 19 18	6 3 7 20 19	6 19 20
7	7 9 1	7 9 1 10 4 2	7 20 19 6 3	7 9 1 10 4	7 20 19 18 5	7 3 6	—	7 9 1 10 8	7 2 4 10 1 9	7 20 19 18 5 8 10	7 9 13 17 16 11	7 9 13 17 12	7 2 4 10 1 12 17 13	7 20 19 18 14	7 20 19 18 14 15	7 20 19 18 14 15 11 16	7 2 4 10 1 12 17	7 20 19 18	7 20 19	7 3 6 19 20
8	8 5 18 19 20 7 9 1	8 10 1 9 7 2	8 10 1 9 7 3	8 10 4	8 10 1 9 7 20 19 18 5	8 10 1 9 7 3 6	8 10 1 9 7	—	8 5 18 19 20 7 9	8 5 18 19 20 7 9 1 10	8 5 18 14 15 11	8 5 18 19 20 7 9 1 12	8 5 18 19 20 7 9 13	8 10 1 12 17 16 11 15 14	8 5 18 14 15	8 5 18 19 20 7 9 13 17 16	8 5 18 14 15 11 16 17	8 10 4 2 7 20 19 18	8 10 4 2 7 20 19	8 5 18 19 20
9	9 13 17 12 1	9 7 2	9 1 10 8 5 18 19 6 3	9 7 20 19 18 5 8 10 4	9 1 10 8 5	9 1 10 8 5 18 19 6	9 1 10 4 2 7	9 7 20 19 18 5 8	—	9 7 2 4 10	9 13 17 16 11	9 13 17 12	9 1 12 17 13	9 13 17 16 11 15 14	9 13 17 16 11 15	9 7 20 19 18 14 15 11 16	9 1 12 17	9 13 17 16 11 15 14 18	9 1 10 8 5 18 19	9 1 10 8 5 18 19 20
10	10 4 2 7 9 1	10 4 2	10 8 5 18 19 6 3	10 1 9 7 2 4	10 8 5	10 1 9 7 3 6	10 8 5 18 19 20 7	10 1 9 7 20 19 18 5 8	10 4 2 7 9	—	10 1 12 17 16 11	10 1 12	10 1 9 13	10 1 12 17 16 11 15 14	10 1 12 17 16 11 15	10 1 12 17 16	10 1 9 13 17	10 1 9 7 20 19 18	10 1 9 7 20 19	10 8 5 18 19 20
11	11 16 17 12 1	11 16 17 13 9 7 2	11 15 14 18 19 6 3	11 16 17 13 9 7 2 4	11 15 14 18 5	11 15 14 18 19 6	11 16 17 13 9 7	11 15 14 18 5 8	11 16 17 13 9	11 16 17 12 1 10	—	11 16 17 12	11 16 17 13	11 16 17 12 1 10 8 5 18 14	11 16 17 12 1 10 8 5 18 14 15	11 15 14 18 5 8 10 1 12 17 16	11 16 17	11 16 17 12 1 10 8 5 18	11 16 17 13 9 7 20 19	11 15 14 18 19 20
12	12 17 13 9 1	12 17 13 9 7 2	12 17 13 9 7 3	12 1 9 7 2 4	12 1 9 7 20 19 18 5	12 17 13 9 7 20 19 6	12 17 13 9 7	12 1 9 7 20 19 18 5 8	12 17 13 9	. 12 1 10	12 17 16 11	—	12 17 13	12 1 10 8 5 18 14	12 1 10 8 5 18 14 15	12 17 16	12 1 9 13 17	12 17 16 11 15 14 18	12 17 13 9 7 20 19	12 17 16 11 15 14 18 19 20
13	13 17 12 1	13 17 16 11 15 14 18 19 20 7 2	13 17 16 11 15 14 18 19 6 3	13 9 7 2 4	13 17 12 1 10 8 5	13 17 16 11 15 14 18 19 6	13 17 12 1 10 4 2 7	13 9 7 20 19 18 5 8	13 17 12 1 9	13 9 1 10	13 17 16 11	13 17 12	—	13 9 7 20 19 18 14	13 9 7 20 19 18 14 15	13 9 7 20 19 18 14 15 11 16	13 9 1 12 17	13 17 16 11 15 14 18	13 17 16 11 15 14 18 19	13 17 16 11 15 14 18 19 20
14	14 15 11 16 17 12 1	14 18 19 20 7 2	14 18 19 6 3	14 18 19 20 7 2 4	14 18 5	14 18 19 6	14 18 19 20 7	14 15 11 16 17 12 1 10 8	14 15 11 16 17 13 9	14 15 11 16 17 12 1 10	14 18 5 8 10 1 12 17 16 11	14 18 5 8 10 1 12	14 18 19 20 7 9 13	—	14 18 5 8 10 1 12 17 16 11 15	14 18 5 8 10 1 12 17 16	14 18 19 20 7 9 13 17	14 15 11 16 17 12 1 10 8 5 18	14 15 11 16 17 13 9 7 20 19	14 15 11 16 17 13 9 7
15	15 11 16 17 12 1	15 14 18 19 20 7 2	15 14 18 19 6 3	15 11 16 17 12 1 10 4	15 14 18 5	15 14 18 19 6	15 14 18 19 20 7	15 14 18 5 8	15 11 16 17 13 9	15 11 16 17 12 1 10	15 14 18 5 8 10 1 12 17 16 11	15 14 18 5 8 10 1 12	15 14 18 19 20 7 9 13	15 11 16 17 12 1 10 8 5 18 14	—	15 14 18 5 8 10 1 12 17 16	15 14 18 19 20 7 9 13 17	15 11 16 17 12 1 10 8 5 18	15 11 16 17 13 9 7 20 19	15 11 16 17 13 9 7 20
16	16 17 12 1	16 17 13 9 7 2	16 17 13 9 7 3	16 17 13 9 7 2 4	16 17 13 9 7 20 19 18 5	16 17 13 9 7 3 6	16 11 15 14 18 19 20 7	16 17 13 9 7 20 19 18 5 8	16 11 15 14 18 19 20 7 9	16 17 12 1 10	16 17 12 1 10 8 5 18 14 15 11	16 17 12	16 11 15 14 18 19 20 7 9 13	16 17 12 1 10 8 5 18 14	16 17 12 1 10 8 5 18 14 15	—	16 11 15 14 18 5 8 10 1 12 17	16 17 12 1 10 8 5 18	16 17 13 9 7 20 19	16 11 15 14 18 19 20
17	17 13 9 1	17 13 9 7 2	17 13 9 7 3	17 13 9 7 2 4	17 16 11 15 14 18 5	17 16 11 15 14 18 19 6	17 12 1 10 4 2 7	17 16 11 15 14 18 5 8	17 12 1 9	17 13 9 1 10	17 16 11	17 13 9 1 12	17 12 1 9 13	17 13 9 7 20 19 18 14	17 13 9 7 20 19 18 14 15	17 12 1 10 8 5 18 14 15 11 16	—	17 16 11 15 14 18	17 16 11 15 14 18 19	17 16 11 15 14 18 19 20
18	18 19 20 7 9 1	18 19 20 7 2	18 19 6 3	18 19 20 7 2 4	18 19 20 7 2 4 10 8 5	18 19 6	18 19 20 7	18 19 20 7 2 4 10 8	18 14 15 11 16 17 13 9	18 19 20 7 9 1 10	18 5 8 10 1 12 17 16 11	18 14 15 11 16 17 12	18 14 15 11 16 17 13	18 5 8 10 1 12 17 16 11 15 14	18 5 8 10 1 12 17 16 11 15	18 5 8 10 1 12 17 16	18 14 15 11 16 17	—	18 5 8 10 4 2 7 20 19	18 5 8 10 4 2 7 20
19	19 20 7 9 1	19 20 7 2	19 20 7 3	19 20 7 2 4	19 18 5	19 20 7 3 6	19 20 7	19 20 7 2 4 10 8	19 18 5 8 10 1 9	19 20 7 9 1 10	19 20 7 9 13 17 16 11	19 20 7 9 13 17 12	19 18 14 15 11 16 17 13	19 20 7 9 13 17 16 11 15 14	19 20 7 9 13 17 16 11 15	19 20 7 9 13 17 16	19 18 14 15 11 16 17	19 20 7 2 4 10 8 5 18	—	19 6 3 7 20
20	20 19 18 5 8 10 1	20 19 18 5 8 10 4 2	20 19 6 3	20 19 18 5 8 10 4	20 19 18 5	20 19 6	20 19 6 3 7	20 19 18 5 8	20 19 18 5 8 10 1 9	20 19 18 5 8 10	20 19 18 14 15 11	20 19 18 14 15 11 16 17 12	20 19 18 14 15 11 16 17 13	20 7 9 13 17 16 11 15 14	20 7 9 13 17 16 11 15	20 19 18 14 15 11 16	20 19 18 14 15 11 16 17	20 7 2 4 10 8 5 18	20 7 3 6 19	—

Backup Paths of The 20-Node Network - Case III

Table 9.8 Backup Paths of The 20-Node Network with Node-and-Link Failure Tolerance (Case III)

Appendix D

Tables and Figures for Case IV, V, and VI

This appendix includes tables and figures for Networks 1,2,3, and 4. It includes the backup paths and figures for Case IV, V, and Case VI for Networks 1,2,3, and 4.

The six optimization cases mentioned in the appendices are:

- Case I: link-failure with spare capacity optimization criteria
- Case II: node-failure with spare capacity optimization criteria
- Case III: link-or-node failure with spare capacity optimization criteria
- Case IV: link-failure with minimum network cost optimization criteria
- Case V: node-failure with minimum network cost optimization criteria
- Case VI: link-or-node failure with minimum network cost optimization criteria

Node	1	2	3	4	5	6	7	8	9	10	11	12	13
1	---	1 10 4 2	1 9 7 6 5 3	1 10 4	1 9 7 6 5	1 9 7 6	1 9 7	1 10 12 11 8	1 10 12 13 9	1 9 13 12 10	1 9 13 12 11	1 10 12	1 10 12 13
2	2 4 10 1	---	2 4 10 12 11 8 5 3	2 3 5 8 11 12 10 4	2 4 10 12 11 8 5	2 4 10 1 9 7 6	2 3 5 6 7	2 3 5 8	2 3 5 6 7 9	2 4 10	2 3 5 6 7 9 13 12 11	2 4 10 12	2 4 10 12 13
3	3 5 6 7 9 1	3 5 8 11 12 10 4 2	---	3 5 8 11 12 10 4	3 2 4 10 12 11 8 5	3 5 6	3 5 6 7	3 2 4 10 12 11 8	3 2 4 10 1 9	3 5 8 11 12 10	3 2 4 10 12 11	3 5 8 11 12	3 2 4 10 12 13
4	4 10 1	4 10 12 11 8 5 3 2	4 10 12 11 8 5 3	---	4 2 3 5	4 10 1 9 7 6	4 10 1 9 7	4 2 3 5 8	4 10 12 13 9	4 2 3 5 8 11 12 10	4 10 12 11	4 2 3 5 8 11 12	4 2 3 5 6 7 9 13
5	5 6 7 9 1	5 8 11 12 10 4 2	5 8 11 12 10 4 2 3	5 3 2 4	---	5 8 11 12 13 9 7 6	5 6 7	5 3 2 4 10 12 11 8	5 8 11 12 13 9	5 8 11 12 10	5 3 2 4 10 12 11	5 8 11 12	5 8 11 12 13
6	6 7 9 1	6 7 9 1 10 4 2	6 5 3	6 7 9 1 10 4	6 7 9 13 12 11 8 5	---	6 5 8 11 12 13 9 7	6 7 9 13 12 11 8	6 5 8 11 12 13 9	6 7 9 1 10	6 7 9 13 12 11	6 5 8 11 12	6 5 8 11 12 13
7	7 9 1	7 6 5 3 2	7 6 5 3	7 9 1 10 4	7 6 5	7 9 13 12 11 8 5 6	---	7 6 5 8	7 6 5 8 11 12 13 9	7 9 13 12 10	7 9 13 12 11	7 9 13 12	7 6 5 8 11 12 13
8	8 11 12 10 1	8 5 3 2	8 11 12 10 4 2 3	8 5 3 2 4	8 11 12 10 4 2 3 5	8 11 12 13 9 7 6	8 5 6 7	---	8 5 6 7 9	8 11 12 10	8 5 3 2 4 10 12 11	8 5 3 2 4 10 12	8 5 6 7 9 13
9	9 13 12 10 1	9 7 6 5 3 2	9 1 10 4 2 3	9 13 12 10 4	9 13 12 11 8 5	9 13 12 11 8 5 6	9 13 12 11 8 5 6 7	9 7 6 5 8	---	9 13 12 10	9 13 12 11	9 13 12	9 1 10 12 13
10	10 12 13 9 1	10 4 2	10 12 11 8 5 3	10 12 11 8 5 3 2 4	10 12 11 8 5	10 1 9 7 6	10 12 13 9 7	10 12 11 8	10 12 13 9	---	10 12 11	10 1 9 13 12	10 1 9 13
11	11 12 13 9 1	11 12 13 9 7 6 5 3 2	11 12 10 4 2 3	11 12 10 4	11 12 10 4 2 3 5	11 12 13 9 7 6	11 12 13 9 7	11 12 10 4 2 3 5 8	11 12 13 9	11 12 10	---	11 8 5 3 2 4 10 12	11 8 5 6 7 9 13
12	12 10 1	12 10 4 2	12 11 8 5 3	12 11 8 5 3 2 4	12 11 8 5	12 11 8 5 6	12 13 9 7	12 10 4 2 3 5 8	12 13 9	12 13 9 1 10	12 10 4 2 3 5 8 11	---	12 10 1 9 13
13	13 12 10 1	13 12 10 4 2	13 12 10 4 2 3	13 9 7 6 5 3 2 4	13 12 11 8 5	13 12 11 8 5 6	13 12 11 8 5 6 7	13 9 7 6 5 8	13 12 10 1 9	13 9 1 10	13 9 7 6 5 8 11	13 9 1 10 12	---

Backup Paths of The 13-Node - Case IV

Table 9.9 Backup Paths of The 13-Node Network with Link-Failure Tolerance (Case IV)

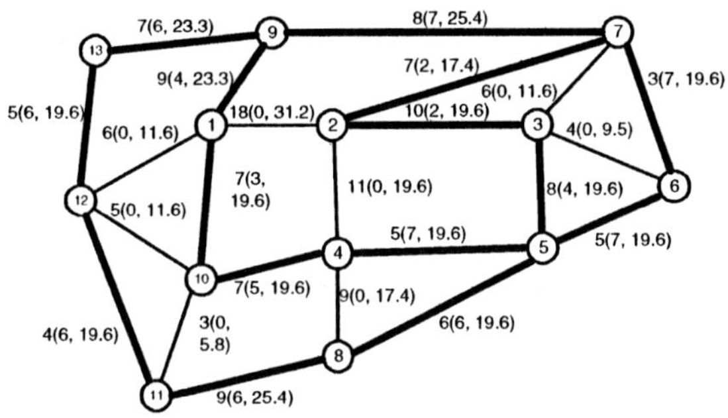

Figure 9.7 13-Node Network (Network 1) with Node-Failure Tolerance (Case V)

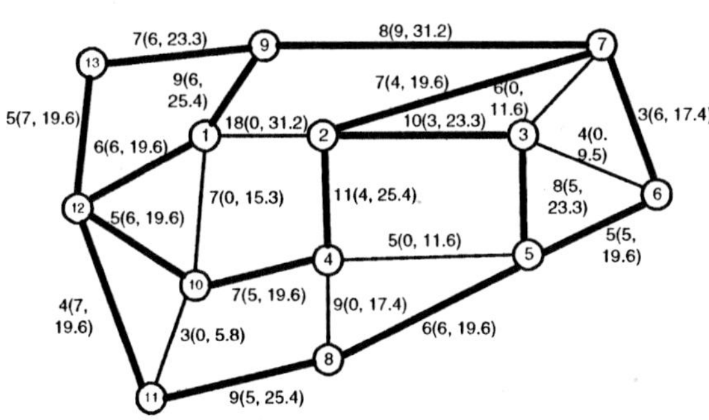

Figure 9.8 13-Node Network (Network 1) with Link-and-Node-Failure Tolerance (Case VI)

Node	1	2	3	4	5	6	7	8	9	10	11	12	13
1	—	1 9 7 2	1 10 4 5 3	1 10 4	1 10 4 5	1 9 7 6	1 9 7	1 9 7 6 5 8	1 10 4 5 6 7 9	1 9 7 6 5 4 10	1 9 13 12 11	1 9 13 12	1 10 4 5 8 11 12 13
2	2 7 9 1	—	2 7 6 5 3	2 3 5 4	2 7 6 5	2 7 6	2 3 5 6 7	2 3 5 8	2 7 9	2 3 5 4 10	2 7 9 13 12 11	2 7 9 13 12	2 3 5 8 11 12 13
3	3 5 4 10 1	3 5 6 7 2	—	3 5 4	3 2 7 6 5	3 5 6	3 2 7	3 2 7 9 13 12 11 8	3 5 4 10 1 9	3 5 4 10	3 2 7 9 13 12 11	3 5 8 11 12	3 5 8 11 12 13
4	4 10 1	4 5 3 2	4 5 3	—	4 10 1 9 7 6 5	4 10 1 9 7 6	4 5 6 7	4 5 8	4 5 6 7 9	4 5 6 7 9 1 10	4 10 1 9 13 12 11	4 5 8 11 12	4 5 6 7 9 13
5	5 4 10 1	5 6 7 2	5 6 7 2 3	5 6 7 9 1 10 4	—	5 3 2 7 6	5 6 7	5 6 7 9 13 12 11 8	5 4 10 1 9	5 6 7 9 1 10	5 6 7 9 13 12 11	5 8 11 12	5 8 11 12 13
6	6 7 9 1	6 7 2	6 5 3	6 7 9 1 10 4	6 7 2 3 5	—	6 5 3 2 7	6 7 9 13 12 11 8	6 5 4 10 1 9	6 7 9 1 10	6 7 9 13 12 11	6 5 8 11 12	6 5 8 11 12 13
7	7 9 1	7 6 5 3 2	7 2 3	7 6 5 4	7 6 5	7 2 3 5 6	—	7 6 5 8	7 6 5 4 10 1 9	7 6 5 4 10	7 9 13 12 11	7 9 13 12	7 6 5 8 11 12 13
8	8 5 6 7 9 1	8 5 3 2	8 11 12 13 9 7 2 3	8 5 4	8 11 12 13 9 7 6 5	8 11 12 13 9 7 6	8 5 6 7	—	8 5 6 7 9	8 5 6 7 9 1 10	8 5 6 7 9 13 12 11	8 5 6 7 9 13 12	8 5 6 7 9 13
9	9 7 6 5 4 10 1	9 7 2	9 1 10 4 5 3	9 7 6 5 4	9 1 10 4 5	9 1 10 4 5 6	9 1 10 4 5 6 7	9 7 6 5 8	—	9 7 6 5 4 10	9 13 12 11	9 13 12	9 7 6 5 8 11 12 13
10	10 4 5 6 7 9 1	10 4 5 3 2	10 4 5 3	10 1 9 7 6 5 4	10 1 9 7 6 5	10 1 9 7 6	10 4 5 6 7	10 1 9 7 6 5 8	10 4 5 6 7 9	—	10 4 5 8 11	10 1 9 13 12	10 1 9 13
11	11 12 13 9 1	11 12 13 9 7 2	11 12 13 9 7 2 3	11 12 13 9 1 10 4	11 12 13 9 7 6 5	11 12 13 9 7 6	11 12 13 9 7	11 12 13 9 7 6 5 8	11 12 13 9	11 8 5 4 10	—	11 8 5 6 7 9 13 12	11 8 5 6 7 9 13
12	12 13 9 1	12 13 9 7 2	12 11 8 5 3	12 11 8 5 4	12 11 8 5	12 11 8 5 6	12 13 9 7	12 13 9 7 6 5 8	12 13 9	12 13 9 1 10	12 13 9 7 6 5 8 11	—	12 11 8 5 6 7 9 13
13	13 12 11 8 5 4 10 1	13 12 11 8 5 3 2	13 12 11 8 5 3	13 9 7 6 5 4	13 12 11 8 5	13 12 11 8 5 6	13 12 11 8 5 6 7	13 9 7 6 5 8	13 12 11 8 5 6 7 9	13 9 1 10	13 9 7 6 5 8 11	13 9 7 6 5 8 11 12	—

Backup Paths of The 13-Node Network - Case V

Table 9.10 Backup Paths of The 13-Node Network with Node-Failure Tolerance (Case V)

Node	1	2	3	4	5	6	7	8	9	10	11	12	13
1	---	1 9 7 2	1 9 7 6 5 3	1 12 10 4	1 9 7 6 5	1 9 7 6	1 9 7	1 12 11 8	1 12 13 9	1 12 10	1 12 11	1 9 13 12	1 12 13
2	2 7 9 1	---	2 7 6 5 3	2 7 9 1 12 10 4	2 7 6 5	2 7 6	2 3 5 6 7	2 3 5 8	2 7 9	2 4 10	2 7 9 1 12 11	2 4 10 12	2 4 10 12 13
3	3 5 6 7 9 1	3 5 6 7 2	---	3 5 8 11 12 10 4	3 2 7 6 5	3 5 6	3 2 7	3 2 4 10 12 11 8	3 2 4 10 12 1 9	3 5 8 11 12 10	3 2 4 10 12 11	3 5 8 11 12	3 2 4 10 12 13
4	4 10 12 1	4 10 12 1 9 7 2	4 10 12 11 8 5 3	---	4 2 3 5	4 2 7 6	4 10 12 1 9 7	4 2 3 5 8	4 10 12 13 9	4 2 7 9 1 12 10	4 10 12 11	4 2 7 9 1 12	4 2 7 9 13
5	5 6 7 9 1	5 6 7 2	5 6 7 2 3	5 3 2 4	---	5 3 2 7 6	5 6 7	5 6 7 9 1 12 11 8	5 8 11 12 1 9	5 8 11 12 10	5 6 7 9 1 12 11	5 8 11 12	5 8 11 12 13
6	6 7 9 1	6 7 2	6 5 3	6 7 2 4	6 7 2 3 5	---	6 5 3 2 7	6 7 9 1 12 11 8	6 5 8 11 12 1 9	6 7 9 1 12 10	6 7 9 1 12 11	6 5 8 11 12	6 5 8 11 12 13
7	7 9 1	7 6 5 3 2	7 2 3	7 9 1 12 10 4	7 6 5	7 2 3 5 6	---	7 6 5 8	7 2 4 10 12 1 9	7 9 13 12 10	7 9 1 12 11	7 9 13 12	7 2 4 10 12 13
8	8 11 12 1	8 5 3 2	8 11 12 10 4 2 3	8 5 3 2 4	8 11 12 1 9 7 6 5	8 11 12 1 9 7 6	8 5 6 7	---	8 5 6 7 9	8 11 12 10	8 5 6 7 9 1 12 11	8 5 6 7 9 1 12	8 5 6 7 9 13
9	9 13 12 1	9 7 2	9 1 12 10 4 2 3	9 13 12 10 4	9 1 12 11 8 5	9 1 12 11 8 5 6	9 1 12 10 4 2 7	9 7 6 5 8	---	9 13 12 10	9 13 12 11	9 13 12	9 1 12 13
10	10 12 1	10 4 2	10 12 11 8 5 3	10 12 1 9 7 2 4	10 12 11 8 5	10 12 1 9 7 6	10 12 13 9 7	10 12 11 8	10 12 13 9	---	10 12 11	10 4 2 7 9 1 12	10 4 2 7 9 13
11	11 12 1	11 12 1 9 7 2	11 12 10 4 2 3	11 12 10 4	11 12 1 9 7 6 5	11 12 1 9 7 6	11 12 1 9 7	11 12 1 9 7 6 5 8	11 12 13 9	11 12 10	---	11 8 5 6 7 9 1 12	11 8 5 6 7 9 13
12	12 13 9 1	12 10 4 2	12 11 8 5 3	12 1 9 7 2 4	12 11 8 5	12 11 8 5 6	12 13 9 7	12 1 9 7 6 5 8	12 13 9	12 1 9 7 2 4 10	12 1 9 7 6 5 8 11	---	12 1 9 13
13	13 12 1	13 12 10 4 2	13 12 10 4 2 3	13 9 7 2 4	13 12 11 8 5	13 12 11 8 5 6	13 12 10 4 2 7	13 9 7 6 5 8	13 12 1 9	13 9 7 2 4 10	13 9 7 6 5 8 11	13 9 1 12	---

Backup Paths of The 13-Node Network - Case VI

Table 9.11 Backup Paths of The 13-Node Network with Node-and-Link Failure Tolerance (Case VI)

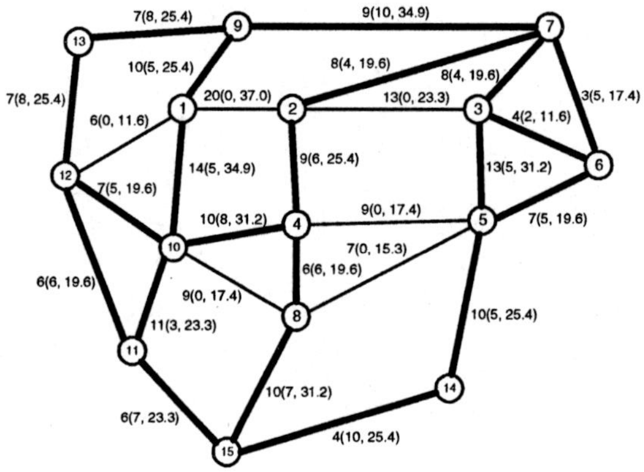

Figure 9.9 15-Node Network (Network 2) with Link-Failure Tolerance (Case IV)

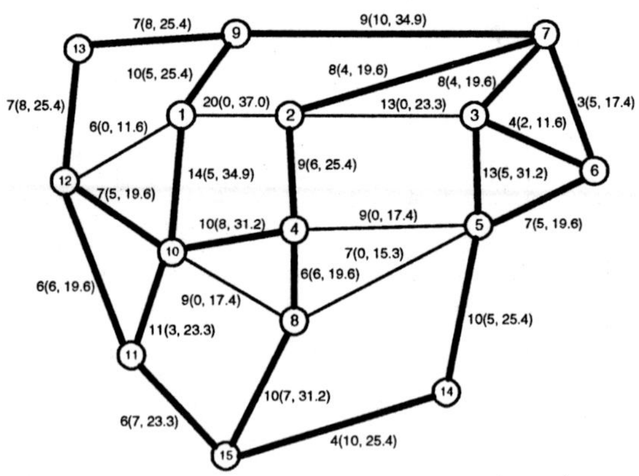

Figure 9.10 15-Node Network (Network 2) with Node-Failure Tolerance (Case V)

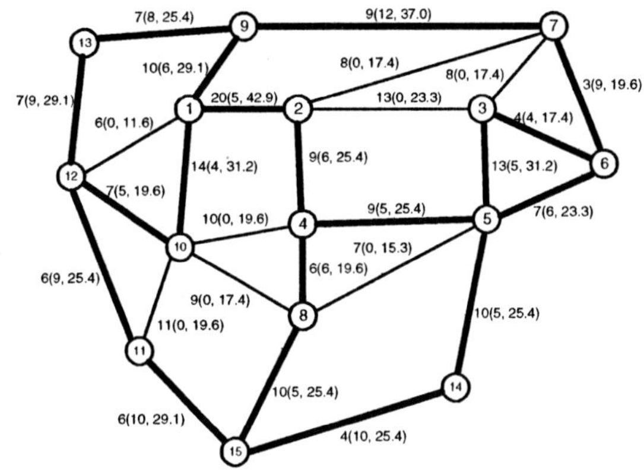

Figure 9.11 15-Node Network (Network 2) with Link-and-Node-Failure Tolerance (Case VI)

Node	1	2	3	4	5	6	7	8	9	10	11	12	13	14	15
1	---	1 10 4 2	1 9 7 3	1 10 4	1 9 7 6 5	1 9 7 6	1 9 7	1 9 7 2 4 8	1 10 12 13 9	1 9 13 12 10	1 9 13 12 11	1 10 12	1 10 12 13	1 10 11 15 14	1 9 13 12 11 15
2	2 4 10 1	---	2 7 3	2 7 9 1 10 4	2 7 6 5	2 7 6	2 4 10 1 9 7	2 7 3 5 14 15 8	2 7 9	2 4 10	2 4 10 12 11	2 4 10 12	2 4 10 12 13	2 4 8 15 14	2 7 3 5 14 15
3	3 7 9 1	3 7 2	---	3 5 14 15 8 4	3 6 5	3 5 6	3 6 7	3 7 2 4 8	3 6 7 2 4 10 1 9	3 7 2 4 10	3 5 14 15 11	3 7 9 13 12	3 5 14 15 11 12 13	3 7 2 4 8 15 14	3 6 5 14 15
4	4 10 1	4 10 1 9 7 2	4 8 15 14 5 3	---	4 2 7 3 5	4 2 7 6	4 10 1 9 7	4 10 11 15 8	4 10 12 13 9	4 8 15 11 10	4 8 15 11	4 8 15 11 12	4 2 7 9 13	4 8 15 14	4 10 11 15
5	5 6 7 9 1	5 6 7 2	5 6 3	5 3 7 2 4	---	5 3 6	5 6 7	5 14 15 8	5 14 15 11 10 1 9	5 14 15 11 10	5 14 15 11	5 14 15 11 12	5 14 15 11 12 13	5 3 7 2 4 8 15 14	5 14 15
6	6 7 9 1	6 7 2	6 5 3	6 7 2 4	6 3 5	---	6 3 7	6 7 2 4 8	6 3 7 2 4 10 1 9	6 7 9 1 10	6 7 9 13 12 11	6 7 9 13 12	6 5 14 15 11 12 13	6 7 2 4 8 15 14	6 3 5 14 15
7	7 9 1	7 9 1 10 4 2	7 6 3	7 9 1 10 4	7 6 5	7 3 6	---	7 3 5 14 15 8	7 2 4 10 1 9	7 9 13 12 10	7 9 13 12 11	7 9 13 12	7 2 4 10 12 13	7 2 4 8 15 14	7 3 5 14 15
8	8 4 2 7 9 1	8 15 14 5 3 7 2	8 4 2 7 3	8 15 11 10 4	8 15 14 5	8 4 2 7 6	8 15 14 5 3 7	---	8 4 2 7 9	8 4 10	8 15 11	8 15 11 12	8 4 10 1 9 13	8 15 14	8 4 10 11 15
9	9 13 12 10 1	9 7 2	9 1 10 4 2 7 6 3	9 13 12 10 4	9 1 10 11 15 14 5	9 1 10 4 2 7 3 6	9 1 10 4 2 7	9 7 2 4 8	---	9 13 12 10	9 13 12 11	9 13 12	9 1 10 12 13	9 1 10 11 15 14	9 13 12 11 15
10	10 12 13 9 1	10 4 2	10 4 2 7 3	10 11 15 8 4	10 11 15 14 5	10 1 9 7 6	10 12 13 9 7	10 4 8	10 12 13 9	---	10 12 11	10 11 12	10 1 9 13	10 11 15 14	10 11 15
11	11 12 13 9 1	11 12 10 4 2	11 15 14 5 3	11 15 8 4	11 15 14 5	11 12 13 9 7 6	11 12 13 9 7	11 15 8	11 12 13 9	11 12 10	---	11 10 12	11 10 1 9 13	11 10 4 2 7 3 5 14	11 10 4 8 15
12	12 10 1	12 10 4 2	12 13 9 7 3	12 11 15 8 4	12 11 15 14 5	12 13 9 7 6	12 13 9 7	12 11 15 8	12 13 9	12 11 10	12 10 11	---	12 10 1 9 13	12 13 9 7 3 5 14	12 10 4 8 15
13	13 12 10 1	13 12 10 4 2	13 12 11 15 14 5 3	13 9 7 2 4	13 12 11 15 14 5	13 12 11 15 14 5 6	13 12 10 4 2 7	13 9 1 10 4 8	13 12 10 1 9	13 9 1 10	13 9 1 10 11	13 9 1 10 12	---	13 9 7 3 5 14	13 9 7 2 4 8 15
14	14 15 11 10 1	14 15 8 4 2	14 15 8 4 2 7 3	14 15 8 4	14 15 8 4 2 7 3 5	14 15 8 4 2 7 6	14 15 8 4 2 7	14 15 8	14 15 11 10 1 9	14 15 11 10	14 5 3 7 2 4 10 11	14 5 3 7 9 13 12	14 5 3 7 9 13	---	14 5 3 7 2 4 8 15
15	15 11 12 13 9 1	15 14 5 3 7 2	15 14 5 6 3	15 11 10 4	15 14 5	15 14 5 3 6	15 14 5 3 7	15 11 10 4 8	15 11 12 13 9	15 11 10	15 8 4 10 11	15 8 4 10 12	15 8 4 2 7 9 13	15 8 4 2 7 3 5 14	---

Backup Paths of The 15-Node Network - Case IV

Table 9.12 Backup Paths of The 15-Node Network with Link-Failure Tolerance (Case IV)

Backup Paths of The 15-Node Network - Case V

Node	1	2	3	4	5	6	7	8	9	10	11	12	13	14	15
1	---	1 12 11 15 8 4 2	1 12 11 15 14 5 3	1 12 11 15 8 4	1 12 11 15 14 5	1 12 13 9 7 6	1 12 13 9 7	1 2 4 8	1 12 13 9	1 12 10	1 12 11	1 2 4 8 15 11 12	1 12 13	1 12 11 15 14	1 12 11 15
2	2 4 8 15 11 12 1	---	2 4 5 3	2 3 5 4	2 4 5	2 4 5 6	2 3 5 6 7	2 1 12 11 15 8	2 3 5 6 7 9	2 4 8 15 11 10	2 4 8 15 11	2 4 8 15 11 12	2 4 8 15 11 12 13	2 4 8 15 14	2 1 12 11 15
3	3 5 14 15 11 12 1	3 5 4 2	---	3 5 4	3 2 4 5	3 5 6	3 5 6 7	3 2 4 8	3 2 1 12 13 9	3 5 14 15 11 10	3 5 14 15 11	3 5 14 15 11 12	3 2 1 12 13	3 2 4 8 15 14	3 2 1 12 11 15
4	4 8 15 11 12 1	4 5 3 2	4 5 3	---	4 2 3 5	4 2 1 12 13 9 7 6	4 5 6 7	4 5 14 15 8	4 5 6 7 9	4 8 15 11 10	4 8 15 11	4 2 1 12	4 5 6 7 9 13	4 8 15 14	4 5 14 15
5	5 14 15 11 12 1	5 4 2	5 4 2 3	5 3 2 4	---	5 3 2 1 12 13 9 7 6	5 6 7	5 4 8	5 4 2 1 12 13 9	5 14 15 11 10	5 14 15 11	5 3 2 1 12	5 4 2 1 12 13	5 4 8 15 14	5 14 15
6	6 7 9 13 12 1	6 5 4 2	6 5 3	6 7 9 13 12 1 2 4	6 7 9 13 12 1 2 3 5	---	6 5 3 2 1 12 13 9 7	6 7 9 13 12 11 15 8	6 5 3 2 1 12 13 9	6 7 9 13 12 10	6 7 9 13 12 11	6 7 9 13 12	6 5 3 2 1 12 13	6 7 9 13 12 11 15 14	6 7 9 13 12 11 15
7	7 9 13 12 1	7 6 5 3 2	7 6 5 3	7 6 5 4	7 6 5	7 9 13 12 1 2 3 5 6	---	7 6 5 14 15 8	7 6 5 3 2 1 12 13 9	7 9 13 12 10	7 9 13 12 11	7 9 13 12	7 6 5 3 2 1 12 13	7 9 13 12 11 15 14	7 6 5 14 15
8	8 4 2 1	8 15 11 12 1 2	8 4 2 3	8 15 14 5 4	8 4 5	8 15 11 12 13 9 7 6	8 15 14 5 6 7	---	8 4 5 6 7 9	8 15 11 10	8 15 11	8 15 11 12	8 4 5 6 7 9 13	8 15 14	8 4 5 14 15
9	9 13 12 1	9 7 6 5 3 2	9 13 12 1 2 3	9 7 6 5 4	9 13 12 1 2 4 5	9 13 12 1 2 3 5 6	9 13 12 1 2 3 5 6 7	9 7 6 5 4 8	---	9 13 12 10	9 13 12 11	9 13 12	9 7 6 5 3 2 1 12 13	9 13 12 11 15 14	9 13 12 11 15
10	10 12 1	10 11 15 8 4 2	10 11 15 14 5 3	10 11 15 8 4	10 11 15 14 5	10 12 13 9 7 6	10 12 13 9 7	10 11 15 8	10 12 13 9	---	10 12 11	10 11 12	10 11 15 14 5 6 7 9 13	10 11 15 14	10 11 15
11	11 12 1	11 15 8 4 2	11 15 14 5 3	11 15 8 4	11 15 14 5	11 12 13 9 7 6	11 12 13 9 7	11 15 8	11 12 13 9	11 12 10	---	11 10 12	11 15 14 5 6 7 9 13	11 12 1 2 3 5 14	11 12 1 2 4 8 15
12	12 11 15 8 4 2 1	12 11 15 8 4 2	12 11 15 14 5 3	12 1 2 4	12 1 2 3 5	12 13 9 7 6	12 13 9 7	12 11 15 8	12 13 9	12 11 10	12 10 11	---	12 1 2 3 5 6 7 9 13	12 1 2 3 5 14	12 1 2 4 8 15
13	13 12 1	13 12 11 15 8 4 2	13 12 1 2 3	13 9 7 6 5 4	13 12 1 2 4 5	13 12 1 2 3 5 6	13 12 1 2 3 5 6 7	13 9 7 6 5 4 8	13 12 1 2 3 5 6 7 9	13 9 7 6 5 14 15 11 10	13 9 7 6 5 14 15 11	13 9 7 6 5 3 2 1 12	---	13 9 7 6 5 14	13 9 7 6 5 14 15
14	14 15 11 12 1	14 15 8 4 2	14 15 8 4 2 3	14 15 8 4	14 15 8 4 5	14 15 11 12 13 9 7 6	14 15 11 12 13 9 7	14 15 8	14 15 11 12 13 9	14 15 11 10	14 5 3 2 1 12 11	14 5 3 2 1 12	14 5 6 7 9 13	---	14 5 4 8 15
15	15 11 12 1	15 11 12 1 2	15 11 12 1 2 3	15 14 5 4	15 14 5	15 11 12 13 9 7 6	15 14 5 6 7	15 14 5 4 8	15 11 12 13 9	15 11 10	15 8 4 2 1 12 11	15 8 4 2 1 12	15 14 5 6 7 9 13	15 8 4 5 14	---

Table 9.13 Backup Paths of The 15-Node Network with Node-Failure Tolerance (Case V)

Backup Paths of The 15-Node Network - Case VI

Node	1	2	3	4	5	6	7	8	9	10	11	12	13	14	15
1	---	1 9 7 6 5 4 2	1 9 7 6 3	1 9 7 6 5 4	1 9 7 6 5	1 9 7 6	1 9 7	1 2 4 8	1 10 12 13 9	1 9 13 12 10	1 9 13 12 11	1 10 12	1 10 12 13	1 10 12 11 15 14	1 9 13 12 11 15
2	2 4 5 6 7 9 1	---	2 4 5 3	2 1 9 7 6 5 4	2 4 5	2 4 5 6	2 1 9 7	2 1 10 12 11 15 8	2 4 5 6 7 9	2 4 8 15 11 12 10	2 4 8 15 11	2 4 8 15 11 12	2 4 8 15 11 12 13	2 4 8 15 14	2 1 10 12 11 15
3	3 6 7 9 1	3 5 4 2	---	3 5 4	3 6 5	3 5 6	3 6 7	3 6 7 9 1 2 4 8	3 5 4 2 1 9	3 5 14 15 11 12 10	3 5 14 15 11	3 5 14 15 11 12	3 5 14 15 11 12 13	3 6 7 9 13 12 11 15 14	3 6 7 9 13 12 11 15
4	4 5 6 7 9 1	4 5 6 7 9 1 2	4 5 3	---	4 8 15 14 5	4 2 1 9 7 6	4 5 6 7	4 5 14 15 8	4 5 6 7 9	4 2 1 10	4 8 15 11	4 8 15 11 12	4 2 1 9 13	4 8 15 14	4 5 14 15
5	5 6 7 9 1	5 4 2	5 6 3	5 14 15 8 4	---	5 3 6	5 6 7	5 4 8	5 4 2 1 9	5 6 7 9 1 10	5 14 15 11	5 14 15 11 12	5 14 15 11 12 13	5 4 8 15 14	5 14 15
6	6 7 9 1	6 5 4 2	6 5 3	6 7 9 1 2 4	6 3 5	---	6 5 4 2 1 9 7	6 7 9 1 2 4 8	6 5 4 2 1 9	6 7 9 1 10	6 7 9 13 12 11	6 7 9 13 12	6 5 14 15 11 12 13	6 7 9 13 12 11 15 14	6 7 9 13 12 11 15
7	7 9 1	7 9 1 2	7 6 3	7 6 5 4	7 6 5	7 9 1 2 4 5 6	---	7 6 5 14 15 8	7 6 5 4 2 1 9	7 9 13 12 10	7 9 13 12 11	7 9 13 12	7 6 5 14 15 11 12 13	7 9 13 12 11 15 14	7 6 5 14 15
8	8 4 2 1	8 15 11 12 10 1 2	8 4 2 1 9 7 6 3	8 15 14 5 4	8 4 5	8 4 2 1 9 7 6	8 15 14 5 6 7	---	8 4 5 6 7 9	8 4 2 1 10	8 15 11	8 15 11 12	8 4 2 1 9 13	8 15 14	8 4 5 14 15
9	9 13 12 10 1	9 7 6 5 4 2	9 1 2 4 5 3	9 7 6 5 4	9 1 2 4 5	9 1 2 4 5 6	9 1 2 4 5 6 7	9 7 6 5 4 8	---	9 13 12 10	9 13 12 11	9 13 12	9 1 10 12 13	9 13 12 11 15 14	9 13 12 11 15
10	10 12 13 9 1	10 12 11 15 8 4 2	10 12 11 15 14 5 3	10 1 2 4	10 1 9 7 6 5	10 1 9 7 6	10 12 13 9 7	10 1 2 4 8	10 12 13 9	---	10 12 11	10 1 9 13 12	10 1 9 13	10 12 11 15 14	10 12 11 15
11	11 12 13 9 1	11 15 8 4 2	11 15 14 5 3	11 15 8 4	11 15 14 5	11 12 13 9 7 6	11 12 13 9 7	11 15 8	11 12 13 9	11 12 10	---	11 15 8 4 2 1 10 12	11 15 8 4 2 1 9 13	11 12 10 1 2 4 5 14	11 12 10 1 2 4 8 15
12	12 10 1	12 11 15 8 4 2	12 11 15 14 5 3	12 11 15 8 4	12 11 15 14 5	12 13 9 7 6	12 13 9 7	12 11 15 8	12 13 9	12 13 9 1 10	12 10 1 2 4 8 15 11	---	12 10 1 9 13	12 10 1 2 4 5 14	12 10 1 2 4 8 15
13	13 12 10 1	13 12 11 15 8 4 2	13 12 11 15 14 5 3	13 9 1 2 4	13 12 11 15 14 5	13 12 11 15 14 5 6	13 12 11 15 14 5 6 7	13 9 1 2 4 8	13 12 10 1 9	13 9 1 10	13 9 1 2 4 8 15 11	13 9 1 10 12	---	13 9 7 6 5 14	13 9 1 2 4 8 15
14	14 15 11 12 10 1	14 15 8 4 2	14 15 11 12 13 9 7 6 3	14 15 8 4	14 15 8 4 5	14 15 11 12 13 9 7 6	14 15 11 12 13 9 7	14 15 8	14 15 11 12 13 9	14 15 11 12 10	14 5 4 2 1 10 12 11	14 5 4 2 1 10 12	14 5 6 7 9 13	---	14 5 4 8 15
15	15 11 12 13 9 1	15 11 12 10 1 2	15 11 12 13 9 7 6 3	15 14 5 4	15 14 5	15 11 12 13 9 7 6	15 14 5 6 7	15 14 5 4 8	15 11 12 13 9	15 11 12 10	15 8 4 2 1 10 12 11	15 8 4 2 1 10 12	15 8 4 2 1 9 13	15 8 4 5 14	---

Table 9.14 Backup Paths of The 15-Node Network with Link-and-Node Failure Tolerance (Case VI)

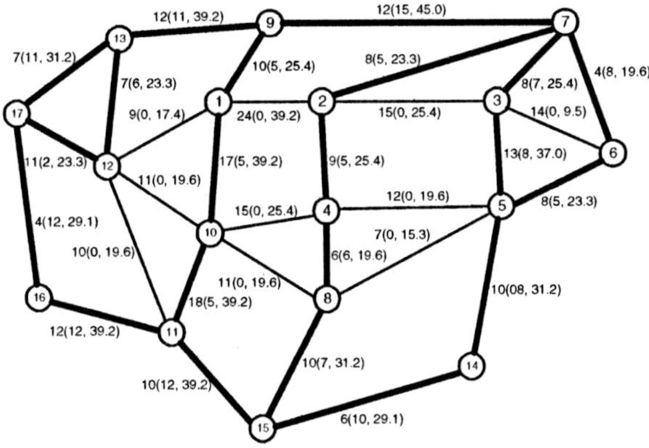

Figure 9.12 17-Node Network (Network 3) with Link-Failure Tolerance (Case IV)

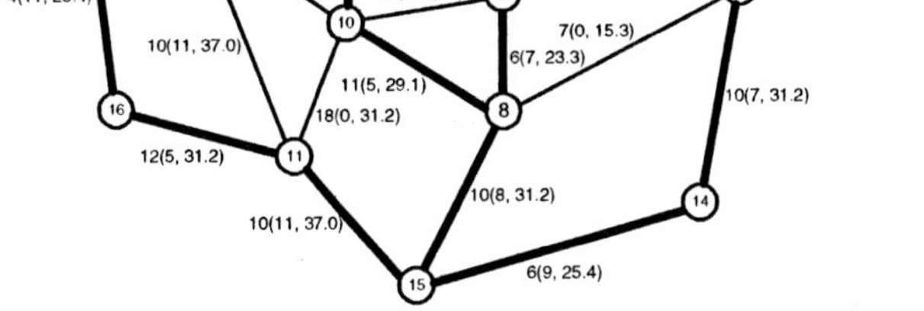

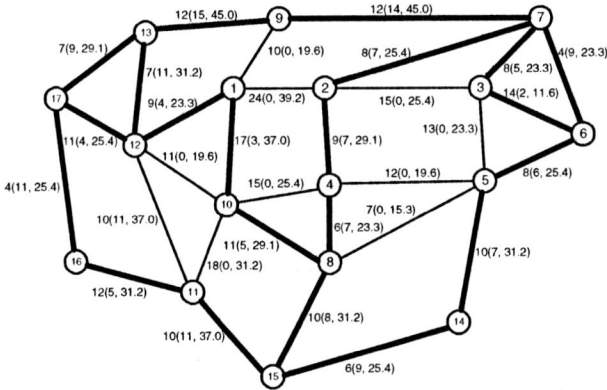

Figure 9.13 17-Node Network (Network 3) with Node-Failure Tolerance (Case V)

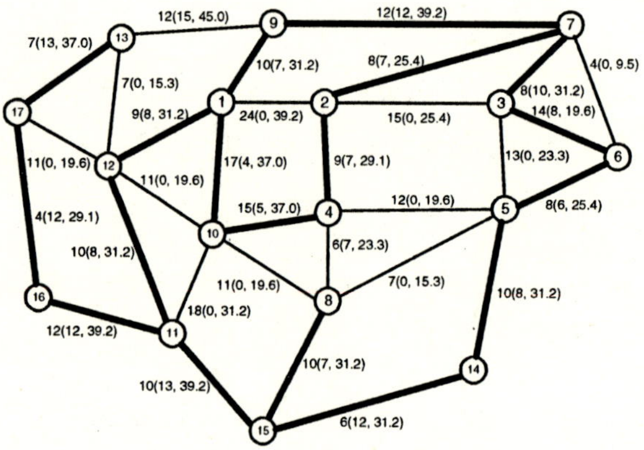

Figure 9.14 17-Node Network (Network 3) with Link-and-Node-Failure Tolerance (Case VI)

Backup Paths of The 17-Node Network - Case IV

From / To	1	2	3	4	5	6	7	8	9	10	11	12	13	14	15	16	17
1	---	1 9 7 2	1 9 7 3	1 10 11 15 8 4	1 9 7 6 5	1 9 7 6	1 9 7	1 9 7 2 4 8	1 10 11 16 17 13 9	1 9 13 17 16 11 10	1 9 13 17 16 11	1 9 13 12	1 10 11 16 17 13	1 10 11 15 14	1 9 13 17 16 11 15	1 9 13 17 16	1 9 13 17
2	2 7 9 1	---	2 7 3	2 7 3 5 14 15 8 4	2 7 6 5	2 7 6	2 4 8 15 14 5 3 7	2 7 3 5 14 15 8	2 7 9	2 4 8 15 11 10	2 4 8 15 11	2 7 9 13 12	2 4 8 15 11 16 17 13	2 4 8 15 14	2 7 3 5 14 15	2 7 9 13 17 16	2 7 9 13 17
3	3 7 9 1	3 7 2	---	3 5 14 15 8 4	3 7 6 5	3 5 6	3 5 6 7	3 7 2 4 8	3 5 14 15 11 10 1 9	3 5 14 15 11 10	3 5 14 15 11	3 7 9 13 12	3 5 14 15 11 16 17 13	3 7 2 4 8 15 14	3 7 6 5 14 15	3 7 9 13 17 16	3 7 9 13 17
4	4 8 15 11 10 1	4 8 15 14 5 3 7 2	4 8 15 14 5 3	---	4 2 7 3 5	4 2 7 6	4 8 15 14 5 3 7	4 2 7 3 5 14 15 8	4 8 15 14 5 3 7 9	4 8 15 11 10	4 8 15 11	4 2 7 9 13 12	4 2 7 9 13	4 8 15 14	4 2 7 3 5 14 15	4 2 7 9 13 17 16	4 2 7 9 13 17
5	5 6 7 9 1	5 6 7 2	5 6 7 3	5 3 7 2 4	---	5 3 7 6	5 6 7	5 14 15 8	5 14 15 11 10 1 9	5 14 15 11 10	5 14 15 11	5 3 7 9 13 12	5 14 15 11 16 17 13	5 3 7 2 4 8 15 14	5 14 15	5 3 7 9 13 17 16	5 3 7 9 13 17
6	6 7 9 1	6 7 2	6 5 3	6 7 2 4	6 7 3 5	---	6 5 3 7	6 7 2 4 8	6 5 14 15 11 10 1 9	6 7 9 1 10	6 7 2 4 8 15 11	6 7 9 13 12	6 5 14 15 11 16 17 13	6 7 2 4 8 15 14	6 7 3 5 14 15	6 7 9 13 17 16	6 5 14 15 11 16 17
7	7 9 1	7 3 5 14 15 8 4 2	7 6 5 3	7 3 5 14 15 8 4	7 6 5	7 3 5 6	---	7 3 5 14 15 8	7 2 4 8 15 11 10 1 9	7 3 5 14 15 11 10	7 3 5 14 15 11	7 9 13 12	7 2 4 8 15 11 16 17 13	7 2 4 8 15 14	7 3 5 14 15	7 2 4 8 15 11 16	7 2 4 8 15 11 16 17
8	8 4 2 7 9 1	8 15 14 5 3 7 2	8 4 2 7 3	8 15 14 5 3 7 2 4	8 15 14 5	8 4 2 7 6	8 15 14 5 3 7	---	8 4 2 7 9	8 15 11 10	8 15 11	8 15 11 16 17 12	8 4 2 7 9 13	8 15 14	8 4 2 7 3 5 14 15	8 4 2 7 9 13 17 16	8 15 11 16 17
9	9 13 17 16 11 10 1	9 7 2	9 1 10 11 15 14 5 3	9 7 3 5 14 15 8 4	9 1 10 11 15 14 5	9 1 10 11 15 14 5 6	9 1 10 11 15 8 4 2 7	9 7 2 4 8	---	9 13 17 16 11 10	9 13 17 16 11	9 13 12	9 1 10 11 16 17 13	9 1 10 11 15 14	9 13 17 16 11 15	9 1 10 11 16	9 1 10 11 16 17
10	10 11 16 17 13 9 1	10 11 15 8 4 2	10 11 15 14 5 3	10 11 15 8 4	10 11 15 14 5	10 1 9 7 6	10 11 15 14 5 3 7	10 11 15 8	10 11 16 17 13 9	---	10 1 9 13 17 16 11	10 1 9 13 12	10 1 9 13	10 11 15 14	10 11 15	10 1 9 13 17 16	10 11 16 17
11	11 16 17 13 9 1	11 15 8 4 2	11 15 14 5 3	11 15 8 4	11 15 14 5	11 15 8 4 2 7 6	11 15 14 5 3 7	11 15 8	11 16 17 13 9	11 16 17 13 9 1 10	---	11 16 17 12	11 16 17 13	11 10 1 9 7 3 5 14	11 10 1 9 7 2 4 8 15	11 10 1 9 13 17 16	11 16 17
12	12 13 9 1	12 13 9 7 2	12 13 9 7 3	12 13 9 7 2 4	12 13 9 7 3 5	12 13 9 7 6	12 13 9 7	12 17 16 11 15 8	12 13 9	12 13 9 1 10	12 17 16 11	---	12 17 13	12 13 9 7 3 5 14	12 13 9 7 2 4 8 15	12 17 16	12 13 17
13	13 17 16 11 10 1	13 17 16 11 15 8 4 2	13 17 16 11 15 14 5 3	13 9 7 2 4	13 17 16 11 15 14 5	13 17 16 11 15 14 5 6	13 17 16 11 15 8 4 2 7	13 9 7 2 4 8	13 17 16 11 10 1 9	13 9 1 10	13 17 16 11	13 17 12	---	13 9 7 3 5 14	13 9 7 2 4 8 15	13 9 1 10 11 16	13 12 17
14	14 15 11 10 1	14 15 8 4 2	14 15 8 4 2 7 3	14 15 8 4	14 15 8 4 2 7 3 5	14 15 8 4 2 7 6	14 15 8 4 2 7	14 15 8	14 15 11 10 1 9	14 15 11 10	14 5 3 7 9 1 10 11	14 5 3 7 9 13 12	14 5 3 7 9 13	---	14 5 3 7 2 4 8 15	14 5 3 7 9 13 17 16	14 5 3 7 9 13 17
15	15 11 16 17 13 9 1	15 14 5 3 7 2	15 14 5 6 7 3	15 14 5 3 7 2 4	15 14 5	15 14 5 3 7 6	15 14 5 3 7	15 14 5 3 7 2 4 8	15 11 16 17 13 9	15 11 10	15 8 4 2 7 9 1 10 11	15 8 4 2 7 9 13 12	15 8 4 2 7 9 13	15 8 4 2 7 3 5 14	---	15 8 4 2 7 9 13 17 16	15 8 4 2 7 9 13 17
16	16 17 13 9 1	16 17 13 9 7 2	16 17 13 9 7 3	16 17 13 9 7 2 4	16 17 13 9 7 3 5	16 17 13 9 7 6	16 11 15 8 4 2 7	16 17 13 9 7 2 4 8	16 11 10 1 9	16 17 13 9 1 10	16 17 13 9 1 10 11	16 17 12	16 11 10 1 9 13	16 17 13 9 7 3 5 14	16 17 13 9 7 2 4 8 15	---	16 11 10 1 9 13 17
17	17 13 9 1	17 13 9 7 2	17 13 9 7 3	17 13 9 7 2 4	17 13 9 7 3 5	17 16 11 15 14 5 6	17 16 11 15 8 4 2 7	17 16 11 15 8	17 16 11 10 1 9	17 16 11 10	17 16 11	17 13 12	17 12 13	17 13 9 7 3 5 14	17 13 9 7 2 4 8 15	17 13 9 1 10 11 16	---

Table 9.15 Backup Paths of The 17-Node Network with Link-Failure Tolerance (Case IV)

Backup Paths of The 17-Node Network - Case V

From / To	1	2	3	4	5	6	7	8	9	10	11	12	13	14	15	16	17
1	---	1 10 8 4 2	1 12 13 9 7 3	1 10 8 4	1 10 8 15 14 5	1 12 13 9 7 6	1 12 13 9 7	1 12 11 15 8	1 12 13 9	1 12 11 15 8 10	1 12 11	1 10 8 15 11 12	1 12 13	1 10 8 15 14	1 12 11 15	1 12 17 16	1 10 8 15 11 16 17
2	2 4 8 10 1	---	2 7 3	2 7 6 5 14 15 8 4	2 7 6 5	2 7 6	2 4 8 15 14 5 6 7	2 7 6 5 14 15 8	2 7 9	2 4 8 10	2 4 8 15 11	2 7 9 13 12	2 4 8 15 11 12 13	2 4 8 15 14	2 7 6 5 14 15	2 7 9 13 17 16	2 7 9 13 17
3	3 7 9 13 12 1	3 7 2	---	3 6 5 14 15 8 4	3 6 5	3 7 6	3 6 7	3 7 2 4 8	3 6 5 14 15 11 12 13 9	3 6 5 14 15 8 10	3 7 9 13 12 11	3 7 9 13 12	3 6 5 14 15 11 12 13	3 7 2 4 8 15 14	3 7 9 13 12 11 15	3 7 9 13 17 16	3 7 9 13 17
4	4 8 10 1	4 8 15 14 5 6 7 2	4 8 15 14 5 6 3	---	4 2 7 6 5	4 2 7 6	4 8 15 14 5 6 7	4 2 7 6 5 14 15 8	4 8 15 11 12 13 9	4 8 10	4 8 15 11	4 8 15 11 12	4 2 7 9 13	4 8 15 14	4 2 7 6 5 14 15	4 2 7 9 13 17 16	4 2 7 9 13 17
5	5 14 15 8 10 1	5 6 7 2	5 6 3	5 6 7 2 4	---	5 14 15 8 4 2 7 6	5 6 7	5 14 15 8	5 14 15 11 12 13 9	5 14 15 8 10	5 14 15 11	5 14 15 11 12	5 14 15 11 12 13	5 6 7 2 4 8 15 14	5 14 15	5 6 7 9 13 17 16	5 6 7 9 13 17
6	6 7 9 13 12 1	6 7 2	6 7 3	6 7 2 4	6 7 2 4 8 15 14 5	---	6 3 7	6 7 2 4 8	6 5 14 15 11 12 13 9	6 7 9 13 12 1 10	6 7 9 13 12 11	6 7 9 13 12	6 5 14 15 11 12 13	6 7 2 4 8 15 14	6 7 9 13 12 11 15	6 7 9 13 17 16	6 5 14 15 11 12 17
7	7 9 13 12 1	7 6 5 14 15 8 4 2	7 6 3	7 6 5 14 15 8 4	7 6 5	7 3 6	---	7 6 5 14 15 8	7 2 4 8 10 1 12 13 9	7 6 5 14 15 8 10	7 9 13 12 11	7 9 13 12	7 2 4 8 10 1 12 13	7 2 4 8 15 14	7 6 5 14 15	7 2 4 8 15 11 16	7 2 4 8 10 1 12 17
8	8 15 11 12 1	8 15 14 5 6 7 2	8 4 2 7 3	8 15 14 5 6 7 2 4	8 15 14 5	8 4 2 7 6	8 15 14 5 6 7	---	8 4 2 7 9	8 15 11 12 1 10	8 15 11	8 15 11 12	8 4 2 7 9 13	8 15 14	8 10 1 12 11 15	8 4 2 7 9 13 17 16	8 15 11 16 17
9	9 13 12 1	9 7 2	9 13 12 11 15 14 5 6 3	9 13 12 11 15 8 4	9 13 12 11 15 14 5	9 13 12 11 15 14 5 6	9 13 12 1 10 8 4 2 7	9 7 2 4 8	---	9 7 2 4 8 10	9 13 12 11	9 13 12	9 7 2 4 8 10 1 12 13	9 13 12 11 15 14	9 13 12 11 15	9 7 2 4 8 15 11 16	9 7 2 4 8 10 1 12 17
10	10 8 15 11 12 1	10 8 4 2	10 8 15 14 5 6 3	10 8 4	10 8 15 14 5	10 1 12 13 9 7 6	10 8 15 14 5 6 7	10 1 12 11 15 8	10 8 4 2 7 9	---	10 1 12 11	10 1 12	10 8 4 2 7 9 13	10 8 15 14	10 1 12 11 15	10 1 12 17 16	10 8 15 11 16 17
11	11 12 1	11 15 8 4 2	11 12 13 9 7 3	11 15 8 4	11 15 14 5	11 12 13 9 7 6	11 12 13 9 7	11 15 8	11 12 13 9	11 12 1 10	---	11 16 17 12	11 16 17 13	11 12 13 9 7 6 5 14	11 12 1 10 8 15	11 12 17 16	11 16 17
12	12 11 15 8 10 1	12 13 9 7 2	12 13 9 7 3	12 11 15 8 4	12 11 15 14 5	12 13 9 7 6	12 13 9 7	12 11 15 8	12 13 9	12 1 10	12 17 16 11	---	12 17 13	12 13 9 7 6 5 14	12 1 10 8 15	12 17 16	12 13 17
13	13 12 1	13 12 11 15 8 4 2	13 12 11 15 14 5 6 3	13 9 7 2 4	13 12 11 15 14 5	13 12 11 15 14 5 6	13 12 1 10 8 4 2 7	13 9 7 2 4 8	13 12 1 10 8 4 2 7 9	13 9 7 2 4 8 10	13 17 16 11	13 17 12	---	13 9 7 6 5 14	13 9 7 2 4 8 15	13 12 11 16	13 12 17
14	14 15 8 10 1	14 15 8 4 2	14 15 8 4 2 7 3	14 15 8 4	14 15 8 4 2 7 6 5	14 15 8 4 2 7 6	14 15 8 4 2 7	14 15 8	14 15 11 12 13 9	14 15 8 10	14 5 6 7 9 13 12 11	14 5 6 7 9 13 12	14 5 6 7 9 13	---	14 5 6 7 2 4 8 15	14 5 6 7 9 13 17 16	14 5 6 7 9 13 17
15	15 11 12 1	15 14 5 6 7 2	15 11 12 13 9 7 3	15 14 5 6 7 2 4	15 14 5	15 11 12 13 9 7 6	15 14 5 6 7	15 11 12 1 10 8	15 11 12 13 9	15 11 12 1 10	15 8 10 1 12 11	15 8 10 1 12	15 8 4 2 7 9 13	15 8 4 2 7 6 5 14	---	15 8 10 1 12 17 16	15 8 4 2 7 9 13 17
16	16 17 12 1	16 17 13 9 7 2	16 17 13 9 7 3	16 17 13 9 7 2 4	16 17 13 9 7 6 5	16 17 13 9 7 6	16 11 15 8 4 2 7	16 17 13 9 7 2 4 8	16 11 15 8 4 2 7 9	16 17 12 1 10	16 17 12 11	16 17 12	16 11 12 13	16 17 13 9 7 6 5 14	16 17 12 1 10 8 15	---	16 11 12 17
17	17 16 11 15 8 10 1	17 13 9 7 2	17 13 9 7 3	17 13 9 7 2 4	17 13 9 7 6 5	17 12 11 15 14 5 6	17 12 1 10 8 4 2 7	17 16 11 15 8	17 12 1 10 8 4 2 7 9	17 16 11 15 8 10	17 16 11	17 13 12	17 12 13	17 13 9 7 6 5 14	17 13 9 7 2 4 8 15	17 12 11 16	---

Table 9.16 Backup Paths of The 17-Node Network with Node-Failure Tolerance (Case V)

From / To	1	2	3	4	5	6	7	8	9	10	11	12	13	14	15	16	17
1	---	1 10 4 2	1 9 7 3	1 10 4	1 12 11 15 14 5	1 12 11 15 14 5 6	1 9 7	1 12 11 15 8	1 10 4 2 7 9	1 9 7 2 4 10	1 12 11	1 10 4 8 15 11 12	1 12 11 16 17 13	1 12 11 15 14	1 12 11 15	1 9 13 17 16	1 9 13 17
2	2 4 10 1	---	2 7 3	2 7 9 1 10 4	2 4 8 15 14 5	2 4 8 15 14 5 6	2 4 10 1 9 7	2 7 9 1 12 11 15 8	2 7 9	2 4 10	2 4 8 15 11	2 4 8 15 11 12	2 4 8 15 11 16 17 13	2 4 8 15 14	2 7 9 1 12 11 15	2 7 9 13 17 16	2 7 9 13 17
3	3 7 9 1	3 7 2	---	3 7 9 1 10 4	3 6 5	3 7 2 4 8 15 14 5 6	3 6 5 14 15 8 4 2 7	3 7 2 4 8	3 6 5 14 15 11 12 1 9	3 6 5 14 15 8 4 10	3 6 5 14 15 11	3 6 5 14 15 11 12	3 6 5 14 15 11 16 17 13	3 7 2 4 8 15 14	3 7 9 1 12 11 15	3 7 9 13 17 16	3 7 9 13 17
4	4 10 1	4 10 1 9 7 2	4 10 1 9 7 3	---	4 8 15 14 5	4 2 7 3 6	4 10 1 9 7	4 10 1 12 11 15 8	4 8 15 11 16 17 13 9	4 2 7 9 1 10	4 8 15 11	4 8 15 11 12	4 2 7 9 13	4 8 15 14	4 10 1 12 11 15	4 2 7 9 13 17 16	4 2 7 9 13 17
5	5 14 15 11 12 1	5 14 15 8 4 2	5 6 3	5 14 15 8 4	---	5 14 15 8 4 2 7 3 6	5 14 15 8 4 2 7	5 14 15 8	5 14 15 11 12 1 9	5 6 3 7 9 1 10	5 14 15 11	5 14 15 11 12	5 14 15 11 16 17 13	5 6 3 7 2 4 8 15 14	5 14 15	5 6 3 7 9 13 17 16	5 14 15 11 16 17
6	6 5 14 15 11 12 1	6 5 14 15 8 4 2	6 5 14 15 8 4 2 7 3	6 3 7 2 4	6 3 7 2 4 8 15 14 5	---	6 3 7	6 3 7 2 4 8	6 5 14 15 11 12 1 9	6 3 7 9 1 10	6 3 7 9 1 12 11	6 5 14 15 11 12	6 5 14 15 11 16 17 13	6 3 7 2 4 8 15 14	6 3 7 9 1 12 11 15	6 3 7 9 13 17 16	6 5 14 15 11 16 17
7	7 9 1	7 9 1 10 4 2	7 2 4 8 15 14 5 6 3	7 9 1 10 4	7 2 4 8 15 14 5	7 3 6	---	7 9 1 12 11 15 8	7 2 4 10 1 9	7 3 6 5 14 15 8 4 10	7 9 13 17 16 11	7 9 13 17 16 11 12	7 2 4 8 15 11 16 17 13	7 2 4 8 15 14	7 9 1 12 11 15	7 2 4 8 15 11 16	7 2 4 8 15 11 16 17
8	8 15 11 12 1	8 15 11 12 1 9 7 2	8 4 2 7 3	8 15 11 12 1 10 4	8 15 14 5	8 4 2 7 3 6	8 15 11 12 1 9 7	---	8 4 2 7 9	8 4 10	8 15 11	8 15 11 12	8 4 2 7 9 13	8 15 14	8 4 10 1 12 11 15	8 4 2 7 9 13 17 16	8 15 11 16 17
9	9 7 2 4 10 1	9 7 2	9 1 12 11 15 14 5 6 3	9 13 17 16 11 15 8 4	9 1 12 11 15 14 5	9 1 12 11 15 14 5 6	9 1 10 4 2 7	9 7 2 4 8	---	9 7 2 4 10	9 13 17 16 11	9 13 17 16 11 12	9 1 12 11 16 17 13	9 1 12 11 15 14	9 13 17 16 11 15	9 1 12 11 16	9 1 12 11 16 17
10	10 4 2 7 9 1	10 4 2	10 4 8 15 14 5 6 3	10 1 9 7 2 4	10 1 9 7 3 6 5	10 1 9 7 3 6	10 4 8 15 14 5 6 3 7	10 4 8	10 4 2 7 9	---	10 1 12 11	10 1 12	10 1 9 13	10 1 12 11 15 14	10 1 12 11 15	10 1 9 13 17 16	10 1 9 13 17
11	11 12 1	11 15 8 4 2	11 15 14 5 6 3	11 15 8 4	11 15 14 5	11 12 1 9 7 3 6	11 16 17 13 9 7	11 15 8	11 16 17 13 9	11 12 1 10	---	11 16 17 13 9 1 12	11 16 17 13	11 12 1 9 7 3 6 5 14	11 12 1 10 4 8 15	11 12 1 9 13 17 16	11 16 17
12	12 11 15 8 4 10 1	12 11 15 8 4 2	12 11 15 14 5 6 3	12 11 15 8 4	12 11 15 14 5	12 11 15 14 5 6	12 11 16 17 13 9 7	12 11 15 8	12 11 16 17 13 9	12 1 10	12 1 9 13 17 16 11	---	12 1 9 13	12 1 9 7 3 6 5 14	12 1 10 4 8 15	12 1 9 13 17 16	12 11 16 17
13	13 17 16 11 12 1	13 17 16 11 15 8 4 2	13 17 16 11 15 14 5 6 3	13 9 7 2 4	13 17 16 11 15 14 5	13 17 16 11 15 14 5 6	13 17 16 11 15 8 4 2 7	13 9 7 2 4 8	13 17 16 11 12 1 9	13 9 1 10	13 17 16 11	13 9 1 12	---	13 9 7 3 6 5 14	13 9 7 2 4 8 15	13 9 1 12 11 16	13 9 1 12 11 16 17
14	14 15 11 12 1	14 15 8 4 2	14 15 8 4 2 7 3	14 15 8 4	14 15 8 4 2 7 3 6 5	14 15 8 4 2 7 3 6	14 15 8 4 2 7	14 15 8	14 15 11 12 1 9	14 15 11 12 1 10	14 5 6 3 7 9 1 12 11	14 5 6 3 7 9 1 12	14 5 6 3 7 9 13	---	14 5 6 3 7 2 4 8 15	14 5 6 3 7 9 13 17 16	14 5 6 3 7 9 13 17
15	15 11 12 1	15 11 12 1 9 7 2	15 11 12 1 9 7 3	15 11 12 1 10 4	15 14 5	15 11 12 1 9 7 3 6	15 11 12 1 9 7	15 11 12 1 10 4 8	15 11 16 17 13 9	15 11 12 1 10	15 8 4 10 1 12 11	15 8 4 10 1 12	15 8 4 2 7 9 13	15 8 4 2 7 3 6 5 14	---	15 8 4 10 1 9 13 17 16	15 8 4 10 1 9 13 17
16	16 17 13 9 1	16 17 13 9 7 2	16 17 13 9 7 3	16 17 13 9 7 2 4	16 17 13 9 7 3 6 5	16 17 13 9 7 3 6	16 11 15 8 4 2 7	16 17 13 9 7 2 4 8	16 11 12 1 9	16 17 13 9 1 10	16 17 13 9 1 12 11	16 17 13 9 1 12	16 11 12 1 9 13	16 17 13 9 7 3 6 5 14	16 17 13 9 1 10 4 8 15	---	16 11 12 1 9 13 17
17	17 13 9 1	17 13 9 7 2	17 13 9 7 3	17 13 9 7 2 4	17 16 11 15 14 5	17 16 11 15 14 5 6	17 16 11 15 8 4 2 7	17 16 11 15 8	17 16 11 12 1 9	17 13 9 1 10	17 16 11	17 16 11 12	17 16 11 12 1 9 13	17 13 9 7 3 6 5 14	17 13 9 1 10 4 8 15	17 13 9 1 12 11 16	---

Backup Paths of The 17-Node Network - Case VI

Table 9.17 Backup Paths of The 17-Node Network with Link-and-Node Failure Tolerance (Case VI)

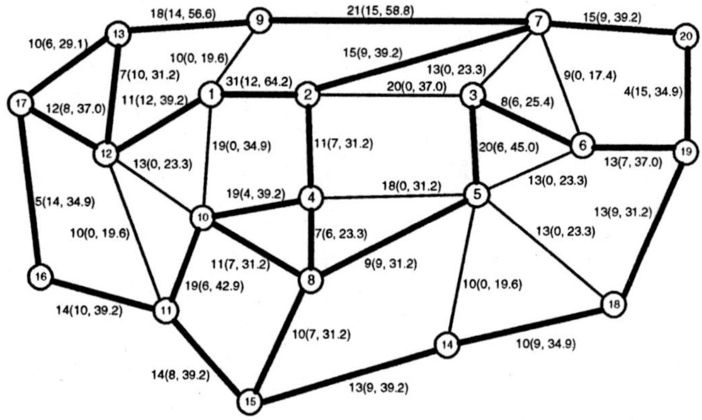

Figure 9.15 20-Node Network (Network 4) with Link-Failure Tolerance (Case IV)

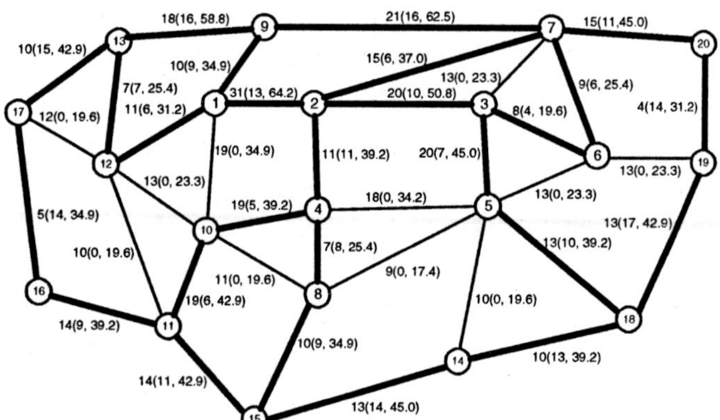

Figure 9.16 20-Node Network (Network 4) with Node-Failure Tolerance (Case V)

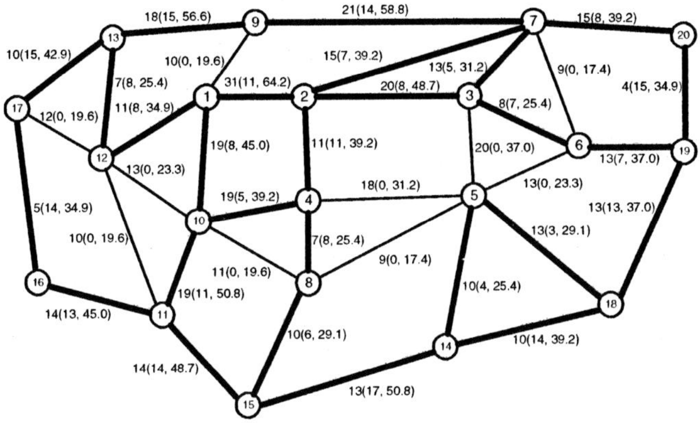

Figure 9.17 20-Node Network (Network 4) with Link-and-Node-Failure Tolerance (Case VI)

From / To	1	2	3	4	5	6	7	8	9	10	11	12	13	14	15	16	17	18	19	20
1	–	1 12 13 9 7 2	1 12 17 16 11 10 8 5 3	1 12 17 16 11 10 4	1 12 17 16 11 10 8 5	1 12 13 9 7 20 19 6	1 12 13 9 7	1 2 4 8	1 2 7 9	1 2 4 10	1 12 17 16 11	1 2 7 9 13 12	1 12 13	1 12 17 16 11 15 14	1 2 4 10 11 15	1 12 17 16	1 2 7 9 13 17	1 12 17 16 11 15 14 18	1 12 13 9 7 20 19	1 12 17 16 11 15 14 18 19 20
2	2 7 9 13 12 1	–	2 4 8 5 3	2 1 12 17 16 11 10 4	2 4 8 5	2 7 20 19 6	2 1 12 13 9 7	2 7 20 19 6 3 5 8	2 7 9	2 4 10	2 4 8 15 11	2 7 9 13 12	2 4 10 11 16 17 13	2 4 8 15 14	2 1 12 17 16 11 15	2 7 9 13 17 16	2 7 9 13 17	2 7 20 19 18	2 7 20 19	2 4 8 5 3 6 19 20
3	3 5 8 10 11 16 17 12 1	3 5 8 4 2	–	3 5 8 4	3 6 19 18 14 15 8 5	3 5 8 15 14 18 19 6	3 6 19 20 7	3 6 19 18 14 15 8	3 5 8 4 2 1 12 13 9	3 5 8 10	3 5 8 15 11	3 6 19 20 7 9 13 12	3 5 8 4 2 1 12 13	3 6 19 18 14	3 6 19 18 14 15	3 6 19 20 7 9 13 17 16	3 5 8 10 11 16 17	3 6 19 18	3 5 8 15 14 18 19	3 6 19 20
4	4 10 11 16 17 12 1	4 10 11 16 17 12 1 2	4 8 5 3	–	4 8 5	4 8 5 3 6	4 10 11 16 17 13 9 7	4 10 8	4 10 11 16 17 13 9	4 8 10	4 8 15 11	4 2 1 12	4 2 7 9 13	4 8 15 14	4 10 11 15	4 2 1 12 17 16	4 2 7 9 13 17	4 8 15 14 18	4 2 7 20 19	4 8 5 3 6 19 20
5	5 8 10 11 16 17 12 1	5 8 4 2	5 8 15 14 18 19 6 3	5 8 4	–	5 3 6	5 8 4 2 7	5 3 6 19 18 14 15 8	5 8 4 2 1 12 13 9	5 8 10	5 8 15 11	5 8 4 2 1 12	5 8 4 2 1 12 13	5 8 15 14	5 3 6 19 18 14 15	5 8 4 2 1 12 17 16	5 8 10 11 16 17	5 8 15 14 18	5 8 15 14 18 19	5 8 15 14 18 19 20
6	6 19 20 7 9 13 12 1	6 19 20 7 2	6 19 18 14 15 8 5 3	6 3 5 8 4	6 3 5	–	6 19 20 7	6 19 18 14 15 8	6 19 20 7 2 1 12 13 9	6 3 5 8 10	6 3 5 8 15 11	6 19 20 7 9 13 12	6 19 20 7 2 1 12 13	6 19 18 14	6 19 18 14 15	6 19 20 7 9 13 17 16	6 19 20 7 2 1 12 17	6 19 18	6 3 5 8 15 14 18 19	6 19 20
7	7 9 13 12 1	7 9 13 12 1 2	7 20 19 6 3	7 9 13 17 16 11 10 4	7 2 4 8 5	7 20 19 6	–	7 20 19 6 3 5 8	7 2 1 12 13 9	7 9 13 17 16 11 10	7 9 13 17 16 11	7 9 13 12	7 2 1 12 13	7 20 19 18 14	7 20 19 18 14 15	7 2 4 10 11 16	7 2 1 12 17	7 20 19 18	7 20 19	7 2 4 8 5 3 6 19 20
8	8 4 2 1	8 5 3 6 19 20 7 2	8 15 14 18 19 6 3	8 10 4	8 15 14 18 19 6 3 5	8 15 14 18 19 6	8 5 3 6 19 20 7	–	8 4 2 7 9	8 4 10	8 15 11	8 4 2 1 12	8 4 2 7 9 13	8 15 14	8 10 11 15	8 4 2 1 12 17 16	8 15 11 16 17	8 15 14 18	8 15 14 18 19	8 5 3 6 19 20
9	9 7 2 1	9 7 2	9 13 12 1 2 4 8 5 3	9 13 17 16 11 10 4	9 13 12 1 2 4 8 5	9 13 12 1 2 7 20 19 6	9 13 12 1 2 7	9 7 2 4 8	–	9 7 2 4 10	9 13 17 16 11	9 13 12	9 7 2 1 12 13	9 13 17 16 11 15 14	9 13 17 16 11 15	9 7 2 4 10 11 16	9 7 2 1 12 17	9 13 17 16 11 15 14 18	9 13 12 1 2 7 20 19	9 13 17 16 11 15 14 18 19 20
10	10 4 2 1	10 4 2	10 8 5 3	10 8 4	10 8 5	10 8 5 3 6	10 11 16 17 13 9 7	10 4 8	10 4 2 7 9	–	10 8 15 11	10 4 2 1 12	10 11 16 17 13	10 8 15 14	10 11 15	10 4 2 1 12 17 16	10 11 16 17	10 8 15 14 18	10 8 15 14 18 19	10 8 5 3 6 19 20
11	11 16 17 12 1	11 15 8 4 2	11 15 8 5 3	11 15 8 4	11 15 8 5	11 15 8 5 3 6	11 16 17 13 9 7	11 15 8	11 16 17 13 9	11 15 8 10	–	11 16 17 12	11 16 17 13	11 10 8 5 3 6 19 18 14	11 10 8 15	11 10 4 2 1 12 17 16	11 16 17	11 10 8 5 3 6 19 18	11 10 8 5 3 6 19	11 15 14 18 19 20
12	12 13 9 7 2 1	12 13 9 7 2	12 13 9 7 20 19 6 3	12 1 2 4	12 1 2 4 8 5	12 13 9 7 20 19 6	12 13 9 7	12 1 2 4 8	12 13 9	12 1 2 4 10	12 17 16 11	–	12 17 13	12 1 2 7 20 19 18 14	12 1 2 4 8 15	12 17 16	12 13 17	12 17 16 11 15 14 18	12 13 9 7 20 19	12 17 16 11 15 14 18 19 20
13	13 12 1	13 17 16 11 10 4 2	13 12 1 2 4 8 5 3	13 9 7 2 4	13 12 1 2 4 8 5	13 12 1 2 7 20 19 6	13 12 1 2 7	13 9 7 2 4 8	13 12 1 2 7 9	13 17 16 11 10	13 17 16 11	13 17 12	–	13 9 7 20 19 18 14	13 9 7 2 4 8 15	13 12 1 2 4 10 11 16	13 12 17	13 17 16 11 15 14 18	13 12 1 2 7 20 19	13 17 16 11 15 14 18 19 20
14	14 15 11 16 17 12 1	14 15 8 4 2	14 18 19 6 3	14 15 8 4	14 15 8 5	14 18 19 6	14 18 19 20 7	14 15 8	14 15 11 16 17 13 9	14 15 8 10	14 18 19 6 3 5 8 10 11	14 18 19 20 7 2 1 12	14 18 19 20 7 9 13	–	14 18 19 6 3 5 8 15	14 18 19 20 7 9 13 17 16	14 18 19 20 7 9 13 17	14 15 8 5 3 6 19 18	14 15 8 5 3 6 19	14 15 8 4 2 7 20
15	15 11 10 4 2 1	15 11 16 17 12 1 2	15 14 18 19 6 3	15 11 10 4	15 14 18 19 6 3 5	15 14 18 19 6	15 14 18 19 20 7	15 11 10 8	15 11 16 17 13 9	15 11 10	15 8 10 11	15 8 4 2 1 12	15 8 4 2 7 9 13	15 8 5 3 6 19 18 14	–	15 8 4 2 1 12 17 16	15 8 10 11 16 17	15 8 5 3 6 19 18	15 8 5 3 6 19	15 8 4 2 7 20
16	16 17 12 1	16 17 13 9 7 2	16 17 13 9 7 20 19 6 3	16 17 12 1 2 4	16 17 12 1 2 4 8 5	16 17 13 9 7 20 19 6	16 11 10 4 2 7	16 17 12 1 2 4 8	16 11 10 4 2 7 9	16 17 12 1 2 4 10	16 17 12 1 2 4 10 11	16 17 12	16 11 10 4 2 1 12 13	16 17 13 9 7 20 19 18 14	16 17 12 1 2 4 8 15	–	16 11 10 4 2 1 12 17	16 17 13 9 7 20 19 18	16 17 13 9 7 20 19	16 11 15 14 18 19 20
17	17 13 9 7 2 1	17 13 9 7 2	17 16 11 10 8 5 3	17 13 9 7 2 4	17 16 11 10 8 5	17 12 1 2 7 20 19 6	17 12 1 2 7	17 16 11 15 8	17 12 1 2 7 9	17 16 11 10	17 16 11	17 13 12	17 12 13	17 13 9 7 20 19 18 14	17 16 11 10 8 15	17 12 1 2 4 10 11 16	–	17 16 11 15 14 18	17 16 11 15 14 18 19	17 16 11 15 14 18 19 20
18	18 14 15 11 16 17 12 1	18 19 20 7 2	18 19 6 3	18 14 15 8 4	18 14 15 8 5	18 19 6	18 19 20 7	18 14 15 8	18 14 15 11 16 17 13 9	18 14 15 8 10	18 19 6 3 5 8 10 11	18 14 15 11 16 17 12	18 14 15 11 16 17 13	18 19 6 3 5 8 15 14	18 19 6 3 5 8 15	18 19 20 7 9 13 17 16	18 14 15 11 16 17	–	18 14 15 8 5 3 6 19	18 14 15 8 4 2 7 20
19	19 20 7 9 13 12 1	19 20 7 2	19 18 14 15 8 5 3	19 20 7 2 4	19 18 14 15 8 5	19 18 14 15 8 5 3 6	19 20 7	19 18 14 15 8	19 20 7 2 1 12 13 9	19 18 14 15 8 10	19 6 3 5 8 10 11	19 20 7 9 13 12	19 20 7 2 1 12 13	19 6 3 5 8 15 14	19 6 3 5 8 15	19 20 7 9 13 17 16	19 18 14 15 11 16 17	19 6 3 5 8 15 14 18	–	19 6 3 5 8 4 2 7 20
20	20 19 18 14 15 11 16 17 12 1	20 19 6 3 5 8 4 2	20 19 6 3	20 19 6 3 5 8 4	20 19 18 14 15 8 5	20 19 6	20 19 6 3 5 8 4 2 7	20 19 6 3 5 8	20 19 18 14 15 11 16 17 13 9	20 19 6 3 5 8 10	20 19 18 14 15 11	20 19 18 14 15 11 16 17 12	20 19 18 14 15 11 16 17 13	20 7 2 4 8 15 14	20 7 2 4 8 15	20 19 18 14 15 11 16	20 19 18 14 15 11 16 17	20 7 2 4 8 15 14 18	20 7 2 4 8 5 3 6 19	–

Backup Paths of The 20-Node Network - Case IV

Table 9.18 Backup Paths of The 20-Node Network with Link-Failure Tolerance (Case IV)

From / To	1	2	3	4	5	6	7	8	9	10	11	12	13	14	15	16	17	18	19	20
1	---	1 9 7 2	1 9 7 6 3	1 9 13 17 16 11 10 4	1 9 7 20 19 18 5	1 9 7 6	1 9 7	1 2 4 8	1 2 7 9	1 2 4 10	1 2 4 8 15 11	1 9 13 12	1 12 13	1 9 7 20 19 18 14	1 9 13 17 16 11 15	1 9 13 17 16	1 9 13 17	1 9 7 20 19 18	1 9 7 20 19	1 9 13 17 16 11 15 14 18 19 20
2	2 7 9 1	---	2 7 6 3	2 3 5 18 14 15 8 4	2 7 20 19 18 5	2 7 6	2 3 6 7	2 3 5 18 14 15 8	2 7 9	2 4 10	2 4 8 15 11	2 7 9 13 12	2 4 10 11 16 17 13	2 4 8 15 14	2 3 5 18 14 15	2 7 9 13 17 16	2 7 9 13 17	2 7 20 19 18	2 7 20 19	2 3 5 18 19 20
3	3 6 7 9 1	3 6 7 2	---	3 5 18 14 15 8 4	3 2 7 20 19 18 5	3 2 7 6	3 2 7	3 2 4 8	3 2 1 9	3 5 18 14 15 11 10	3 5 18 14 15 11	3 6 7 9 13 12	3 2 1 12 13	3 2 4 8 15 14	3 2 4 10 11 15	3 6 7 9 13 17 16	3 6 7 9 13 17	3 2 7 20 19 18	3 5 18 19	3 5 18 19 20
4	4 10 11 16 17 13 9 1	4 8 15 14 18 5 3 2	4 8 15 14 18 5 3	---	4 2 3 5	4 2 3 6	4 10 11 16 17 13 9 7	4 10 11 15 8	4 10 11 16 17 13 9	4 8 15 11 10	4 8 15 11	4 2 1 12	4 2 1 9 13	4 8 15 14	4 10 11 15	4 2 1 9 13 17 16	4 2 1 9 13 17	4 8 15 14 18	4 2 7 20 19	4 8 15 14 18 19 20
5	5 18 19 20 7 9 1	5 18 19 20 7 2	5 18 19 20 7 2 3	5 3 2 4	---	5 3 6	5 18 19 20 7	5 3 2 4 8	5 18 14 15 8 4 2 1 9	5 18 14 15 11 10	5 18 14 15 11	5 3 2 1 12	5 18 14 15 11 16 17 13	5 18 14	5 18 14 15	5 3 2 1 9 13 17 16	5 3 2 1 9 13 17	5 3 2 7 20 19 18	5 18 19	5 18 19 20
6	6 7 9 1	6 7 2	6 7 2 3	6 3 2 4	6 3 5	---	6 3 2 7	6 3 2 4 8	6 3 2 1 9	6 7 9 13 17 16 11 10	6 7 9 13 17 16 11	6 7 9 13 12	6 3 2 1 12 13	6 7 20 19 18 14	6 3 2 4 10 11 15	6 7 9 13 17 16	6 3 2 4 10 11 16 17	6 7 20 19 18	6 7 20 19	6 3 5 18 19 20
7	7 9 1	7 6 3 2	7 2 3	7 9 13 17 16 11 10 4	7 20 19 18 5	7 2 3 6	---	7 20 19 18 14 15 8	7 2 1 9	7 9 13 17 16 11 10	7 9 13 17 16 11	7 9 13 12	7 2 1 12 13	7 20 19 18 14	7 20 19 18 14 15	7 2 4 10 11 16	7 2 4 10 11 16 17	7 20 19 18	7 20 19	7 2 3 5 18 19 20
8	8 4 2 1	8 15 14 18 5 3 2	8 4 2 3	8 15 11 10 4	8 4 2 3 5	8 4 2 3 6	8 15 14 18 19 20 7	---	8 4 2 7 9	8 4 10	8 15 11	8 4 2 1 12	8 4 2 1 9 13	8 15 14	8 4 10 11 15	8 4 2 1 9 13 17 16	8 15 11 16 17	8 15 14 18	8 15 14 18 19	8 15 14 18 19 20
9	9 7 2 1	9 7 2	9 1 2 3	9 13 17 16 11 10 4	9 1 2 4 8 15 14 18 5	9 1 2 3 6	9 1 2 7	9 7 2 4 8	---	9 7 2 4 10	9 13 17 16 11	9 13 12	9 1 12 13	9 1 2 4 8 15 14	9 13 17 16 11 15	9 1 2 4 10 11 16	9 1 2 4 10 11 16 17	9 1 2 4 8 15 14 18	9 1 2 3 5 18 19	9 1 2 3 5 18 19 20
10	10 4 2 1	10 4 2	10 11 15 14 18 5 3	10 11 15 8 4	10 11 15 14 18 5	10 11 16 17 13 9 7 6	10 11 16 17 13 9 7	10 4 8	10 4 2 7 9	---	10 4 8 15 11	10 4 2 1 12	10 11 16 17 13	10 11 15 14	10 11 15	10 4 2 1 9 13 17 16	10 11 16 17	10 11 15 14 18	10 11 15 14 18 19	10 11 15 14 18 19 20
11	11 15 8 4 2 1	11 15 8 4 2	11 15 14 18 5 3	11 15 8 4	11 15 14 18 5	11 16 17 13 9 7 6	11 16 17 13 9 7	11 15 8	11 16 17 13 9	11 15 8 4 10	---	11 16 17 13 12	11 16 17 13	11 10 4 2 3 5 18 14	11 10 4 8 15	11 10 4 2 1 9 13 17 16	11 16 17	11 10 4 2 3 5 18	11 10 4 2 7 20 19	11 15 14 18 19 20
12	12 13 9 1	12 13 9 7 2	12 13 9 7 6 3	12 1 2 4	12 1 2 3 5	12 13 9 7 6	12 13 9 7	12 1 2 4 8	12 13 9	12 1 2 4 10	12 13 17 16 11	---	12 1 9 13	12 1 2 3 5 18 14	12 1 2 4 8 15	12 13 17 16	12 13 17	12 1 2 7 20 19 18	12 13 9 7 20 19	12 13 17 16 11 15 14 18 19 20
13	13 12 1	13 17 16 11 10 4 2	13 12 1 2 3	13 9 1 2 4	13 17 16 11 15 14 18 5	13 12 1 2 3 6	13 12 1 2 7	13 9 1 2 4 8	13 12 1 9	13 17 16 11 10	13 17 16 11	13 9 1 12	---	13 9 7 20 19 18 14	13 9 1 2 4 8 15	13 9 1 2 4 10 11 16	13 9 1 2 4 10 11 16 17	13 17 16 11 15 14 18	13 12 1 2 3 5 18 19	13 12 1 2 3 5 18 19 20
14	14 18 19 20 7 9 1	14 15 8 4 2	14 15 8 4 2 3	14 15 8 4	14 18 5	14 18 19 20 7 6	14 18 19 20 7	14 15 8	14 15 8 4 2 1 9	14 15 11 10	14 18 5 3 2 4 10 11	14 18 5 3 2 1 12	14 18 19 20 7 9 13	---	14 18 5 3 2 4 8 15	14 18 19 20 7 9 13 17 16	14 18 19 20 7 9 13 17	14 15 8 4 2 3 5 18	14 15 8 4 2 7 20 19	14 15 8 4 2 7 20
15	15 11 16 17 13 9 1	15 14 18 5 3 2	15 11 10 4 2 3	15 11 10 4	15 14 18 5	15 11 10 4 2 3 6	15 14 18 19 20 7	15 11 10 4 8	15 11 16 17 13 9	15 11 10	15 8 4 10 11	15 8 4 2 1 12	15 8 4 2 1 9 13	15 8 4 2 3 5 18 14	---	15 8 4 2 1 9 13 17 16	15 8 4 2 1 9 13 17	15 8 4 2 3 5 18	15 8 4 2 7 20 19	15 8 4 2 7 20
16	16 17 13 9 1	16 17 13 9 7 2	16 17 13 9 7 6 3	16 17 13 9 1 2 4	16 17 13 9 1 2 3 5	16 17 13 9 7 6	16 11 10 4 2 7	16 17 13 9 1 2 4 8	16 11 10 4 2 1 9	16 17 13 9 1 2 4 10	16 17 13 9 1 2 4 10 11	16 17 13 12	16 11 10 4 2 1 9 13	16 17 13 9 7 20 19 18 14	16 17 13 9 1 2 4 8 15	---	16 11 10 4 2 1 9 13 17	16 17 13 9 7 20 19 18	16 17 13 9 7 20 19	16 11 15 14 18 19 20
17	17 13 9 1	17 13 9 7 2	17 13 9 7 6 3	17 13 9 1 2 4	17 13 9 1 2 3 5	17 16 11 10 4 2 3 6	17 16 11 10 4 2 7	17 16 11 15 8	17 16 11 10 4 2 1 9	17 16 11 10	17 16 11	17 13 12	17 16 11 10 4 2 1 9 13	17 13 9 7 20 19 18 14	17 13 9 1 2 4 8 15	17 13 9 1 2 4 10 11 16	---	17 16 11 15 14 18	17 16 11 15 14 18 19	17 16 11 15 14 18 19 20
18	18 19 20 7 9 1	18 19 20 7 2	18 19 20 7 2 3	18 14 15 8 4	18 19 20 7 2 3 5	18 19 20 7 6	18 19 20 7	18 14 15 8	18 14 15 8 4 2 1 9	18 14 15 11 10	18 5 3 2 4 10 11	18 19 20 7 2 1 12	18 14 15 11 16 17 13	18 5 3 2 4 8 15 14	18 5 3 2 4 8 15	18 19 20 7 9 13 17 16	18 14 15 11 16 17	---	18 5 3 2 7 20 19	18 5 3 2 7 20
19	19 20 7 9 1	19 20 7 2	19 18 5 3	19 20 7 2 4	19 18 5	19 20 7 6	19 20 7	19 18 14 15 8	19 18 5 3 2 1 9	19 18 14 15 11 10	19 20 7 2 4 10 11	19 20 7 9 13 12	19 18 5 3 2 1 12 13	19 20 7 2 4 8 15 14	19 20 7 2 4 8 15	19 20 7 9 13 17 16	19 18 14 15 11 16 17	19 20 7 2 3 5 18	---	19 18 5 3 2 7 20
20	20 19 18 14 15 11 16 17 13 9 1	20 19 18 5 3 2	20 19 18 5 3	20 19 18 14 15 8 4	20 19 18 5	20 19 18 5 3 6	20 19 18 5 3 2 7	20 19 18 14 15 8	20 19 18 5 3 2 1 9	20 19 18 14 15 11 10	20 19 18 14 15 11	20 19 18 14 15 11 16 17 13 12	20 19 18 5 3 2 1 12 13	20 7 2 4 8 15 14	20 7 2 4 8 15	20 19 18 14 15 11 16	20 19 18 14 15 11 16 17	20 7 2 3 5 18	20 7 2 3 5 18 19	---

Backup Paths of The 20-Node Network - Case V

Table 9.19 Backup Paths of The 20-Node Network with Node-Failure Tolerance (Case V)

From / To	1	2	3	4	5	6	7	8	9	10	11	12	13	14	15	16	17	18	19	20
1	—	1 10 4 2	1 12 13 9 7 3	1 10 4	1 10 11 15 14 5	1 10 11 15 14 18 19 6	1 12 13 9 7	1 2 4 8	1 2 7 9	1 2 4 10	1 2 4 8 15 11	1 2 7 9 13 12	1 12 13	1 10 11 15 14	1 12 13 17 16 11 15	1 12 13 17 16	1 10 11 16 17	1 10 11 15 14 18	1 10 11 15 14 18 19	1 10 11 15 14 18 19 20
2	2 4 10 1	—	2 7 3	2 1 10 4	2 4 8 15 14 5	2 7 20 19 6	2 3 7	2 1 10 11 15 8	2 7 9	2 4 10	2 4 8 15 11	2 7 9 13 12	2 4 10 11 16 17 13	2 4 8 15 14	2 1 10 11 15	2 7 9 13 17 16	2 7 9 13 17	2 7 20 19 18	2 7 20 19	2 3 6 19 20
3	3 7 9 13 12 1	3 7 2	—	3 6 19 18 14 15 8 4	3 6 19 18 5	3 7 20 19 6	3 2 7	3 2 4 8	3 2 1 12 13 9	3 6 19 18 14 15 11 10	3 6 19 18 14 15 11	3 7 9 13 12	3 2 1 12 13	3 6 19 18 14	3 2 1 10 11 15	3 7 9 13 17 16	3 7 9 13 17	3 6 19 18	3 7 20 19	3 6 19 20
4	4 10 1	4 10 1 2	4 8 15 14 18 19 6 3	—	4 8 15 14 5	4 2 3 6	4 10 1 12 13 9 7	4 10 11 15 8	4 10 11 16 17 13 9	4 2 1 10	4 8 15 11	4 2 1 12	4 2 7 9 13	4 8 15 14	4 10 11 15	4 2 7 9 13 17 16	4 2 7 9 13 17	4 8 15 14 18	4 2 7 20 19	4 8 15 14 18 19 20
5	5 14 15 11 10 1	5 14 15 8 4 2	5 18 19 6 3	5 14 15 8 4	—	5 18 19 6	5 18 19 20 7	5 14 15 8	5 14 15 11 16 17 13 9	5 14 15 11 10	5 14 15 11	5 18 19 6 3 2 1 12	5 14 15 11 16 17 13	5 18 14	5 14 15	5 18 19 20 7 9 13 17 16	5 14 15 11 16 17	5 14 18	5 18 19	5 18 19 20
6	6 19 18 14 15 11 10 1	6 19 20 7 2	6 19 20 7 3	6 3 2 4	6 19 18 5	—	6 3 7	6 3 2 4 8	6 3 2 1 12 13 9	6 3 2 1 10	6 19 18 14 15 11	6 19 20 7 9 13 12	6 3 2 1 12 13	6 19 18 14	6 19 18 14 15	6 3 7 9 13 17 16	6 3 2 1 10 11 16 17	6 19 18	6 3 7 20 19	6 19 20
7	7 9 13 12 1	7 3 2	7 2 3	7 9 13 12 1 10 4	7 20 19 18 5	7 3 6	—	7 20 19 18 14 15 8	7 2 1 12 13 9	7 9 13 17 16 11 10	7 9 13 17 16 11	7 9 13 12	7 2 1 12 13	7 20 19 18 14	7 20 19 18 14 15	7 2 1 10 11 16	7 2 1 10 11 16 17	7 20 19 18	7 20 19	7 3 6 19 20
8	8 4 2 1	8 15 11 10 1 2	8 4 2 3	8 15 11 10 4	8 15 14 5	8 4 2 3 6	8 15 14 18 19 20 7	—	8 4 2 7 9	8 4 10	8 15 11	8 4 2 1 12	8 4 2 7 9 13	8 15 14	8 4 10 11 15	8 4 2 7 9 13 17 16	8 15 11 16 17	8 15 14 18	8 15 14 18 19	8 15 14 18 19 20
9	9 7 2 1	9 7 2	9 13 12 1 2 3	9 13 17 16 11 10 4	9 13 17 16 11 15 14 5	9 13 12 1 2 3 6	9 13 12 1 2 7	9 7 2 4 8	—	9 7 2 4 10	9 13 17 16 11	9 13 12	9 7 2 1 12 13	9 13 17 16 11 15 14	9 13 17 16 11 15	9 7 2 1 10 11 16	9 7 2 1 10 11 16 17	9 13 17 16 11 15 14 18	9 13 17 16 11 15 14 18 19	9 13 12 1 2 3 6 19 20
10	10 4 2 1	10 4 2	10 11 15 14 18 19 6 3	10 1 2 4	10 11 15 14 5	10 1 2 3 6	10 11 16 17 13 9 7	10 4 8	10 4 2 7 9	—	10 4 8 15 11	10 1 12	10 11 16 17 13	10 11 15 14	10 11 15	10 1 12 13 17 16	10 11 16 17	10 11 15 14 18	10 11 15 14 18 19	10 11 15 14 18 19 20
11	11 15 8 4 2 1	11 15 8 4 2	11 15 14 18 19 6 3	11 15 8 4	11 15 14 5	11 15 14 18 19 6	11 16 17 13 9 7	11 15 8	11 16 17 13 9	11 15 8 4 10	—	11 10 1 12	11 16 17 13	11 10 1 2 3 6 19 18 14	11 10 4 8 15	11 10 1 12 13 17 16	11 16 17	11 10 1 2 3 6 19 18	11 10 1 2 3 6 19	11 15 14 18 19 20
12	12 13 9 7 2 1	12 13 9 7 2	12 13 9 7 3	12 1 2 4	12 1 2 3 6 19 18 5	12 13 9 7 20 19 6	12 13 9 7	12 1 2 4 8	12 13 9	12 1 10	12 1 10 11	—	12 1 2 7 9 13	12 1 2 3 6 19 18 14	12 1 2 4 8 15	12 13 17 16	12 13 17	12 1 2 3 6 19 18	12 13 9 7 20 19	12 13 17 16 11 15 14 18 19 20
13	13 12 1	13 17 16 11 10 4 2	13 12 1 2 3	13 9 7 2 4	13 17 16 11 15 14 5	13 12 1 2 3 6	13 12 1 2 7	13 9 7 2 4 8	13 12 1 2 7 9	13 17 16 11 10	13 17 16 11	13 9 7 2 1 12	—	13 9 7 20 19 18 14	13 9 7 2 4 8 15	13 12 1 10 11 16	13 12 1 10 11 16 17	13 17 16 11 15 14 18	13 17 16 11 15 14 18 19	13 12 1 2 3 6 19 20
14	14 15 11 10 1	14 15 8 4 2	14 18 19 6 3	14 15 8 4	14 18 5	14 18 19 6	14 18 19 20 7	14 15 8	14 15 11 16 17 13 9	14 15 11 10	14 18 19 6 3 2 1 10 11	14 18 19 6 3 2 1 12	14 18 19 20 7 9 13	—	14 18 19 6 3 2 4 8 15	14 18 19 20 7 9 13 17 16	14 18 19 20 7 9 13 17	14 5 18	14 15 8 4 2 3 6 19	14 15 8 4 2 7 20
15	15 11 16 17 13 12 1	15 11 10 1 2	15 11 10 1 2 3	15 11 10 4	15 14 5	15 14 18 19 6	15 14 18 19 20 7	15 11 10 4 8	15 11 16 17 13 9	15 11 10	15 8 4 10 11	15 8 4 2 1 12	15 8 4 2 7 9 13	15 8 4 2 3 6 19 18 14	—	15 8 4 2 7 9 13 17 16	15 8 4 2 7 9 13 17	15 8 4 2 3 6 19 18	15 8 4 2 3 6 19	15 8 4 2 7 20
16	16 17 13 12 1	16 17 13 9 7 2	16 17 13 9 7 3	16 17 13 9 7 2 4	16 17 13 9 7 20 19 18 5	16 17 13 9 7 3 6	16 11 10 1 2 7	16 17 13 9 7 2 4 8	16 11 10 1 2 7 9	16 17 13 12 1 10	16 17 13 12 1 10 11	16 17 13 12	16 11 10 1 12 13	16 17 13 9 7 20 19 18 14	16 17 13 9 7 2 4 8 15	—	16 11 10 1 12 13 17	16 17 13 9 7 20 19 18	16 17 13 9 7 20 19	16 11 15 14 18 19 20
17	17 16 11 10 1	17 13 9 7 2	17 13 9 7 3	17 13 9 7 2 4	17 16 11 15 14 5	17 16 11 10 1 2 3 6	17 16 11 10 1 2 7	17 16 11 15 8	17 16 11 10 1 2 7 9	17 16 11 10	17 16 11	17 13 12	17 16 11 10 1 12 13	17 13 9 7 20 19 18 14	17 13 9 7 2 4 8 15	17 13 12 1 10 11 16	—	17 16 11 15 14 18	17 16 11 15 14 18 19	17 16 11 15 14 18 19 20
18	18 14 15 11 10 1	18 19 20 7 2	18 19 6 3	18 14 15 8 4	18 14 5	18 19 6	18 19 20 7	18 14 15 8	18 14 15 11 16 17 13 9	18 14 15 11 10	18 19 6 3 2 1 10 11	18 19 6 3 2 1 12	18 14 15 11 16 17 13	18 5 14	18 19 6 3 2 4 8 15	18 19 20 7 9 13 17 16	18 14 15 11 16 17	—	18 14 15 8 4 2 3 6 19	18 14 15 8 4 2 7 20
19	19 18 14 15 11 10 1	19 20 7 2	19 20 7 3	19 20 7 2 4	19 18 5	19 20 7 3 6	19 20 7	19 18 14 15 8	19 18 14 15 11 16 17 13 9	19 18 14 15 11 10	19 6 3 2 1 10 11	19 20 7 9 13 12	19 18 14 15 11 16 17 13	19 6 3 2 4 8 15 14	19 6 3 2 4 8 15	19 20 7 9 13 17 16	19 18 14 15 11 16 17	19 6 3 2 4 8 15 14 18	—	19 6 3 7 20
20	20 19 18 14 15 11 10 1	20 19 6 3 2	20 19 6 3	20 19 18 14 15 8 4	20 19 18 5	20 19 6	20 19 6 3 7	20 19 18 14 15 8	20 19 6 3 2 1 12 13 9	20 19 18 14 15 11 10	20 19 18 14 15 11	20 19 18 14 15 11 16 17 13 12	20 19 6 3 2 1 12 13	20 7 2 4 8 15 14	20 7 2 4 8 15	20 19 18 14 15 11 16	20 19 18 14 15 11 16 17	20 7 2 4 8 15 14 18	20 7 3 6 19	—

Backup Paths of The 20-Node Network - Case VI

Table 9.20 Backup Paths of The 20-Node Network with Link-and-Node Failure Tolerance (Case VI)

Appendix E

Tables for Non-Symmetrical Traffic Load and QoS

To \ From	1	2	3	4	5	6	7	8	9	10	11	12	13
1	—	1 10 4 2	1 12 13 9 7 3	1 10 4	1 12 11 8 5	1 12 11 8 5 6	1 12 13 9 7	1 12 11 8	1 12 13 9	1 12 10	1 12 11	1 10 12	1 12 13
2	2 4 10 1	—	2 4 10 12 13 9 7 3	2 3 7 9 13 12 10 4	2 4 10 12 11 8 5	2 4 10 12 11 8 5 6	2 3 7	2 3 7 6 5 8	2 3 7 9	2 4 10	2 3 7 9 13 12 11	2 4 10 12	2 4 10 12 13
3	3 7 9 13 12 1	3 7 9 13 12 10 4 2	—	3 7 9 13 12 10 4	3 7 6 5	3 7 6	3 2 4 10 12 13 9 7	3 2 4 10 12 11 8	3 2 4 10 12 13 9	3 7 9 13 12 10	3 2 4 10 12 11	3 7 9 13 12	3 2 4 10 12 13
4	4 10 1	4 10 12 13 9 7 3 2	4 10 12 13 9 7 3	—	4 2 3 7 6 5	4 2 3 7 6	4 10 12 13 9 7	4 10 12 11 8	4 10 12 13 9	4 2 3 7 9 13 12 10	4 10 12 11	4 2 3 7 9 13 12	4 2 3 7 9 13
5	5 8 11 12 1	5 8 11 12 10 4 2	5 6 7 3	5 6 7 3 2 4	—	5 8 11 12 13 9 7 6	5 6 7	5 6 7 9 13 12 11 8	5 8 11 12 13 9	5 8 11 12 10	5 6 7 9 13 12 11	5 8 11 12	5 8 11 12 13
6	6 5 8 11 12 1	6 5 8 11 12 10 4 2	6 7 3	6 7 3 2 4	6 7 9 13 12 11 8 5	—	6 5 8 11 12 13 9 7	6 7 9 13 12 11 8	6 5 8 11 12 13 9	6 7 9 13 12 10	6 7 9 13 12 11	6 5 8 11 12	6 5 8 11 12 13
7	7 9 13 12 1	7 3 2	7 9 13 12 10 4 2 3	7 9 13 12 10 4	7 6 5	7 9 13 12 11 8 5 6	—	7 6 5 8	7 3 2 4 10 12 13 9	7 3 2 4 10	7 9 13 12 11	7 9 13 12	7 3 2 4 10 12 13
8	8 11 12 1	8 5 6 7 3 2	8 11 12 10 4 2 3	8 11 12 10 4	8 11 12 13 9 7 6 5	8 11 12 13 9 7 6	8 5 6 7	—	8 5 6 7 9	8 11 12 10	8 5 6 7 9 13 12 11	8 5 6 7 9 13 12	8 5 6 7 9 13
9	9 13 12 1	9 7 3 2	9 13 12 10 4 2 3	9 13 12 10 4	9 13 12 11 8 5	9 13 12 11 8 5 6	9 13 12 10 4 2 3 7	9 7 6 5 8	—	9 13 12 10	9 13 12 11	9 13 12	9 7 3 2 4 10 12 13
10	10 12 1	10 4 2	10 12 13 9 7 3	10 12 13 9 7 3 2 4	10 12 11 8 5	10 12 13 9 7 6	10 4 2 3 7	10 12 11 8	10 12 13 9	—	10 12 11	10 1 12	10 4 2 3 7 9 13
11	11 12 1	11 12 13 9 7 3 2	11 12 10 4 2 3	11 12 10 4	11 12 13 9 7 6 5	11 12 13 9 7 6	11 12 13 9 7	11 12 13 9 7 6 5 8	11 12 13 9	11 12 10	—	11 8 5 6 7 9 13 12	11 8 5 6 7 9 13
12	12 10 1	12 10 4 2	12 13 9 7 3	12 13 9 7 3 2 4	12 11 8 5	12 11 8 5 6	12 13 9 7	12 13 9 7 6 5 8	12 13 9	12 1 10	12 13 9 7 6 5 8 11	—	12 10 4 2 3 7 9 13
13	13 12 1	13 12 10 4 2	13 12 10 4 2 3	13 9 7 3 2 4	13 12 11 8 5	13 12 11 8 5 6	13 12 10 4 2 3 7	13 9 7 6 5 8	13 12 10 4 2 3 7 9	13 9 7 3 2 4 10	13 9 7 6 5 8 11	13 9 7 3 2 4 10 12	—

Backup Paths of The 13-Node Network with Non-Symmetrical Traffic Load

Table 10.1 Backup Paths of The 13-Node Network with Non-Symmetrical Traffic Load and Link-Failure Tolerance

Node	1	2	3	4	5	6	7	8	9	10	11	12	13
1	---	1 9 7 2	1 10 4 5 3	1 10 4	1 10 4 5	1 9 7 6	1 9 7	1 10 11 8	1 12 13 9	1 12 11 10	1 12 11	1 10 11 12	1 12 13
2	2 7 9 1	---	2 7 6 3	2 3 5 4	2 7 6 5	2 7 6	2 3 6 7	2 3 5 8	2 7 9	2 3 5 4 10	2 7 9 1 10 11	2 7 9 13 12	2 7 9 1 12 13
3	3 5 4 10 1	3 6 7 2	---	3 5 4	3 6 5	3 5 6	3 2 7	3 6 5 4 10 11 8	3 5 4 10 1 9	3 5 4 10	3 6 5 4 10 11	3 5 8 11 12	3 5 8 11 12 13
4	4 10 1	4 5 3 2	4 5 3	---	4 10 11 8 5	4 10 1 9 7 6	4 5 6 7	4 5 8	4 5 6 7 9	4 5 8 11 10	4 10 11	4 5 8 11 12	4 5 6 7 9 13
5	5 4 10 1	5 6 7 2	5 6 3	5 8 11 10 4	---	5 3 6	5 6 7	5 4 10 11 8	5 4 10 1 9	5 8 11 10	5 4 10 11	5 8 11 12	5 8 11 12 13
6	6 7 9 1	6 7 2	6 5 3	6 7 9 1 10 4	6 3 5	---	6 3 2 7	6 7 9 1 10 11 8	6 5 4 10 1 9	6 7 9 1 10	6 7 9 1 10 11	6 5 8 11 12	6 5 8 11 12 13
7	7 9 1	7 6 3 2	7 2 3	7 6 5 4	7 6 5	7 2 3 6	---	7 6 5 8	7 6 5 4 10 1 9	7 6 5 4 10	7 9 1 10 11	7 9 13 12	7 6 5 8 11 12 13
8	8 11 10 1	8 5 3 2	8 11 10 4 5 6 3	8 5 4	8 11 10 4 5	8 11 10 1 9 7 6	8 5 6 7	---	8 5 6 7 9	8 11 10	8 5 4 10 11	8 5 4 10 1 12	8 5 6 7 9 13
9	9 13 12 1	9 7 2	9 1 10 4 5 3	9 7 6 5 4	9 1 10 4 5	9 1 10 4 5 6	9 1 10 4 5 6 7	9 7 6 5 8	---	9 13 12 11 10	9 13 12 11	9 13 12	9 1 12 13
10	10 11 12 1	10 4 5 3 2	10 4 5 3	10 11 8 5 4	10 11 8 5	10 1 9 7 6	10 4 5 6 7	10 11 8	10 11 12 13 9	---	10 1 12 11	10 1 12	10 1 9 13
11	11 12 1	11 10 1 9 7 2	11 10 4 5 6 3	11 10 4	11 10 4 5	11 10 1 9 7 6	11 10 1 9 7	11 10 4 5 8	11 12 13 9	11 12 1 10	---	11 10 1 12	11 10 1 9 13
12	12 11 10 1	12 13 9 7 2	12 11 8 5 3	12 11 8 5 4	12 11 8 5	12 11 8 5 6	12 13 9 7	12 1 10 4 5 8	12 13 9	12 1 10	12 1 10 11	---	12 1 9 13
13	13 12 1	13 12 1 9 7 2	13 12 11 8 5 3	13 9 7 6 5 4	13 12 11 8 5	13 12 11 8 5 6	13 12 11 8 5 6 7	13 9 7 6 5 8	13 12 1 9	13 9 1 10	13 9 1 10 11	13 9 1 12	---

Backup Paths of The 13-Node Network Satisfying QoS Constraints

Table 10.2 Backup Paths of The 13-Node Network with Link-Failure Tolerance Satisfying QoS Constraints

Appendix F

Large-Scale Networks

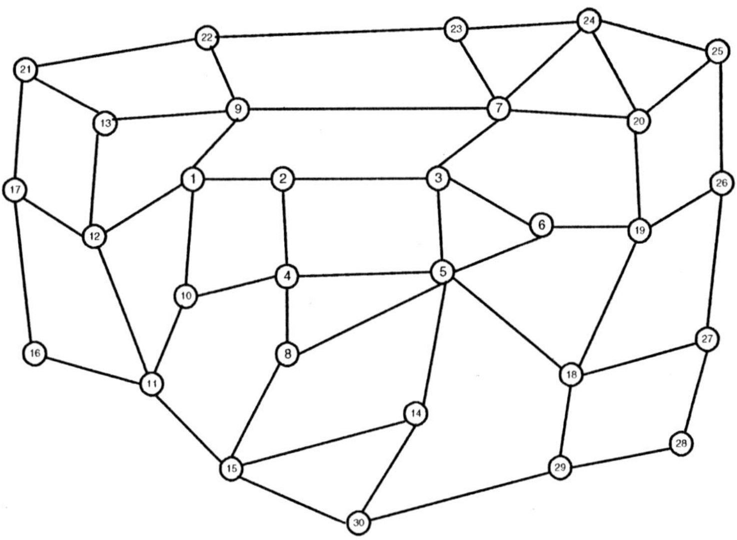

Figure 11.1 30-Node Network (Network 5)

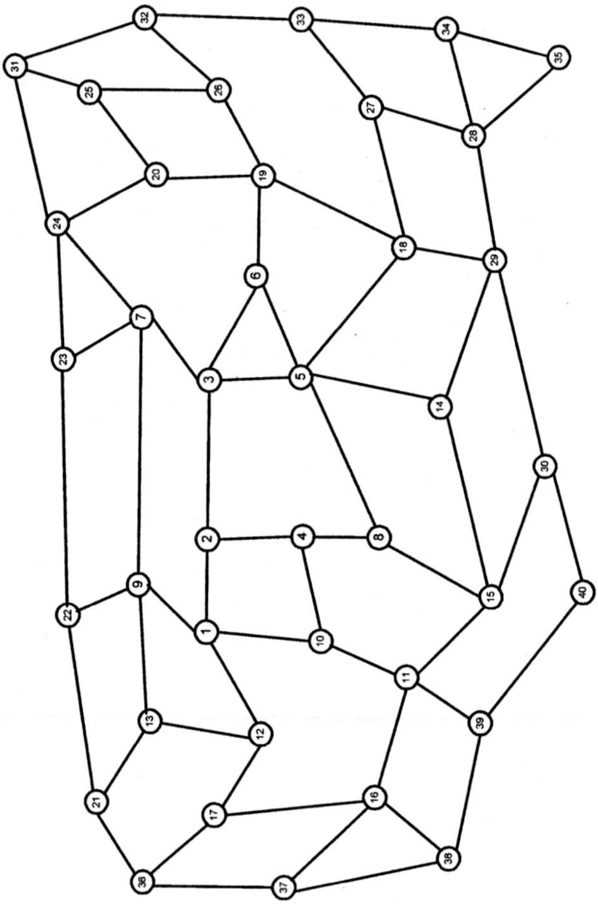

Figure 11.2 40-Node Network (Network 6)

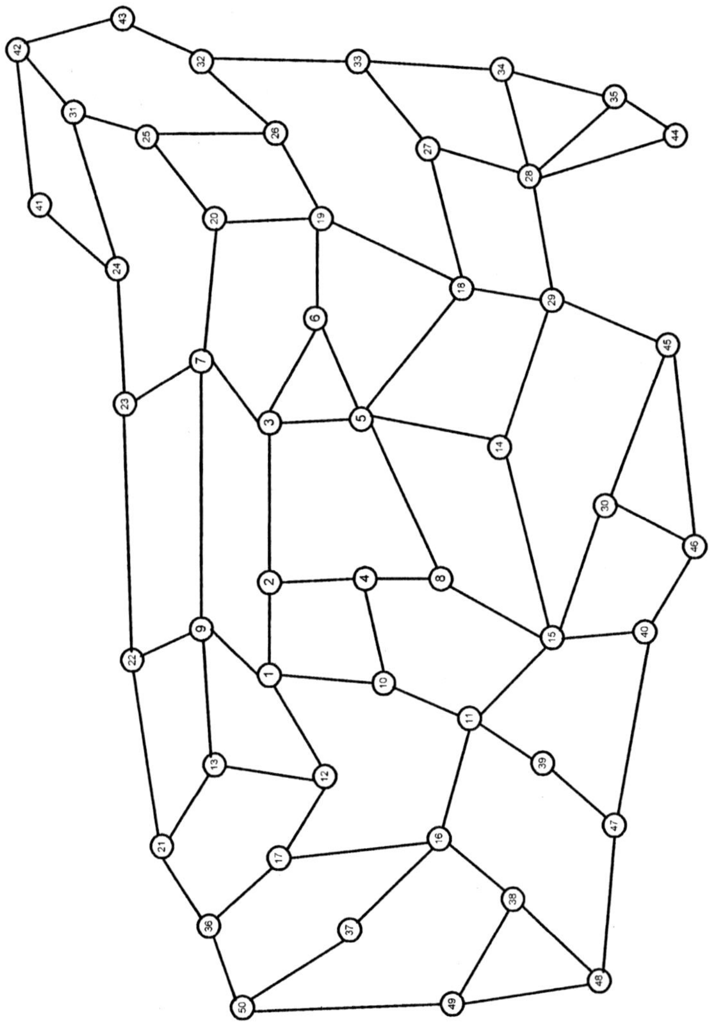

Figure 11.3 50-Node Network (Network 7)

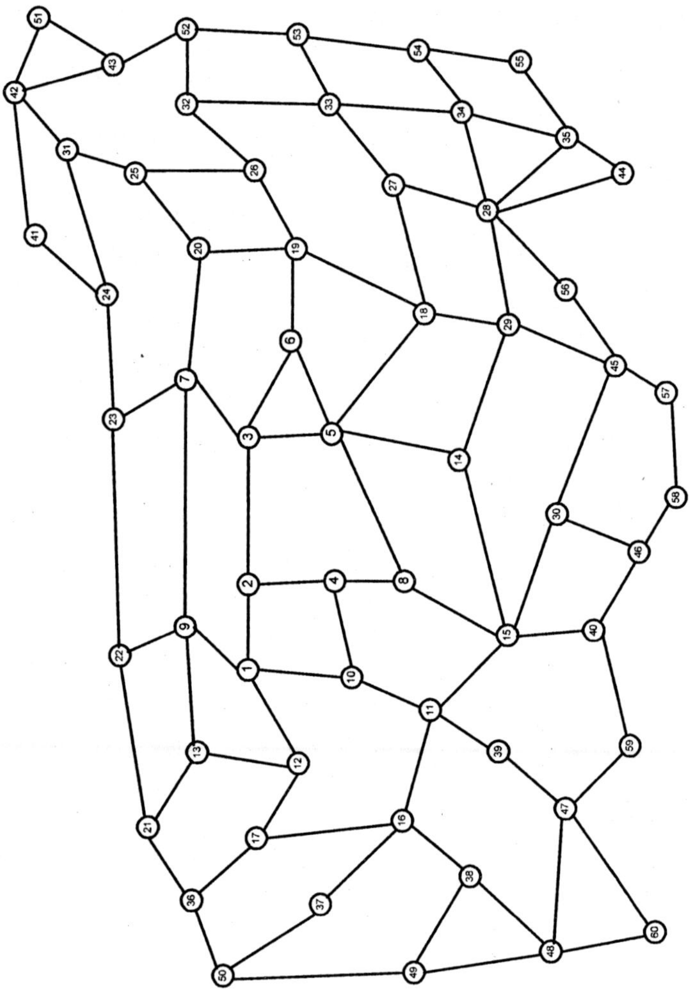

Figure 11.4 60-Node Network (Network 8)

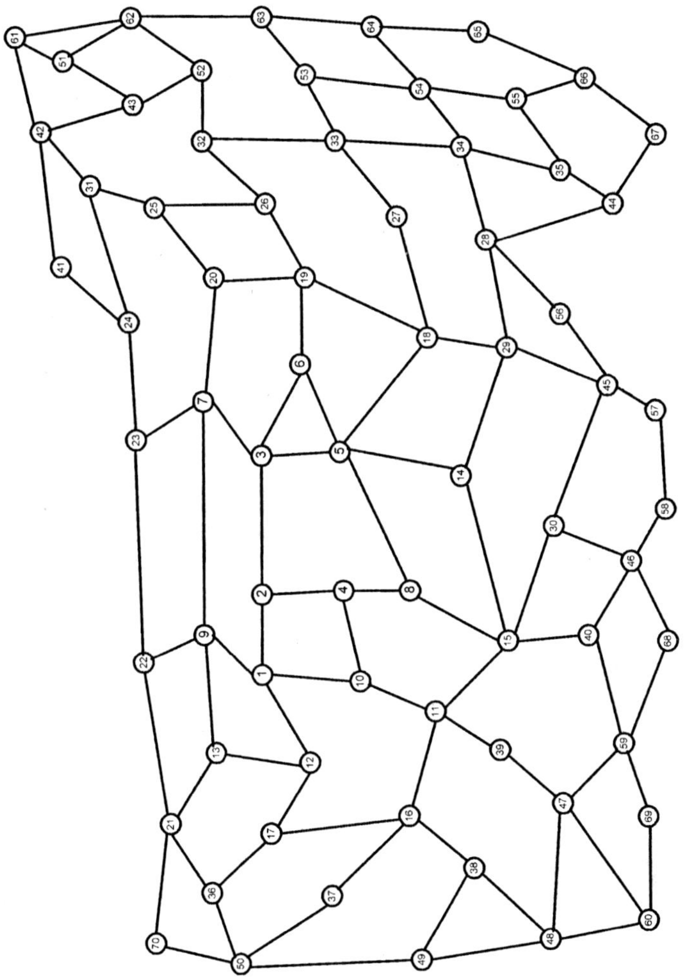

Figure 11.5 70-Node Network (Network 9)

Bibliography

[1] C. Byrne, "Fault Management," in *Telecommunications Network Management into 21st Century - Techniques, Standards, Technologies, and Applications*, S. Aidarous and T. Plevyak, Eds. New York, NY: IEEE Press, 1994, pp. 286-302.

[2] D. Kuhn, "Sources of Failure in the Public Switched Telephone Network," *IEEE Computer*, pp. 31-36, April 1997.

[3] G. Phillip and K. Watkin, "National Information Infrastructure (NII) Reliability and Survivability Initiatives," presented at IEEE Global Conference on Communications, November 1994.

[4] President's Commission on Critical Infrastructure Protection, http://www.pccip.gov.

[5] J. McDonald, "Public Network Integrity," *IEEE Journal on Selected Areas in Communications*, vol. 12, pp. 5-12, January 1994.

[6] T.-H. Wu and D. Kolar, "High-Speed Self-Healing Ring Architectures for Future Interoffice Networks," presented at IEEE Global Conference on Communications, November 1989.

[7] C. Yang and S. Hasegawa, "FITNESS: Failure Immunization Technology for Network Service Survivability," , IEEE Global Conference on Communications, December 1988.

[8] W. Grover, B. Venables, J. Sandham, and A. Milne, "Performance Studies of a Self-healing Network Protocol in Telecom Canada Long Haul Networks," presented at IEEE Global Conference on Communications.

[9] R. Doverspike and B. Wilson, "Comparison of Capacity Efficiency of DCS Network Restoration Routing Techniques," *Journal of Network and System Management*, vol. 2, pp. 95-123, 1994.

[10] M. Herzberg, S. Bye, and A. Utano, "The Hop-limit Approach for Spare Capacity Assignment in Survivable Networks," *IEEE/ACM Transactions on Networking*, vol. 2, December 1995.

[11] W. Grover, T. Bilodean, and B. Vernbles, "Near Optimal Spare Capacity Planning in a Mesh Restorable Network," presented at IEEE Global Conference on Communications, November 1991.

[12] M. MacGregor, W. Grover, and K. Ryhorchuk, "Optimal Spare Capacity Preconfiguration for Faster Restoration of Mesh Networks," *Journal of Network and Systems Management*, vol. 52, pp. 159-171, June 1997.

[13] R. Iraschko, M. MacGregor, and K. Ryhorchuk, "Optimal Capacity Placement for Path Restoration of Mesh Survivable Networks," presented at IEEE Global Conference on Communications, November 1996.

[14] D. Tipper, J. Hammond, S. Sharma, A. Khetan, K. Balakrishnan, and S. Menon, "An Analysis of the Congestion Effects of Link Failures in Wide Area Networks," *IEEE Journal on Selected Areas in Communications*, vol. 12, pp. 179-191, January 1994.

[15] L. Nederlot, K. Struyre, C. O'Shen, H. Misser, Y. Du, and B. Tamayo, "End-to-End Survivable Broadband Networks," *IEEE Communications Magazine*, pp. 63-70, September 1995.

[16] D. Medhi, "A Unified Framework for Survivable Telecommunications Network Design," presented at IEEE International Conference on Communications, June 1992.

[17] K. Laretto, "Sprint Network Survivability," presented at IEEE Global Conference on Communications, November 1994.

[18] "A Technical Report on Network Survivability Performance," Exchange Carrier Standard Association, T1A1 Committee T1A1.2/93-001R3, October 1993.

[19] A. Tanenbaum, *Computer Networks*, 3 ed: Prentice Hall, 1996.

[20] M. Herzberg and S. Bye, "An Optimal Spare-Capacity Assignment Model for Survivable Networks with Hop Limits," presented at IEEE Global Conference on Communications, November 1994.

[21] H. Sakauchi, Y. Nishimura, and S. Hasegawa, "A Self-Healing Network with an Economical Spare-Channel Assignment," presented at IEEE Global Conference on Communications, November 1990.

[22] T.-H. Wu, "Emerging Technologies for Fiber Network Survivability," *IEEE Communications Magazine*, pp. 58-74, February 1995.

[23] R. Cardwell and G. Brush, "Meeting the Challenge of Assuring Dependable Telecommunications Service in the 90's," *IEEE Communications Magazine*, pp. 40-45, June 1990.

[24] "Bellcore Generic Requirements, GR-1400-CORE, SONET Dual-Fed unidirectional, Path Switched Ring (UPSR) Equipment Generic Criteria," Bellcore March 1994.

[25] W. Grover, "Distributed Restoration of the Transport Network," in *Telecommunications Network Management into 21st Century - Techniques, Standards, Technologies, and Applications.* New York, NY: IEEE Press, 1994, pp. 337-419.

[26] A. Orda and R. Rom, "Multihoming in Computer Networks: A Topology-design Approach," *Computer Networks and ISDN Systems*, vol. 18, pp. 133-141, 1990.

[27] "SONET Bidirectional Line Switched Rings Standard Working Document," T1X1.5/92-004, February 3, 1992.

[28] T. Flanagan, "Fiber Network Survivability," *IEEE Communications Magazine*, pp. 46-53, June 1990.

[29] G. Ash, "Dynamic Network Evolution, with Examples from AT&T's Evolving Dynamic Network," *IEEE Communications Magazine*, pp. 26-39, July 1995.

[30] L. Stark and J. Scholl, "AT&T Worldwide Intelligent Network: Reliability, Restoration, and Special Survivability Initiatives," presented at IEEE Global Conference on Communications, November 1994.

[31] D. Dunn and W. Grover, "Comparison of k-Shortest Paths and Maximum Flow Routing for Network Facility Restoration," *IEEE Journal on Selected Areas in Communications*, vol. 12, January 1994.

[32] B. Venables, W. Grover, and M. MacGregor, "Two Strategies for Spare Capacity Placement in Mesh Restorable Networks," presented at IEEE Global Conference on Communications, November 1993.

[33] L. Ford and D. Fulkerson, *Flows in Network.* Princeton, NJ: Princeton University Press, 1962.

[34] R. Iraschko, M. MacGregor, and K. Ryhorchuk, "Optimal Capacity Placement for Path Restoration in STM or ATM Mesh-Survivable Networks," *IEEE/ACM Transactions on Networking*, vol. 6, pp. 325-336, June 1998.

[35] J. Yamada, "A Spare Capacity Design Method for Restorable Networks," presented at IEEE Global Conference on Communications, November 1995.

[36] B. Caenegem, N. Wauters, and P. Demeester, "Spare Capacity Assignment for Different Restoration Strategies in Mesh Survivable Networks," presented at International Conference on Communications, June 1997.

[37] T. Chujo, H. Komine, K. Miyazaki, T. Ogura, and T. Soejima, "The Design and Simulation of an Intelligent Transport Network with Distributed Control," presented at IEEE Network Operations and Management Symposium, February 1990.

[38] W. Wang, D. Tipper, B. Jaeger, and D. Medhi, "Fault Recovery Routing in Wide Area Packet Networks," presented at 15th International Teletraffic Congress, Washington, DC, June 1997.

[39] R. Cotter, D. Medhi, and D. Tipper, "Traffic Backlog and Impact on Network Dimensioning for Survivability for Wide-Area VP-based ATM Networks," presented at 15th International Teletraffic Congress, Washington, DC, June 1997.

[40] K.-T. Ko, K.-S. Tang, C.-Y. Chan, K.-F. Man, and S. Kwong, "Using Genetic Algorithms to Design Mesh Networks," *IEEE Computer*, pp. 56-60, August 1997.

[41] A. Al-Rumaih, R. Ahmed, and S. Bakry, "A Methodology for Network Topology Design with Link and Node Failure Tolerance," *International Journal of Network Management*, vol. 6, January 1996.

[42] S. Chen, S. Cheng, B. Chen, and J. Chen, "Definitions of Restoration Mechanism Availability and Their Applications," presented at IEEE International Conference on Communications, June 1997.

[43] A. B. Hadj-Alouane and J. Bean, "A Genetic Algorithm for the Multiple Choice Integer Program," *Operations Research*, pp. 92-101, Jan-Feb. 1997.

[44] D. Goldberg, *Genetic Algorithms in Search, Optimization, and Machine Learning*: Addison-Wesley Publishing Co, Inc., 1989.

[45] J. Stender, E. Hillebrand, and J. Kingdon, *Genetic Algorithms in Optimisation, Simulation, and Modeling*. Amsterdam, Netherlands: IOS Press, 1994.

[46] L. Kleinrock, *Queueing Systems Volume II: Computer Applications*. New York, NY: John Wiley And Sons, 1976.

[47] E. Horowitz and S. Sahri, *Fundamentals of Computer Algorithms*. Rochville:Maryland: Computer Science Press, 1984.

[48] J. H. Holland, *Adaptation in Nutural and Artificial Systems*. Ann Arbor: Michigan: University of Michigan Press, 1975.

[49] G. Rawlins, "Introduction to Foundation of Genetic Algoithms," . San Mateo: CA: Mogan Kaufmann Publishers, 1991, pp. 1-10.

[50] L. Davis, "Handbook of Genetic Algorithms," . New York: Van Nostrand Reinhold, 1991.

[51] M. Srinivas and L. Patraik, "Genetic Algorithms: A survey," *Computer*, vol. 27, pp. 17-26, 1994.

[52] D. Tate and A. Smith, "A Genetic Approach to the Quadratic Assignment Problem," *Computer and Operations Research*, vol. 22, pp. 73-83, 1995.

[53] C. Reeves, *Modern Heurstic Techniques for Combinatorial Problems*. New York: John Wiley & Sons, 1993.

[54] T. Starkweather, S. McDaniel, K. Mathias, D. Whitley, and C. Whitley, "A Comparison of Genetic Sequencing Operators," presented at Fourth Conference on Genetic Algorithms, San Diego, July 1991.

[55] P. Jensen, *Students' Guide to Operations Research*. Oakland: CA: Hold-Day, Inc., 1986.

[56] "CPLEX 5.0 User Documentation," CPLEX Optimization Inc., www.cplex.com 1998.

[57] E. McDysan and D. L. Spohn, *Hands on ATM*. New York: McGraw-Hill, 1998.

[58] "MathCad version 7.0," http://www.mathsoft.com 1998.

9 781581 120462